Winning the people wars

Talent and the battle
for human capital

Winning the people wars

Talent and the battle for human capital

MIKE JOHNSON

London · New York · San Francisco · Toronto · Sydney
Tokyo · Singapore · Hong Kong · Cape Town · Madrid
Paris · Milan · Munich · Amsterdam

PEARSON EDUCATION LIMITED

Head Office:
Edinburgh Gate
Harlow CM20 2JE
Tel: +44 (0)1279 623623
Fax: +44 (0)1279 431059

London Office:
128 Long Acre
London WC2E 9AN
Tel: +44 (0)207 447 2000
Fax: +44(0)207 240 5771

Website: www.business-minds.com

First published in Great Britain 2000 © Pearson Education Limited 2000

ISBN 0-273-64197-2

British Library Cataloguing in Publication Data
A catalogue record for this book is available from the British Library.

Library of Congress Cataloging in Publication Data
Applied for.

10 9 8 7 6 5 4 3 2 1

Typeset by M Rules
Printed and bound by Biddles Ltd, Guildford & King's Lynn

The Publishers' policy is to use paper manufactured from sustainable forests.

About the author

Mike Johnson is a consultant, an author and Managing Partner of Johnson & Jones Limited, a corporate communications consultancy, based in Brussels, Belgium and the UK which he founded in 1982; the consultancy works with major multinational corporations and consulting firms. In addition to his consulting activities, he has been the editor of the annual publications *Global Management* and *Global Management Asia Pacific* for the past 17 years and is the author of the best-selling books *Managing in the NEXT Millennium* (translated into 11 languages) and *Getting a GRIP on Tomorrow* (voted one of the 30 best business books in 1996). Two other books on *Teleworking* and *Outsourcing* were published in co-operation with the Institute of Management in 1997. In 1998 he created and developed the highly acclaimed global study *Building and Retaining Global Talent: Towards 2002* for the Economist Intelligence Unit. He is a frequent speaker at business functions, conferences and seminars on HR and communications issues.

Acknowledgements

My thanks to Sultan Kermally, formerly with the Economist Intelligence Unit (EIU) for his encouragement to start researching the business talent issue, and the late Graham Hatton at the EIU for his support, followed by that of Virginia Thorp. Many thanks to all those who helped in the research and no thanks at all to those who said they would, but didn't – I have learned that e-mail is a wonderful electronic 'wall' to hide behind.

To Tom Acuff, Tom McGuire, Mike Staunton, Win Nystrom and Nick Winkfield many thanks – as always – for your input and ideas. To Linda Holbeche at Roffey Park Management Institute for letting me 'steal' from her research one more time and to Rene Cordeiro in Lisbon for arranging interviews. To Richard Stagg at Financial Times Prentice Hall for the opportunity. To my wife Julie a huge thanks for the encouragement, and an even bigger one for knowing me well enough not to ask 'how did it go today?' Finally to my mother Joan, whose undiminished, octogenarian cooking skills sustained both body and soul for three weeks.

Contents

Foreword   *page* xiii

Introduction   xv
Fight the good fight – please!   xv

1 Yes, it really is a war!   1
News from the front line   2
The people wars in microcosm   3
The new seekers of talent   4
IT leads the way   4
Talent famines aren't new   6
A global dearth of professionals   6
More niche players and more graduates   7
All sorts of talent in short supply   8
The lure of the private sector   9
The tight labour market has just begun   10
Too few global managers   10
New heights of cynicism   11
Three into five does go   12
Formulas for involvement   13
Not walking the talk   14
Happy place or hell?   14
Forty per cent of new hires fail   16
Welcome to Cynical Valley   17
Unique methods to hire and hold   18
What CEOs really worry about   19
Surround yourself with excellence   20
Making the same mistakes   21
Who's a winner in the war?   23

Managing at a hectic pace	23
The turn-off factor	24
Getting top management to see the facts	25
What about women?	26
Minorities	28
The 'scrap-heap' generation	28
Voluntary simplicity	29
Businesses converge on same talent	30
More people to go	30
The skill set is vital	31
New-age companies	34

**2   Aspects of war: consternation and
       confusion in the ranks**   **39**

The art of being out of touch	40
Analyze the gaps	41
Making sacrifices	42
The search for true work/life balance	43
What people worry about	44
Trust builders and trust busters	45
The 'no job losses' lie	46
When soft and hard issues collide	47
Let's say hello to human resources	48
Executives for the new corporate age	49
What's holding back HR?	50
HR doesn't deliver	50
Sticking new labels on old corporate baggage	52
Glossy brochure rhetoric	52
Seeking line manager confidence	53
A huge selling job	53
HR strategy must be business strategy	55
An employee eco-system	55
Merger mania or merger mess-up	56
All mergers are acquisitions for somebody	57
Ask questions	58
Four key insights into M&As	58
Learn to explain and motivate or they'll do it themselves	60

You're in a seller's market   60
Motivating – a dying skill?   61
Shell-shocked   62
Be willing to work   65
What defines success?   65

**3   The battle for the best: attracting exciting
     talent to your doorstep**   69
Best practices from other industries   70
Find some new rocks to look under   71
Industry expertise can still count   71
Want a slice of what's hot this month?   73
Do foreign bodies work?   76
Where's cool?   76
Image is all   77
The culture factor   78
Tradition dies hard   79
A sustaining place to develop   82
Shared values   83
Focus on those who ensure your vision works   84
Who's doing what to attract? Some examples   84
What's really new?   86
Corporate turn-offs abound   87
Advice about job-seekers   87
Taking back talent   91
What about Generation X?   91
What do they want?   92
Pressure for companies to respond   93
Attracting graduates to your business   96
Non-negotiable issues   96
Even the advertising changes   97
Is Europe catching up?   98
Levels of cynicism   99
A cautionary tale of the future   100
Women – a waste of talent continues   102
The spouse thing   103
Seeking the global player   104

Location, location, location   105
Excellent infrastructure wins out   106
Taking care of people is taking care of business   107
Going talent shopping   111
Breaking the rules   114

4 Holding the talent line tight   119
Stretch your people   120
Expectation fails to match reality   121
Own the issues   122
I hate the boss   122
Shorter tenures at the top   124
Challenge beats money   124
Opinions count   125
Living for the business   125
A real value shift   126
Whose finger's on the climate control?   127
Ideas to have and to hold   128
A lifestyle example   132
More examples of getting it right   133
Supporting the spouse   135
Expatriation horror   136
Demotivating the repatriates   138
Merger paralysis   139
Advice on the returning expatriate   139
Motivate diverse groups   140
Who do you want to hold onto?   141
Bidding doesn't work   142
Winners, losers and cruisers   143
Retention strategies – more than just a luxury   145

5 Don't follow the rest – play by your own rules   151
More proactivity please   151
No realistic assessment   152
A widening gap   153
The fatal flaw   155
Not the job, the person   156

History lessons   157
Shifting ambitions   158
Building a reputation quietly   158
So let's get some new leaders   161
Identifying the best new leaders   162
Don't hire in your own image   166
Grab a bite and some talent too!   168
Hey oldie! I need you   170
Did we get it wrong?   171
How are employers thinking differently?   173

**6   It's all about development, reward and
     communication**   183
Development – where it's going and why   184
Intellectual capital   185
The right mix of talent   186
A lack of appreciation   186
Miracle management snake oil   187
Flickering lights of sanity   188
Building a global team that delivers   189
Communicate, communicate, communicate   192
Delayering and devolution of power   198
Mergers and acquisitions – the communications
nightmare   199
The intranet as a communications tool   200
Communication isn't what it used to be   203
So what are we going to pay for all this talent?   204
Perception of reward   205
Force-feeding   206
Money for mercenaries   206
Guaranteed net salaries   207
An American pay model   207
Four key trends   208
Global pay rates for global jobs   208
Incentive-based reward   209
A word to the wise   209

7 **Getting your business ready for the**
      battles to come   213
      People issues on the strategic agenda   214
      Look to alliances   216
      Share your talent   216
      A clearly defined balance   217
      Invalid belief   217
      Beyond Generation X   218
      A predictable work schedule   219
      God-like expectations   219
      You have been warned   220
      Those that won't make it   220
      The haunting subject of succession   220
      Where does HR fit in?   224
      What about the shareholders?   225
      Shareholder showdown   226
      We're talking talent   229
      Think like you used to   229

      Bibliography   231
      Index   233

Foreword

In the last decade, working life has changed dramatically, especially for those of us who have spent much of our time in offices or factories. The increased automation and computerization of business has provoked a revolution that the downsizing, rightsizing and flattening of organizational hierarchies and pyramids of power of the early 1990s completed.

We were told that there was a new contract between employer and employee, with a new set of loyalties and working rules to adopt and understand. Corporations would never again be able to offer us guaranteed employment, but – with luck – they would keep us up to date in our chosen skills, so that when they didn't want us anymore, we would be rapidly re-employable. Suddenly, and almost without us noticing, the employer was holding a winning hand with all the aces. They could pick and choose their employees, they could set salaries, they could say who stayed and who would be downsized – again.

In the process, middle managers surrendered their offices, assistants, deputies and secretaries. Those left behind worked in teams, on the road and in clients' organizations. We were rightsized again, told about the wonders of 'horizontal promotion' and many functions were acquired, merged or outsourced to new owners, all the while taking on the tasks of departed colleagues. Life for the survivors was pretty bleak.

Then, in 1998, things began to change, albeit slowly at first. The change began with a talent war for IT specialists, as the growing need for enterprise solutions and the looming threat of the Millennium Bug bit hard. Then other disciplines began to go *supply supercritical* – finance experts, marketers, e-commerce specialists, merger and acquisition professionals, organization development veterans. All of these – and more – were in shorter and shorter supply. The vision that some had predicted, of redundant middle-aged, middle managers becoming five dollar-an-hour hamburger flippers in a fast food chain, was rapidly changing. Having downsized too far and too fast, many corporations were caught out as markets grew and global ambitions pushed the drive for change still further.

Today, the transformation of the employment market is complete. In most job areas and industries, the employees now hold the winning hand – and they are playing it as they have been taught. They are angry, suspicious and cynical. They want the money now and they have little belief in the future. Whether companies can change this situation remains to be seen (although some are trying), but it is not going to be easy. Too many people have too long memories for that.

This book is about what it is going to take in today's climate of mistrust to attract and retain the people that corporations need for their business to succeed. I have called it *Winning the People Wars*. This is an apt phrase. Whether you win those wars is entirely based on just how much ammunition you have and how prepared you are to fight.

This book has a single purpose: to show how the best are gearing up for this battle for business talent – a battle that is only just beginning, and one that will mean severe casualties for those that get it wrong. As with all wars, this one will have a definite outcome – winners and losers.

Mike Johnson,
Hampshire, UK

Introduction

Fight the good fight – please!

There is a new phenomenon sweeping the globe – a battle for the best in business talent. While some see it as a fight to attract high performers to their firms, the street smart know it is something entirely different: having the ability to hold onto the people you want to keep (and *only* those you want to keep) for longer than your competitors. To paraphrase Rudyard Kipling, 'if you can keep your heads when all around are losing theirs, then you are manager, my son'.

But, of course, nothing is ever quite as simple as that. Pressures on certain industries, job skills and geographic regions add thousands of possible permutations as to who you hold onto and when you should let them go. Understanding that some employees need to be successfully managed out of the organization is becoming just as much a core human resource skill as hiring in the right people to meet current needs. Today's corporation isn't made up of a mass of employees that rarely change. Turnover, while not being a good thing if it is sweeping away your best people, is a very good thing if it is clearing out old skills to be replaced with new ones.

Indeed, one thing that is crystal clear after hundreds of interviews with senior executives and management commentators around the globe, is that 'the old days' are just that – consigned to history and to be remembered fondly as a time when change was not the status quo and we could expect our colleagues to be the same people for decades at a time.

In this new world of work, there are – as in anything else – winners and losers. The winners are those firms that recognize that the way we seek out, employ, reward, develop and hold people is a very different (and consequently much more complex) game than ever before. The surprising number of losers are the firms that have not moved on to the new ways of work. They are the corporations with leaders who still exhort their employees to 'think outside the box'. We have news, there is no box anymore. There are no limits. Today, we exist in a world where our opportunities are not circumscribed by organization charts, job descriptions, age or even ability. We are in a new industrial age that has conveniently appeared just as we cross the threshold of a new millennium.

It is a world with less security for some, but with more for those who can take responsibility for their own actions and careers. It is a world where loyalty by both the hirer and the hired is fickle in the extreme and looks set to stay that way for many years to come – despite the books on the subject that urge us to create new contracts based on 'new-look' loyalty. It is a world where reward is increasingly based not just on money (except for those who like it that way, who need to be included as part of the employment permutations of our new work society) but on a balanced lifestyle with a priority based on challenge and personal development. With stress factors in business at an all time high, this work/life balance issue looks set to be one of the defining points of the postindustrial age; clearly delineating between the good, the bad and the just plain ugly employer.

Moreover, as you will see, it is a world where flexibility is paramount for both employer and employee. If you lack flexibility, you're dead. That means from the employer's point of view, creative compensation, reward, skill development and the artful, inventive and total use of technology to effectively solve people issues are going to be the top concerns. For employees, it means that there will not be the option to have the same job for the next ten years, simply because the job won't be there (chances are also high that the company won't be there either). Three-dimensional flexibility across the total organization – up, down, sideways – that is what the business of today really looks like. While it is a revolution that has caught many unawares and has made a great number of people unhappy, it is in reality a tremendous opportunity.

Business life has never been more exciting or more open to new innovation. This book is a guide to the new age of work and what it means for the people in it. It is a guide to winning the people wars that are raging outside your factory gates. Be a winner and you'll survive. Refuse to fight, or even stay neutral and this may be the very last business book you ever read.

1 | Yes, it really is a war!

I have studied the enemy all my life. I have read the memoirs of his generals and his leaders. I have even read his philosophers and listened to his music. I have studied in detail the account of every damned one of his battles. I know exactly how he will react under any given set of circumstances. And he hasn't the slightest idea of what I'm going to do. So when the time comes, I'm going to whip the hell out of him.

General George Patton

If you assign people duties without granting them any rights, you must pay them well.

Goethe

This is the story of the people wars. Not wars where people are killed or maimed, but where there are winners and losers, victors and vanquished all the same. We are in a world where it is estimated that two-thirds of all the executives in Western companies (US and Europe) are expected to change their jobs in the next 36 months. We are in a world where there is a shortfall bordering on a million people to serve the IT industry. We are in a world where experts say there is a shortage of almost a quarter of a million consultants.

The causes of this war are many, but there are two universal issues that are staring everyone in the face and which cannot be ignored. First, there is a shortage of skilled people to fuel the growth ambitions and the complex worlds of the modern corporation. Second, loyalty is at an all time low, and people can be persuaded more easily than ever before to jump ship. And so we begin a giant merry-go-round. You steal my marketing manager, I steal from someone else. The knock-on effect crosses national and regional borders and crosses over industries, turning this war for talent into a multidimensional global conflict.

Demographers now suggest that this shortage is going to last until at least midway through the century, i.e. to at least 2050, when technology will make it possible to rely less and less on people. Anyone who doubts that people are moving in greater and greater numbers isn't reading the newspapers or watching the turnover statistics. During 1998, I interviewed 157 chief executives and organisational development heads in Europe, Asia and the US; by mid-1999, 63 of these had moved. That's a statistic no one can ignore.

It is important to realize that this war is not confined to specific groups (e.g. IT people, although that is a particular short-term issue). This war is being played out at the very top of major organizations as well. When we see that eight of AT&T's top managers (two with 24 and 26 years respectively with the firm) left within a short period for exciting new opportunities, we have to realize that this is a phenomenon that can strike at any of our businesses at any time. Such is the shortage of top talent and such is the pressure on it to deliver results that we must expect turnover rates to soar. Look at General Electric. With the legendary Jack Welsh heading into retirement in2001, you can expect the disappointed who didn't get the big job to be quickly snapped up by predatory headhunters with high-end slots to fill. This is the nature of this war. It is tough, it is bloody and it is going to get very much worse. Corporations that don't have a strategy to deal with it are going to get cut off and encircled. Allowing yourself to be outmanoeuvered in this battle for the best can only result in disaster.

It is no longer enough to look at your traditional competitor in your industry, as the lines between business sectors are blurring more and more each day. Everyone wants an e-commerce expert, everyone wants your best marketing, finance, information systems managers. So you have to put your business on a war footing before it's too late. Cancel all leave, get out the ammunition and prepare to fight. Expect to lose a lot of ground troops when those assaults on your business start, plan to sacrifice some officers, but know those that you would hate to hand over as prisoners in this recruitment war.

News from the front line

This book delivers detailed news from the frontline of the people wars. In doing so, it also provides a guide to what the best firms are doing to ensure a ready supply of top talent and shows how, when you've got it, to hold onto that talent. As you read through this book you will see that there are a great number of examples, ideas and observations all designed to help you and your firm survive the battles to come.

The people wars in microcosm

If you want to know what the action's really like, consider a major railway station, such as London's Waterloo Station. For here the people wars are being fought out daily amongst the great metropolis's commuters. It is also a microcosm of what is happening to our working lives, not just in London, but in New York, Tokyo, Munich and Melbourne. Twenty years ago, the giant arrivals hall would most probably have been host to one of the armed forces (army, navy or air force) on a recruitment drive. Parade ground chic – down to the shiny boots you could see your face in – combined with a salesman's slickness urged passing travellers to consider joining up. With a prescience not always ascribed to the military, slogans such as 'It's a Man's Life in the Modern Army' showed that they knew as much about wars for talent as the more unsavoury conflicts we expect them to engage in.

Fast forward to that same arrivals hall now and we see that the battle to recruit the 'foot soldiers' of today is not so different, only the skills and the rewards have changed. The recruiter might be Cap Gemini, PricewaterhouseCoopers, Deloitte & Touche. Instead of being held in the thrall of 'It's a man's life in the modern army', you will be seduced by the very turn-of-the-millennium lifestyle concept of 'Freedom to be Outstanding' or some other corporate slogan.

Such is the present shortage of technical and software staff that recruiters are pitching jobs in the same way new cars are pitched at a show. 'Come on, look at the brochure and have a cup of coffee in our booth and we'll talk about it. How much money did you say you were earning?

pitching jobs in the same way new cars are pitched at a show

Oh, we can give you 25 per cent better than that.' In Grand Central station in New York, you'll find the same thing. In Tokyo, you won't find it at all because they are more discreet about these things and anyway most IT departments in Japan seem to be exclusively staffed by Indians, Irish and Australians.

But make no mistake about it, this is a war for talent that is being played out more and more in public. The ammunition is twofold: first pay and benefits (which is often enough for those concerned); second, a great project that will broaden or sharpen your skill set so that you are even more marketable to the next bidder.

The new seekers of talent

Still in doubt? Let's leave Waterloo station and take the London Underground (the Tube) to Temple station in the City. Above Temple Underground station is the European headquarters of one of the world's major professional services firms, Andersen Consulting. Hundreds and hundreds of Andersen people stand on the platform at Temple every day waiting for the train. And what do they see? Well, the last time I was there it was a giant advertisement from a major rival with a telephone number to call. Now you can't get much more in your face than that, can you? Indeed, the big five – formerly accounting firms – and the heavyweight consulting outfits are the leaders in the bruising battles for talent.

Although most often of the corporate cannon fodder type, programmers (now called consultants), applications specialists and project managers make up the critical shortage of people who can meet client requirements so that the fights are furious and frequent. And these needs don't get past the organizational humourists, labelling those that work for Andersen 'androids' and corrupting Pricewaterhouse, to Price 'slaughterhouse'. But, laugh if you will, these firms are the new seekers out of talent, they are the leaders in new ways to hook in the hot operators – most other businesses don't come close; they haven't in some cases even dragged themselves to the battle front. For them, the talent wars are still a strange sound of distant gunfire that they have chosen to ignore at their peril.

IT leads the way

There is no doubt that the IT industry leads the way in the people wars that are breaking out around the globe; although it by no means has this phenomenon exclusively to itself. In the US alone, the Bureau of

Labor Statistics has calculated that the number of IT jobs will rise to 2,509,000 over the next nine years – an increase of 108 per cent. The Information Technology Association of America has made an even more dramatic calculation, estimating that there are 3,354,000 IT jobs in the US today and 10 per cent of them (354,000) are unfilled and will seriously affect economic growth. If that looks high, in early 1999 the *Financial Times* estimated that there were 370,000 IT jobs unfilled across Europe. Even Canada has 10,000 software vacancies and is plundering the markets of its big brother, next door neighbour with lucrative offers.

What makes these sort of statistics most disturbing is that most earlier forecasts grossly underestimated reality. As an example, a figure widely quoted in California is that there are always 25,000 job vacancies in Silicon Valley. However, as a recent survey suggests that in Northern Virginia alone there are 20,000 IT vacancies, there is a better than even chance that the Silicon Valley numbers should be revised upwards. Certainly, desperate IT employers in Kansas City know that statistics are working against them: for example, 125 companies came to a job fair where only 100 potential employees showed up. In Salt Lake City, Utah, people capable of writing pro-

in a sellers' market, talent makes its own rules

grammes are so rare they are able to write their own job descriptions and salary profiles. Things are now judged so bad in the local government offices that the County Commissioners drafted a policy requiring new IT hires to commit to the job for two years. Needless to say the idea doesn't work, in a sellers' market talent makes its own rules – maybe we should heed that a lot more.

A widespread issue

This is by no means a problem that the US faces alone. In India – a growing centre of savvy software people – the market is moving at between 50–60 per cent every year, creating a $5 billion business. But the worries of the West are just beginning in India. Highly advantaged in two things, low costs and geographic position (Europe and the US can sleep while Indian software specialists work), the price is beginning to go up, and up and up. Wages are rising at about 25 per cent every year even as retention levels crumble. Again, the shortage of skilled people is at the very heart of the future of this industry. Worse still, there isn't another India hidden behind the Himalayas – there is no Lost Valley packed with programmers waiting to be discovered. There just aren't too many places around the globe with a large cadre of intelligent, highly educated, English-speaking people. Find one if you can and you'll make Bill Gates look like a pauper.

Talent famines aren't new

Of course, talent famines aren't new. Delving into the industrial dark ages you can trace them back to the hiring of mercenaries to fight your wars for you (a slightly different type of war for talent). In more recent times, IT made its first impact when in the mid-to-late 1960s' programmers were at a premium (the same programmers, now aged 50-plus are back in action again for big bucks writing Fortran and Cobol programmes to beat the Millennium Bug), it was areas like engineering after World War Two, nursing and other healthcare roles in the eighties. Wherever there is a shortage, wages rise and people become a lot less likely to stick with their present job – the slightest rumour, or the least little niggle can see them on their way. With loyalty levels at all-time lows and opportunities at all-time highs, retaining talent will soon become a much-prized management skill.

Now, in today's tight market, IT is just the most visible talent conflict taking place in the world. Spend a little time looking at an industry or a region and it doesn't take long to realize that there is a great deal of activity going on under the surface that points to an urgent need for those that want to win to get their people plans in shape to meet the battles to come.

A global dearth of professionals

Certainly, other fast-growth areas like consulting are in head-to-head battles for talent. With a global dearth of professionals who have the twin skills of technical expertise and selling or client service skills, consultants KPMG have estimated that there is a current shortfall of 200,000 consultants worldwide. Much of that has been driven by firms like McKinsey, Roland Berger and Andersen moving into the more technical side of their clients' businesses. This has meant a premium on seeking out engineers with a 'bedside' manner that not only install software and hardware but can charm the client into more investments. In fact, selling on has become a key performance factor in the consulting business, which accounts for much of the boom. Get into the client and begin to build a relationship that will see them acquiring more and more of your 'product' until it is an all-pervading web within the organization.

Such is the shortage that the German Engineering Association estimates a shortfall of 100,000 engineers. Part of the responsibility for that is getting laid at the feet of American corporations who are snatching up newly graduated European engineers to fuel their own needs in the US. And, while it might seem that it is the US that is booming and Europe with its unemployment mountain that is floundering, the facts do not support that view at all. While in Silicon Valley, I was fascinated by software companies like Oracle and Sun Microsystems hiring 15,000 people a year. Later I discovered that Munich-based Siemens had hired 25,000 people in the same period. Sure, they are cutting in the old industries they are getting out of, but they are recruiting for the new businesses they are developing. As with many others in Europe, they find that to be competitive they need new people – retraining doesn't cover every eventuality or opportunity.

The other reason for the shortage is that some years ago – during the toughest downsizing period in Europe's ailing industries – it became clear that becoming an engineer was career suicide. Consequently, enrolment

graduate engineers are getting $100,000 for their first job, say Europe's headhunters

on graduate engineering courses slumped. Companies that downsized in haste are now not only repenting at leisure, but paying through the nose for their actions – in some fields graduate engineers are getting $100,000 for their first job, say Europe's headhunters, double the figure of five years ago.

More niche players and more graduates

Another trend, at the other end of the professional services spectrum is more and more niche players putting a demand on the marketplace. 'Boutique' consultancies with a key, often industry specific, expertise are expanding globally. Elsewhere, headhunters – ever in search of professional respectability and acceptance – are taking on people audits and other human resource assignments that traditionally went to the big consulting firms. The consequence is that they need a new breed of talent too and these people are migrating from once rock-solid industrial operators to new, fast moving firms.

Naturally, the result of all this activity has been escalating salaries and a need to put more emphasis on graduate recruitment to fill in the gaps. Brecker & Merryman, a US consulting firm, reports in a survey that consulting firms increased their campus recruitment of MBAs to 30

a need to put more emphasis on graduate recruitment to fill the gaps

per cent of the graduates from the top 20 business schools – the most active firms were Deloitte & Touche, McKinsey and PricewaterhouseCoopers. To illustrate what the rest of corporate America – and indeed the world – is up against in building a better talent trap, starting base salaries were $90,000 (with a range from $58,000 to $128,000). Average sign-on bonuses were $22,000 (up over 10 per cent on 1997) and guaranteed bonuses were $17,000 – a startling increase of 42 per cent year on year, indicating that graduates are learning negotiation skills at school too!

All sorts of talent in short supply

Shortages come in all shapes and sizes. In Australia, there is a huge demand for workers in the 'well-being' industry, as the Australian Bureau of Statistics classifies it. From 1996–1998 the number of well-being consultants (beauty therapists, natural remedy specialists and weight loss advisers) increased by 50 per cent nationwide. In Sydney, there is also a thriving demand for mobile pedicurists and manicurists.

And employees in traditional industries are not afraid to bet on the future either. In the US, in areas where gambling has been legalized they are losing bank tellers in droves to casino operators. In the construction industry, there is a critical shortage of carpenters (presumably for building all the casinos), with 87 per cent of contractors reporting problems and an average start up on projects of 12 weeks compared to just a week 2 years ago.

In Europe's *de facto* capital Brussels, corporations can't find office receptionists at any price. Quadra-lingual (English, French, Dutch, German), well presented receptionists for multinational corporations can name their price and get it. Next door in The Netherlands the retail industry has a jobs crisis on its hands. Traditionally poorly paid, workers have emigrated to other, better-paid jobs in Holland's booming economy.

Ireland was, for a long time, a country graduates left to seek their fortunes elsewhere. A decade ago an embarrassed Irish development authority had to admit that the photo in their advertisement of a group of Irish graduates ready to take on inward investment challenges was slightly misleading – they had all left to work in Europe or the US. Now there has been a huge resurgence of interest, largely due to special tax legislation. With an influx of financial services groups, it has become a key player in customer call centres, so much so that it is now screaming for talent. Over New Year 1998–9 it even ran a job fair for young people home for the holidays in the hopes of getting them to stay and work. Scotland and Belgium are also experiencing major call centre staff shortages.

The lure of the private sector

In the US, there is an increasing shortage of teachers. Why? Those in areas such as mathematics, science and technology are being lured to high-paying private sector jobs. Things are so bad in Massachusetts that schools are offering incentives to attract and retain top teachers such as scholarships, tax breaks and cash bonuses as high as $20,000. They are also actively recruiting retiring baby-boomers.

The military – in the US at least – is having to get its act together in a major way. In a recent report, consultants Watson Wyatt warned that 'The US Army, Navy and Air Force are facing perhaps the most serious peacetime enlistment shortfalls ever. After falling considerably short of recruiting goals last year, 1999 looks to be even more unsettling.' The main reason for this shortage seems to be that the demographic curve is headed the wrong way. As Watson Wyatt point out, 'signs of an alarming shortage of younger workers [the armed forces recruit heavily in the 17–21 age bracket] began surfacing in certain segments of the private sector' some time ago.

Indeed, concerns that the US would become a 'nation of hamburger flippers', (a view strongly espoused until quite recently) has been consigned to history too. Even four years ago, according to the Watson Wyatt report 'we started to see social security recipients working at McDonald's. Two or three years ago, the demographic wave washed over retail outlets (see the Dutch concern). More recently, we have hit the military and the hi-tech industry.'

The tight labour market has just begun

What this means in human resource terms, is that for most employers the tight labour market – all the way from the unskilled and semi-skilled to the skilled and top managers – has only just begun. Everyone, it would seem, is trading up a rung on the employment food chain. While it leaves serious shortages at top-end, hi-tech jobs, it also takes out and moves up the low paid (often the hourly or part-time worker) and gets them into the regular workforce. Those that pay near the minimum wage need to have an urgent and serious rethink about their future hiring strategy.

Examples abound of areas of industry where wages and salaries are going through the roof. Merchants, a US tyre and car repair chain, have seen starting salaries for auto-technicians head toward $50,000. Master technicians, with six years experience 'can make as much as $100,000', they report. German car manufacturer Audi possibly has the right idea. Over the next five years, it plans to target what it calls the 'misfortunate' and create 250 jobs that will give a new chance to disaffected youth, long-term jobless, immigrants and the hand-icapped. Where Audi lead the rest of us will surely have no choice but to follow.

Of course, those problems pale in comparison with that of China. Frighteningly, it is estimated that they will need upwards of 1.4 million MBAs over the next decade. When you

China needs upwards of 1.4 million MBAs

think that currently, there are less than 30,000 students enrolled on MBA courses (as opposed to 300,000 in the US), the problem of solving the world's biggest business talent shortage becomes clear. In fact, in spite of the Asian economic crisis, there are serious shortages of effective managers across most of the region. Singapore has been advertising for local nationals to come home and Malaysia is plagued with too few executives who can meet modern business needs. Even in Japan, there is a dearth of managers who can lead their companies forward in this new world of work and this becomes particularly acute when looking for managers who understand the strategic implications of IT.

Too few global managers

Another issue, which is causing frown lines on the otherwise smooth faces of the search industry, is that there are just so few global managers around. This, more than anything else, is forcing the current talent battles, particularly those at the top. While some countries seem to have a reasonable supply, others are in less good shape. Countries like Germany, France and Italy have admitted that they can't find enough global talent to meet the needs of the growing internationalization of their businesses. At the risk of alienating a large part of the business world, the American view of going global tends to be: 'for globalization read Americanization'. Ask any European or Asian working for a US corporation to comment on this!

Not surprisingly, in this era of so-called talent famines, there are huge anomalies. While we get the news that industry cannot find enough 'good' people to meet its latest needs, it is also very actively engaged in removing – at a seemingly faster and faster pace – the people who don't fit into the new concept of the corporation. While 1993 was the horror year for downsizing in the West, 1998 turned out to be a banner year as well, with more and more manufacturing positions going on the block. Despite much talk of retraining, most companies are still opting for young, energetic cheaper labour. While this might be something they live to regret as demographics catch up with them (and they end up re-hiring many of the 50 year-olds they just terminated), for the time being they are generally walking the tightrope with only a few wobbles. But that aside, downsizing and other reorganization activity is a bitter pill to swallow, not just for those affected but those left behind too. Loyalty is at a new, historical low. All indicators are that the weather on the loyalty front is set to get worse.

New heights of cynicism

The rise of the Internet and access to all kinds of data at the stroke of a key means that information sharing can raise cynicism to new, unthought of, heights. The American trade union website *www.paywatch.org* is a disloyal employees paradise. Tap in your pay-slip details and find out just how much more than

'toxic workplaces', the only way you'd work there is just for the money

you the CEO earns. The site shows that the average US CEO takes home

$7.8 million – a huge 326 times the pay of the average factory worker! Today it is common to hear the phrase 'toxic workplaces' to describe places where the only way you'd work there was 'just for the money and nothing else'. The trouble is that when you hire mercenaries they are apt to opt for fighting on the other side when you run out of interesting or expensive ammunition they can play with.

In a survey of 10,000 workers in 13 countries, Gemini Consulting encapsulated the unhappiness of our corporate lives in just four questions.

- Were you already affected by a merger, restructuring downsizing or centralization? Yes, said 66 per cent.
- Would you leave your job for advancement opportunity, 10 per cent salary increase and/or more flexible hours? Yes, said 64 per cent.
- Would you leave just for a better advancement opportunity? Yes said 44 per cent.
- Do you know your company's mission statement? No, said 54 per cent. A lot of workers would rightly say that they weren't around long enough to find out what the mission statement was.

Three into five does go

Whilst the US economy remains super-buoyant, the numbers tell another story: according to *The Economist*, 677,795 people were sacked from US firms in 1998, the highest figure this decade. A great deal of that rationalization doesn't mean less work for those left – in fact it is usually the opposite. Recent studies show that in most countries in Europe, three workers or managers are doing jobs that employed five people in the past.

> three workers, or managers are doing jobs that employed five people in the past

At the top, the regime can be even harsher. As Tom Acuff, managing partner of Neumann International in Brussels says, 'I meet senior people with 25 direct reports, that's not only crazy, it's impossible. Worse still, in some cases the people reporting to the manager are not only in different countries but on different continents'. Calling them 'human cinders', Acuff predicts that, 'these people are on a fast track to executive burn-out, they cannot keep up that pace 16 hours a day seven days a week'. But their companies, short of the right talent, cheerfully let them do it. Recently, I met a senior pharmaceutical executive in a Hong Kong hotel. He had responsibility for the whole of Asia *and* South America. Add to that he was expected to fly back to the US for monthly management meetings!

Management writer and commentator Henry Mintzberg, famously pointed out one of the great paradoxes of modern business in an interview I did with him some years ago. 'Just as they started downsizing, companies also said, "hey, we are going to become a service organization". What no one ever worked out was why demoralized, demotivated people, who had seen their colleagues fired would want to smile at people and go the extra mile.' Mintzberg, who has been more than vindicated for his views on downsizing as companies have had to rapidly staff up again, added, 'How can you maintain a change process when the key actors have left? How can you possibly keep the people devoted?'

Formulas for involvement

With mega-mergers the continuing order of the day (the biggest ten mergers in US business history all took place in 1998–9) massive rationalization will surely follow. Some companies are getting it right and seem to have found formulas for employee involvement, but, interestingly, none seem to do the same sorts of things to create these people synergies and successes are in diverse industries with a very mixed bag of ideas. The simplistic, plain vanilla view of this is to offer:

- equitable compensation
- challenging work
- a great work environment
- a flexible approach to employment
- opportunities to grow.

To a greater or lesser extent, a heady cocktail of these ingredients is supposed to ensure success – often it doesn't. So what goes wrong? Mainly, it would seem, it all comes down to humans again. You can set up the systems, but if you don't run them consistently and keep ringing the changes, the whole operation will fail.

Not walking the talk

In hundreds of discussions and interviews, I found the key reason coming up time and time again: management doesn't get fully involved and fails to 'walk the talk'. In short, loyalty begins three levels down and applies to the majority of the workers, but please don't let the top executives have to do this too!

And anyone who thinks this isn't true should have attended three round table sessions I ran in the spring of 1999 in London, Brussels and New York. Attending were young business professionals (youngest 26, eldest 32). The level of cynicism was scary in the extreme. Most had never, ever seen the CEO, several had never met anyone in top management. All understood that their time in the job was a day-to-day affair and could terminate at any moment. Most interesting perhaps was that none of them had any plans to stay in the business they were in. Most in fact, didn't want to be in business having seen how it operates. Said one 28-year-old financial trader, 'if I thought I had to do this every day until I was 60, I think I'd top myself'. They felt that most managers they came into contact with were totally out of touch with the needs of this new generation and they considered anyone over 40 to be 'old'.

How do you expect to motivate and engage a group like this with fake platitudes? They are too intelligent to be fobbed off with mindless corporate speak the way their parents may have been. The half truths, broken promises and unfulfilled expectations are a track record of much of industry at its re-engineering worst. But it just won't wash with a new generation. If management cannot walk the talk and lead by example, employees will head out to a new challenge or more likely a new career. (More on the round table discussions with Generation X in Chapter 3.)

Happy place or hell?

Of course, there are places where the workers are happy, *Fortune* magazine's annual survey of 'the 100 best companies to work for in America' is proof of that. But one of the key issues that comes up is that a place where one individual would be happy would be hell for another. This raises a central theme of this book. Too often in interviews with employees I found much of their unhappiness came from being sold the wrong job in the wrong organisation. Clearly a key point – especially in these days of talent famine – is being able to match the people to your business. Failure to do that can only bring unhappiness all round. However, it is amazing how many companies (and a great number of head-hunters, I keep being told) in their eagerness to hire, make promises they cannot fulfil. Equally people just hire the wrong people for the

a place where one individual would be happy would be hell for another

wrong reasons. 'He's a programmer, get him in here quick, he'll settle down eventually.' Problem is they don't. They hate it, you hate them and you end up spending money to buy out their contract.

One thing we all need to learn to do better in these days when top talent is hard to find, is for goodness sake don't jump in with both feet until you know what the person is like. I compare it to going out and falling in love with a car then driving it home and finding out it won't fit your garage. All the pleasure of ownership somehow vanishes. What seems to be clear from the *Fortune* and other polls is that the matching up of people becomes a paramount activity. Just going out and hiring 200 process engineers doesn't work, unless you are really body-shopping for 200 people that you need for six months to write lines of mindless code, after which they leave and you never see them again.

Some success stories

Munich-based multinational, Siemens have a hugely successful programme in place that tackled the talent drought at the source – they retrained or removed their recruitment people, putting in strict quality controls and making certain that the recruiters were hiring the right people. What they had found was that corporate recruiters weren't truly up-to-speed on the real needs of the business. As their HR head Günther Goth commented, 'people still saw us as an ideal place for mechanical engineers, when in fact over 50 per cent of our global work is in IT today. Our job was to make sure that not only did the outside world know that, but people in our organization were aware too.' Checking out your recruiters sounds like a very good first move.

So, if you want employees to enjoy their time with you, make sure you pick the right ones. The prevailing culture does make a difference. Phone maker Nokia plays strongly on its Finnish roots and the people it hires – now a majority of non-Finns – espouse similar values. Its vice-president of Group HR, Pii Kotilainen says, 'As we add more and more foreigners to our workforce the challenge is to preserve and evolve our culture. We think we have something special called the Nokia culture. It's not one that everyone would enjoy, but that's the same for many organizations.' Nokia's President of Telecommunications operations, Matti Alahunta argues that, 'the biggest challenge we constantly face is the recruitment and integration of new, top-class people – not only the identification and selection, but a proper induction, to share our company values'.

Other Finnish companies like the national airline, Finnair, do the same (it even halved its advertising budget and put the money saved into people development instead: it worked wonders), although it has serious problems getting anyone to go to its high-taxed and remote country (*see* Chapter 3). Indeed, the Scandinavians seem to have developed their own profitable way of managing people. IKEA, the furniture retailer, has a band of totally devoted employees wherever it operates (although it makes even senior managers fly coach class and stay in three star hotels, its 'gimmick' of giving away equally to all employees its world-wide takings for a 24 hour period proved to be a winner), as does Danish hi-fi firm Bang & Olufsen. Many people who would be happy in a Finnish corporation wouldn't dream of working in the brash culture of Southwest Airlines (where the boss is known to serve in-flight meals), or software firm EDS (whose cowboy boot, Texan image delights some and repels others) – but others happily do. It is knowing not just who you need for your business, but how they will fit in that is critical at any time. Right now, you cannot afford to make mistakes.

Forty per cent of new hires fail

But mistakes do happen, not only in getting the wrong people into the business, but just hiring the out and out incompetent. According to the Center for Creative Leadership in North Carolina, '40 per cent of all new executive hires fail within the first 18 months,

> a continual moan from senior managers . . . being sold the wrong kind of people by search firms

being terminated for poor performance, performing significantly below expectations or voluntarily resigning from the position'. In interviews across Europe and the US during 1999, I found a continual moan from senior managers was being 'sold the wrong kind of people' by search firms eager to capitalize on the talent shortage.

In 1979, I carried out a survey of CEO attitudes that showed more than 60 per cent of them had been with the same firm for at least half their career: 42 per cent had been CEO for over ten years. Today that level of tenure would be unthinkable. In fact my own research amongst junior managers shows two interesting trends:

- younger people in business today expect to move every two or three years
- possibly more significant in these talent scarce days – most expect to change not only jobs but industries and job categories as well.

This is a clear indication that today's entrant into the world of business is as skittish as a new born foal. If they don't like your grass they won't stay in your field for very long.

Backing this up is a PricewaterhouseCoopers survey of graduating business students (2,500 students, from 36 universities in 11 countries). Predictably for this group, 57 per cent say that 'balancing work and personal life is their primary career goal' (up from 45 per cent two years ago). The key question for them is not whether personal development is more important than career, but whether these can be achieved in tandem. Prospective employers take note.

Welcome to Cynical Valley

But, as with everything else, this doesn't play out in the same way everywhere. Silicon Valley is already being dubbed 'Cynical Valley' by some. There, the successors to pioneers like Intel's Andy Grove and Apple's Steve Jobs are a lot less rebellious; the religious crusade is not there – the desire to make a lot of loot is. While many of Grove and Jobs' generation eschewed the trappings of wealth, the next generation isn't so backward, causing, amongst other things, a price boom in an already stratospheric house market.

Interestingly enough the next generation seems to be – despite some research – rather split when it comes to wants and needs. Sure they want to make certain that their lifestyle gets in to some kind of balance – having seen the mess many of their parents made of it – but they are also mindful of the need to earn. 'Show-me-the-money' has become the mantra of Generation X-ers (or any other youthful category) the world over. And in a time of talent famine this is another important lesson for employers to learn. The old, 'work hard and we'll make you a manager in two years', just doesn't wash with this group. As one said to me, 'I won't be there and the person that's making the offer doesn't know it but he won't probably be there either.'

Go to Asia and you'll find even more evidence of these attitudes than anywhere else (except Russia). In China mobility is the game to play, spiralling up the earnings table to treble your income in three to four years. In Singapore, US companies have found that offering stock options insults locals who have no plans to stick around until they vest. 'Don't need your stock, give me the money instead', is the cry.

Unique methods to hire and hold

Hard-pressed senior managers, desperate to recruit and retain talent are just having to revise the ways they reward. Fail to do that and doom awaits.

But just how hard are we trying out there? A CEO survey by Deloitte & Touche says that 'while CEOs attribute their success to their high-quality employees, they also recognize scarce human resources as their number one challenge in managing rapid growth'. It goes on, 'the survey results uncovered some unique ways in which technology companies are coping with finding, hiring and retaining employees, including offering sabbaticals and BMW Z3s to outstanding employees on their two-year anniversary'.

These must be good companies. These must be excellent companies. Why? Because the, now famous, 1998 study by McKinsey of 6,000 executives says that only 23 per cent strongly agree that their companies are able to attract highly talented people. Worse still, only 10 per cent questioned think that their companies hold onto the people they should and, in what McKinsey coyly term as 'perhaps more alarmingly', only 16 per cent think that their companies know who their high performers are. The final denouement is that just 3 per cent – that's 180 out of 6,000 – think that their organizations develop people effectively and move low performers out quickly. If ever there was a set of damning statistics to ponder over, these are they.

To that finding by McKinsey, we add those of search firm Korn/Ferry, whose 1998 Executive Demand Index shows demand for senior executives going through the roof and accelerating sharply (so much so that demand in the fourth quarter of 1998 was 44 per cent higher than the previous three months). Reporting on the figures, Korn/Ferry says that, 'this reflects a strong need for talented leadership to steer organizations through uncertain market conditions'. Well if only 16 per cent of 6,000 executives think that their companies know where the talent lies, they certainly need to recruit some new leadership.

What CEOs really worry about

The trouble is, according to a series of new studies, there aren't, surprise, surprise, all that many leaders out there either. When it comes to manpower, we have a global and increasingly critical shortage of everything: no technical talent, no executives, and no leaders.

Without getting into the debate of what is a business leader anyway, there are a few observations that do need to be made, when we consider the chairman or chief executive's contribution to the battle for talent. After hundreds of interviews over the past five years, I have come to one major conclusion: business leaders (those at the very top of their organizations) pay scant attention to people issues. Oh sure, we can read in every last annual report of the past three or four years that epic phrase, 'people are the most important asset of our company'. The proper, carefully considered and accurate response to that is – bullshit. Chief executives – at least those that want to continue being CEO – do not have people as one of the objects on their radar screens. If today's CEO job is a 24-hour affair, then people come into the picture at about 23.55 on a Saturday. Look at it like this:

Concern number one	Share price
Concern number two	Share price
Concern number three	Share price
Concern number four	Who shall we buy next?
Concern number five	Who's trying to buy us?
Concern number six	Getting ready for the next analysts meeting
Concern number seven	Getting ready for the next shareholders meeting

Concern number eight	Integrating the company(s) you just bought
Concern number nine	Keeping the top team happy
Concern number ten	Worrying about your retained hobby from your days as marketing director (tennis, golf or opera)
Concern number eleven	'What do you mean we keep losing good people? Go out and buy some more!'

While you might think this exaggerated, go out and ask a few CEOs to tell you candidly what their priorities are and see where people come in the list. You'll be as surprised as I was.

Surround yourself with excellence

Having spent a long time studying today's corporation, it is pretty clear that the successful CEO just hasn't got the time – in the complex world he or she occupies – to worry about people. Just as few pass judgement on every product, so they expect competent, people-oriented staffers to worry about the talent. The best they can do, it would seem,

the CEO of the global corporation has to delegate people issues

is to ensure that they have surrounded themselves with excellence. The CEO of the global corporation has to delegate people issues. All CEOs can hope to do is make certain that it is a focus of their top teams. But unless it is up there as one of the critical issues it might not get discussed and acted upon until it is too late.

Looked at in this light the McKinsey report makes frightening sense. And, if further evidence were needed, a study I carried out for the Economist Intelligence Unit (EIU) in 1998, *Building and Retaining Global Talent*, paralleled the McKinsey view. Based on face-to-face interviews with more than 150 CEOs and senior HR professionals in Europe, Asia and the US, it revealed what I then described as a 'somewhat depressing picture'. That picture has since got considerably darker as the war clouds have gathered.

What the EIU report did was produce seven pieces of critical evidence that the battles for talent were only just beginning. But there were very clear indications that the skirmishes and guerilla campaigns of today were going to turn into set-piece battles tomorrow. The key findings of the report are as follows.

- Few companies were systematically organized to meet global business challenges.
- Few companies were (despite their protestations and posturing) truly global in their ideas, attitudes, culture or people.
- Organizations were just getting to the starting gate in building global management talent pools. Most reported that it was a hard, uphill task and the tendency was to fudge it slightly and concentrate (in reality) on regionalization.
- Corporations were still failing horribly in their attempts to identify high-flyers in any systematic or consistent way. Even worse, their preparation and re-entry procedures for expatriate managers were still in the organizational stone age.
- Top business executives pay lip-service to the concept of getting new, different kinds of managers into the business to give new, much needed perspectives – but it doesn't happen in reality. Reality is, they hire a young clone of themselves and their colleagues.
- There was a worrying tendency to think that throwing money at a people problem would solve it, despite growing evidence to the contrary. Organizations in a hurry were buying companies and people, without regard to cultural fit. Not surprisingly, people were voting with their feet and leaving – there is no evidence to show that this trend is in any way in remission.
- Firms were failing to secure their people in the longer term and were equally poor in promoting people to challenging, career-stretching jobs. Result? In a tightening talent market, headhunters were sweet-talking them away to new, exciting positions in rival corporations.

Making the same mistakes

Two years on, the talent drought has got considerably worse and little is being done to change it. Corporation after corporation is still making the same fundamental mistakes listed above.

- Succession plans become a joke, because they cannot keep up with departures. Compensation structures creak and groan as all the new hires huddle at the top of the upper quartile, inviting envy and abuse from those below working for a fifth, a quarter or a third less.

- Former downsized middle managers are urged to return as part-time 'consultants' at daily fees that are two and three times their annual salary just a few years ago.

- Headhunters are briefed to scour the globe for people ('as long as they are not too different, of course'). 'We don't have a job for them, but when you find good people, we'll hire them anyway'.

- Managers spend hours in appraisal sessions and 360 degree feedback, to discover no one ever used it and that Charlie Smith, who was universally disliked, was promoted personally by the chairman of the board who met him in the men's toilets! (This is a true story.)

If you think all that is mad, don't dwell on the fact that one of the world's biggest banks has hired personal investment counsellors to help its traders deal with money issues. Don't be amazed, shocked or horrified that a 26-year-old Wall Street dealer committed suicide and was found to own three Mercedes-Benz cars – the most used of which had 150 miles on the clock. Don't feel a sense of 'Wow really!', when you realize that in Silicon Valley geniuses in

former downsized middle managers are urged to return as consultants at daily fees that are two and three times their annual salary of a few years ago

their mid-20s are being bought and sold like baseball stars for the same kind of fees. The reason for this is that you don't just hire someone away with an offer of salary and bonus, you have to buy their stock too. With some of these Valley start-ups splitting stock every six months or so, kids who look almost too young to drive are pocketing $10 million to be 'sprung' from their jobs into new ones, where they will go on earning huge financial rewards until their talent dries up or they 'crash' like their hard drives with the California virus.

Who's a winner in the war?

When lunacy strikes there is always a winner. This time it appears on the surface to be the executive search firms. But a quick look can be very deceptive. Actually, it's those people who always win – the lawyers. Want to hire your rival's CEO? Well the importance of the transaction can be gauged (and a lot of egos massaged into the bargain) by the number of law firms it takes to conclude the deal (which is known in headhunt-speak as 'unsticking' the candidate). If you are not in the big league it takes two firms (one for each side). If you are a mega-buck buy, it takes a minimum of three. The third is hired to ensure fair play by the other two. Perhaps someone should write a book about why law firms are successful. They often appear to be atrociously managed, arrogant and not user-friendly. Or maybe this is the norm for business in general and why loyalty is at such a low ebb and opportunism is the trend.

Managing at a hectic pace

One of the things that seems to have happened is that business has just got too complex for individuals to manage all of the bits and pieces, especially those pieces with heads and hearts. Add to that complexity the greater pressure on time and it is no surprise that even the best intentioned managers don't always (or can't always) follow their own high standards.

Rob Kuijpers, the chief executive of express delivery group DHL is one of the most honest, straightforward managers you will ever meet. Dutch by birth and a terrific sportsman (including playing for his country in Davis Cup matches) he epitomizes the ideal, intelligent, well-rounded manager. But he admits that, in the hectic pace of covering a vast array of countries and offices, people issues can get brushed to the back of the agenda. 'You arrive somewhere and you sit

if the CEO and his team refuse to roll up their sleeves, then problems will be difficult to fix

in an office all day and you fight fires with the local management. About eight at night all the fires are out and you get back on the plane home and say, "we never discussed that succession plan or that performance review". So you do what everyone else often does, but won't admit to, you do it on the plane home, when you are tired and lack objectivity.'

If CEOs and their teams refuse to roll up their sleeves and get their hands dirty and do what one described as 'HR's job', then problems will be difficult to fix. But again, in interview after interview, it is clear to see that senior managers just don't know what the new generations they are trying to entice really want. This is not surprising really. If you are sitting on a couple of million dollars of stock options – as thousands and thousands of 50-year-old managers are – you cannot relate to the lifestyle needs of a bright 23-year-old graduate, who says that he or she wants to work for you but only nine to five and never on weekends. The disconnect between generations is huge and potentially damaging. That is why those that will ultimately win the people wars are those companies with the flexible work patterns to change the way they do business and how the people in their businesses work.

Rob Kuijpers is honest, but in today's hard-charging corporations that sort of late at night, back-of-an-envelope decision making is often the only way to get the job done. So when junior and middle managers say that top managers don't care, and don't know where talent is they are probably right. But, I believe, in many cases it is a sin of omission, based on a lack of time.

However, it would seem that we are running out of time, and unless savvy CEO's in McKinsey's words, 'elevate talent management to a burning corporate priority', many organizations will wallow in the heavy seas forecast for the future, unless people, not just money and marketshare are on the daily agenda for action.

The turn-off factor

As yet another study – this time by the Roffey Park Management Institute in the UK reports, 'it seems clear that the implications of the management of intellectual capital in the post-industrial revolution age have not yet been fully grasped by some managers. The "turn-off" factor of inappropriate management styles is a primary reason for people wishing to leave their organizations. The challenge for managers is to be able to harness employ-ees' initiative and commitment through appropriate support and direction. The increasing complexity of work and the real employability of people with the relevant knowledge skills, suggests that employees will be unlikely to tolerate working conditions which do not satisfy their needs. People are making themselves increasingly employable and many of the respondents to our survey are actively considering leaving their organizations. Their enhanced skills – including strategic thinking – and their recognition of the importance of managing their own career suggest that – more than last year – people believe that they have a choice. Organizations wishing to retain their knowledge workers cannot afford to ignore these messages.'

Getting top management to see the facts

We need to find better, innovative ways to manage this issue if we are going to successfully win the wars to come. A starting place may well be hitting top management over the head with facts that they simply cannot ignore. One person who turned people into a highly emotive issue at her company is Nancy Kravcisin-McClain, divisional vice-president HR for Abbott Laboratories in Chicago. Tired of getting little recognition for people-related issues, she developed the novel idea of putting a price on the head of the top 1,500 people in the company. This got general management's atten-tion as they began to realize just what could happen if top performing talent walked out of the door (in lost business, wobbly alliances, unhappy cus-tomers and cost of replacement). Her idea of turning people into numbers worked, it forced an assessment of reality.

In a similar exercise in a European company, senior managers found to their amazement that one of their top 100 marketers was in fact listed on the succession plan of 17 different people (there had been no cross-checking across countries and regions). The only problem was that he was 63 years old and about to retire. Elsewhere, but only in private, senior managers admit that their succession plans are full of holes. When headhunters are also involved, that plan will soon be unusable – if it is not already.

So what do you do when your succession plan is in tatters and there is no relief in sight? We've already mentioned that the price of graduates is soaring and buying bright, brand new talent is getting ever more expensive and will continue to be so. Women, minorities and the greying population are three sources of talent which may be insufficiently utilised at present.

What about women?

Whatever anyone says, women are still being overlooked for promotion. Put simply, most organizations are refusing to recognize the fact that around 50 per cent of most populations are women. Although we hear stories that women will fit better into the new, kinder, caring organization (which we are still looking for in any numbers, by the way), the truth is that in most industries women do not progress above certain grades. It is so rare that when they do, it makes front page news and cover stories in the business magazines. Carly Fiorina of Hewlett Packard (who was described on her appointment from AT&T in July 1999 as an 'outside the box candidate'), or Marjorie Scardino of Pearson are just two cases in point.

Interestingly, people in industries that seem to naturally reject women in senior positions seem to think it is peculiar to their business alone. This is odd in the extreme, but means that industrial sectors like financial services (especially banking), automobiles, transportation, chemicals, oil and gas, construction and even management consultancy – with a few notable exceptions – are all male dominated.

The glass wall

What this has created is a new phenomenon for women to deal with, that strikes me as very strange in a business world that admits it is critically short of talent. Although a few tough, aggressive women may have broken through the glass-ceiling into the corridors of power, they are now confronted with a new barrier – the glass wall. This is an invisible but very real barrier that prevents women from migrating outside of selected industries and job specs.

But pure male prejudice aside, there are, it seems, very real issues that are preventing most women taking up the reins of power and most come down to the issue of children. Time after time in interviews, executives (all male) will tell you that the child issue is the one that is most difficult to resolve. First women leave the workforce and miss out on changing technologies, which is a more and more critical issue as technology swallows up large pieces of all our jobs. Then, with children, they become reluctant to travel for longer than a few days (a real problem in this business world of cross-cultural project teams and task forces). Other issues are their need to stay at home if a child is sick and their reluctance to work late when their colleagues do. Despite the fact that some companies have made great strides in facing up to these issues in the belief that they will secure talent they would otherwise lose, most organizations are still not trying very hard. Many say that the issue solves itself. Anecdotal evidence suggests that, even today, in marriages of business professionals it is nearly always the woman that sacrifices her career for her partner's advancement. According to Amsterdam-based search consultant for Russell Reynolds, Jacques Bouwens, 'At a certain point it seems that man and wife sit down and decide what happens next. Ninety-nine times out of a hundred they choose to go with the man's career.' Guy Mollett, a management development adviser to Volkswagen, sees the problems of combining a managerial job and raising children but concludes that companies can make it work if they want to. 'Given the facilities today to buy child-minding services and hopefully the help of their male partners, the "real reason" not to promote women to top jobs lies elsewhere.'

The Men's Club

Mollett doesn't say where elsewhere is, but the answer is simple in the extreme. It's just that in some companies (never mind the rights or wrongs of it) the Men's Club is going to take a long, long time to burn down. So amid a battle for talent, business after business is ignoring a large number of potentials. Women, it seems, have their own battle for recognition that even this increasing shortage shows little sign of helping them to win.

> in some companies, the Men's Club is going to take a long, long time to burn down

Minorities

It is a similar story with minorities. Token positions abound, especially in the US. But in Europe – despite decades of so-called guest-workers from countries like Turkey, Greece, Morocco, Algeria and the Southern European countries like Italy, Spain and Portugal – there are still very clear demarcation lines that are not crossed. How this will change remains to be seen as the grandchildren of the first émigrés graduate. At present, they are largely disadvantaged as far as entry to major global corporations goes; advancement is slow – at best.

The 'scrap-heap' generation

Conversely, the 'scrap-heap' generation of former middle managers are hugely back in favour. In fact the fastest growing age group coming into employment in the US is the over 50s. There are two reasons for this:

- the sheer shortage of workers is making companies reluctantly pick up the phone and ask former employees to return
- the discovery that, in their rush to downsize, companies threw the aging babies out with the bathwater and a huge amount of corporate knowledge was sacrificed.

As Liam Fahey, a feisty, outspoken professor at Cranfield School of Management has concluded, 'the most dangerous thing in business these days is a newly qualified MBA with a lap-top full of software – they just don't know enough to make the right decisions'. Adds Didier Pattyn, an HR professional in Europe with white goods maker Whirlpool, 'A lot of companies, aware that they just threw out a lot of knowledge, are bringing these people back as coaches and mentors, because they realize that younger people can learn from them.'

But it isn't all that easy to get people back. As one of Europe's leading outplacement experts, Win Nyström, who has seen more than his share of the hurt that mindless downsizing can bring, says, 'There is no doubt that there are more and more opportunities for the older manager to come back and make a meaningful contribution. The only trouble is that they have probably been hurt at least once before, so they are going to want a lot of guarantees before they sign up.'

Voluntary simplicity

What this has led to is corporations paying through the nose as no longer loyal, former employees exact a premium price for their knowledge and their labour. As many recruiters point out, a lot of these people neither need nor want to return to the status quo they had before they received the pink slip in the mail. Most have a spouse working, most have found another job or set up in business for themselves. They, at age 50 and over, have finally created the lifestyle that Generation X is now demanding. And in case this sounds just too easy, US commentators already have a phrase for it: 'voluntary simplicity'. Workers, right across the age spectrum – largely based on what has been done to them historically – are seeking ways to simplify their lives. They are declining promotions and transfers, refusing to work late and basically earning money on their own terms. Mindless downsizing finally created a new generation of workers that goes all the way from people in their first job experience to those of 50 plus. All expect something better than in the past; and they expect to be paid for it.

So here we have another clue to the people wars – they are going to be expensive.

- *Graduates* – who have a much better sense of their value than their parents ever did – are demanding and getting high start-up salaries and the benefits that *they* want (e.g. time off, a proper work/life balance and challenge).
- *Specialists* – who are intelligent and can read the signs of trouble – are a fluid group who are not disloyal while they are employed by a company, but will move at the drop of a stock price or a better offer – in cash, prestige or work challenges.
- *High potentials* – who, if you can't track their needs and desires on a minimum of a quarterly basis, may well take an offer from a prowling competitor. The motto is 'use them or lose them', and companies that want to win must meet that challenge.
- *The Grey Panthers* – once smart managers whose egos have been battered and bruised by what big business did to them. They will come back to work on their own terms, which will mean flexibility and a price that will have to be paid (also, these grey-hairs may be the only talent you can get in the coming years, so treat them well this time, please).

Businesses converge on same talent

Wherever you look, shortages abound and the prices for talent are going up. Headhunters I talked to say that estimates from their clients forecast that up to 70 per cent of current executives will leave their present employment for pastures new over the next three years (let's hear it for stock options as a way to hold people!). At that pace the only advantages, the only success factors will be how much longer you can keep top talent than your competitors and how quickly you can plug the holes left by the talent that

up to 70 per cent of current executives will leave for pastures new over the next three years

leaves. Remember the human resource cupboards of corporate America and corporate Europe are empty. The days when readymade, well-trained, culturally acceptable successors, who knew the business intimately were waiting in the wings have gone (deputy general managers, assistant directors of marketing and finance, are all gone). And, as the recruiters point out, so many businesses now converge and commingle that it is impossible to recruit in the old ways. Marketers leave Procter & Gamble for bankers HSBC, IBMers head for MasterCard, Heinz' top marketer goes to Citicorp. Moves like these are testament to the fact that anyone can move, almost anywhere. The organizational box has vanished along with a great many of the people.

More people to go

Sadly, there's a great many more people to go. As corporations continue merger mania and restructuring, staff at all levels become vulnerable. BP Amoco, Exxon Mobil, Daimler-Benz Chrysler, Deutsche Bank Bankers Trust, Citicorp Travelers, Total Petrofina, Hoechst Rhone Poulenc, Seagram Polygram, Zeneca Astra, all these and more will mean job losses.

But demographics and the great need for people should suck up most of those who get sidelined very quickly indeed. In fact, not getting in and hiring straight out of some of these corporations may be the greatest folly. Never mind waiting until the outplacement people call you and say they have a bunch of process engineers, go out and look for yourself. While interviewing in Silicon Valley, I was told by the head of Sun Microsystems corporate university Sun U, 'that if we find someone lying outside our offices and they can fog a mirror, meaning they're alive, we'll hire them'. The joke on the streets of New York is that in the old days you always kept to the outside of the sidewalk in case you got mugged from a doorway. Today they say, someone will drag you in that same doorway and put you to work.

The skill set is vital

True there have been many, many situations across America, Asia and Europe where older industries have finally given up trying to keep people in jobs – often with tragic consequences for the people who worked in those one-industry towns. Much of Europe's chronic, lingering unemployment stems from this. Much of the rest – although politicians seem reluctant to admit it – comes from the booming black economy that doesn't file statistics to respective governments of how many people it employs but it's a huge number and is increasing steadily.

But for those of us with skill sets that can be utilized, the year 2000 is an exciting time to be at work.

A few years ago the Dutch aeroplane manufacturer Fokker (then owned by Daimler Benz) finally gave up trying to fight the competition. It was the end of the aircraft industry in the Netherlands. The Dutch government, as a matter of national pride, moved mountains to find a buyer but none appeared. In the Dutch press, it was a tragedy played

> they go the extra mile, they build security and they take away *the fear*

out on the front pages day after day. The reality was very different. Outside the factory gates along with the TV crews were recruiters from all over the globe. Highly trained aircraft technicians and fitters are a rare breed, the competition knew that and moved fast. Recruiters filled the local hotels and had a ball. If you were prepared to move, you had a job within 24 hours.

That's what it is all about, flexibility and seeing opportunity and also dealing with reality. If you don't intend to move ever, well don't go out and play and don't complain either. Survival and success in the new world of work demands flexibility from both sides. It also demands its own kind of

GMs – the real battleground

IT personnel may be at an all-time premium, but the toughest of the talent wars at present is the battle – a few rungs up the hierarchy ladder – for general managers (GMs). Once thought of as has-beens, as specialists from engineers to marketing to finance were seen as the way to go for the thoroughly modern corporation, GMs have had a huge comeback, especially since the world decided that globalization was the way forward. Corporations have quickly discovered that to secure new business ventures, GMs, who have a complete knowledge of the business, are the number one weapon to have on your team. Consequently, businesses the world over are spending vast sums to initially recruit and then develop a cadre of GMs (again, downsizing efforts of a few years ago have taken their toll and often interrupted the supply of new GMs, just as the world placed a new priority label on them).

Why are they so in demand?

- They are the ideal weapon in the corporate armoury for conquering new markets. Knowing all aspects of the business (because they have worked their way through finance, marketing, production, distribution, IT, HR and so forth) they can hit the ground running and just get on with it.

- They know enough about a company's operations that they can cross over from core business to core business. Highly talented GMs are universal operators able to manage in the most diverse operations. This is especially useful in a world governed by mergers and acquisitions.

- They are the ideal ambassadors to forge alliances and joint-venture links, a critical need for most organizations today. Their encyclopedic knowledge of the business is again paramount.

- They are able to be sent out and support the needs of a corporation's customers. So many contracts today call for global support and service. GMs with their overall understanding are ideal for this role.

- They are ably equipped to manage in the modern world governed by complexity and ambiguity.

The only real trouble is that – except in a few companies – GMs are in short supply. This has led to several interesting developments.

First, companies are finding that they are having to 'take on the risk' and move their general managers into positions of real responsibility (running a business unit) earlier and earlier in their careers. You have to have the courage to stretch your people, otherwise they will leave.

Second, they are prize pickings for headhunters, many of whom have permanent assignments from clients to search out and hire as many GMs as they can lay their hands on. The upshot of all this is that you have to constantly prime the pump for new GM talent – knowing that some of them are not going to make it into the places you had planned for them.

With whole industries, not to mention industrial and management associations of nations as diverse as Singapore, Germany and France, publicly stating that they have huge shortages of general managers, especially those that can operate globally, it is hardly surprising that these people can virtually name their price. You had better be able to make them happy, or they won't be around for long.

Mother Duck

I have called this 'the Mother Duck Syndrome.' Assume a mother duck has 12 ducklings, you know that through all kinds of attrition and accident she is only going to end up with two or three – the toughest or the smartest (or a combination of both). The skill lies in looking at those 12 ducklings and deciding which ones you *really* want to keep. If you can do that and you make special provision for their development, and protection, you can afford to lose the rest, hard as it is.

Out in the marketplace, everyone is screaming for candidates with GM potential or experience – they can virtually write their own contracts. But they have a very strong sense of their own worth, so you have to put some sophisticated reward instruments into place if you want them to stay. That doesn't just mean money or other benefits.

Most highly qualified GMs rate the challenge of the job above all else, so that factor must live up to its promise. Flexibility is key. Many organizations are only now coming to grips with the idea that GMs with a major area to cover will live where they choose, not necessarily where the company is located. Additionally, we are seeing the arrival of net compensation (especially in Europe) where a candidate will demand and get a sum net of taxes and other deductions. He or she doesn't mind how that is worked out; that's the company's problem. The candidate just wants to get on with the job.

In winning the people wars a key strategy to take on board is 'make it easy for talent to do the job'. They don't want to worry about pay and conditions, they want to hit the ground running. If you are going to get what you want out of them, you had better make it work – there are always others looking for an unhappy GM to join them.

And a final tip, if you meet a good GM, on a plane, a train or at a conference, you'll know in about five seconds just how good he or she is. Don't hesitate, hire them – or someone else will.

loyalty. The attitude is 'I'll work hard for you as long as you pay me the going rate, challenge me and keep my skills ahead of the marketplace; fail to do that, and I am out of here.' And if you get a little more than that, hiring heaven.

There's a box in the *Fortune* story on the best places to work in America that speaks volumes. It's titled 'Job Security' and it has just three points:

- 3 of the 100 best have formal, no-layoff policies
- another 37 informally maintain such policies
- 74 have never had a mass lay-off.

Now you know why people want to work in these companies. They go the extra mile, they build in security and they take away *the fear. The fear* (i.e. losing your job) is cited as the number one concern and number one stress creator amongst workers at all levels in all sorts of societies and geographies. Remove *the fear* and you are well on the way to really rewriting the employment contract.

New-age companies

Look down the *Fortune* and other 'best of breed' listings and you'll find they have one thing in common. I call them 'new-age' companies. They operate under different rules from the past (and they never read the old command and control, hire and fire rulebook anyway). Few of them carry much in the way of cultural or emotional baggage associated with a long corporate history, that they feel they need to maintain and acts as a constraint to their ability to move quickly and strategically. They and their people are totally at home anywhere. Most of all, they have always had a constant need for talent, because they are growing at a very rapid rate indeed. Some are hi-tech, some are low-tech. All manage in new ways. EDS, DHL, Microsoft, Nike, GAP and SAP are all examples of these new-age knowledge-based companies where people matter because they are the business. Today, they are competing for the best worldwide talent with a host of venerable (and

> they never read the old command and control, hire and fire rulebook anyway

vulnerable) giants like Philips, Siemens, BMW, GM, IBM, Procter & Gamble and Sony. Also in the frame are the major consultants whose growth is astronomic and seemingly endless and whose appetite for warm, thinking bodies is legendary. Behind these groups are the fast-track, exciting start-ups that many want to work for. All of these are competing for talent, not always the same talent, but a lot of it falls into very grey areas these days. Who will win and how they are setting the traps to hire and hold people is revealed in the chapters to come.

It's a killer of a business

Workers secluded in their – or increasingly their client's – offices, or sitting snarled up in the daily commute may feel that life could be improved, but most would say that they are doing better than the toilers of the past. Agrarian workers had it hard in all weathers; physically, it was tough. But, according to polls all over the world, if you want to keep your people productive and happy, you had better carefully consider their wellbeing. To start with, the workplace is a dangerous location to occupy.

First it's literally deadly. According to the International Labor Organization (ILO), every year there are over one million fatalities in the workplace and 250 million job injuries result in sick leave. That translates out to 685,000 injuries a day and 3,000 deaths (two every minute). Asbestos poisoning is the number one killer, causing 10,000 worker's deaths annually.

Stress

Then there's stress. The New York-based American Institute of Stress, say that stress costs at least $200 billion a year to business in the form of reduced productivity, absences and lawsuits.

Findings by management consultants, Runzheimer International, in San Diego, would stop most sane people ever boarding a plane again. Their survey of business travellers revealed that many are stressed out and suffering from fatigue, loss of humour, aching arms and legs, paranoia, memory loss, hyperactivity and crying. Most travellers blame the airlines.

In Germany, the Training, Research and Technology Ministry says that 20 per cent of workers constantly suffer from time stress, while 17 per cent say they work too much overtime and 11 per cent say that their stress is caused by conflicting orders from their bosses. Still in Germany, the Bad Harzburg Manager's Association quizzed 350 German and Austrian executives to discover that a staggering 75 per

▶

cent reported they were under too much pressure. Worse, 83 per cent said they did not understand the reasons for the changes they were being subjected to by their employers. Also in Germany, 25 per cent of the nation's managers have been found to be in poor health after the examination of the medical check-ups of 1,000 managers. Thirty per cent were overweight and 21 per cent complained of poor mental health, including irritability, depression, insomnia and exhaustion.

Next door, the Swiss are in serious trouble too. One study reports that 10–15 per cent of all suicides are due to physiological persecution in the workplace.

In the Netherlands, the statistics bureau found that 10 per cent of Dutch workers are physically and emotionally exhausted, while 25 per cent of construction workers risk falling ill because of excessive workloads.

In the UK, stress on the job is now such an issue that stress counselling is now offered by many companies. The consulting firm, The Hay Group, surveyed 235 companies and found that more than 50 per cent give help on stress issues to their staff, up from 20 per cent eight years ago.

A nationwide survey of 9,000 workers in Canada found that most stress was created in a job where you had no power to change how you worked or who you worked with. Over 40 per cent of the people polled said that this induced high levels of stress.

Points to ponder

- In a sellers' market top talent makes its own recruitment rules – they won't follow yours.

- There is a major need to put more emphasis on graduate recruitment to fill the gaps in the talent line-up.

- The public sector already has been bruised as employees leave for lucrative private sector jobs.

- Reward them, challenge them, be flexible and add a great work environment – then you might just keep them.

- Matching the right people to your business is critical. Don't hire and hope – it doesn't work.

- In the fast moving, show-me-the-money environment, offering promotions if you work hard isn't buying you anything except instant derision and mistrust.

- If only 180 out of 6,000 executives say that their companies develop people effectively, maybe we should ask ourselves, not what are we doing wrong, but are we doing anything right?

- Companies that win big know one thing others don't. They take away *the fear* and replace it with a feeling of security.

2 | Aspects of war

consternation and confusion in the ranks

There is very little difference in people. But that little difference makes a big difference. The little difference is *attitude*. The big difference is whether it is positive or negative.

W Clements Stone, president, Combined Insurance

If the army is confused and suspicious, the neighboring states will surely create trouble . . . this is like saying a confused army provides victory for the enemy

Sun Tze's *The Art of War*

There's a huge paradox confronting large sections of the business world today. It goes something like this: 'we are desperate to seek out the very best people to help us grow and prosper, having done this we then terrorize them, by systematically lying to them and creating an atmosphere of fear and loathing, in which trust is a commodity that is in ever shorter supply'. The upshot of this is that today in many industries we have a bunch of street-wise mercenaries work-

we have a bunch of street-wise mercenaries working for us, who have zero loyalty

ing for us, who have zero loyalty and are ready to flee at the first opportunity.

Does that sound terrible? Of course it does. And while it doesn't apply to every organization it does apply to far too many. Possibly worse still, in my research I have come across the odd fact that you can have wild enthusiasm and super-motivated employees in one division or country and a bunch of whining, clock watchers in another.

This is most in evidence for the average businessperson using an airline. Fly to Frankfurt on the red-eye special with the world's favourite airline and have a super experience. Come back that evening and have a totally different experience that thoroughly depresses you. Two flights, same plane, same seat, same plastic food, totally different service. Reason? One group are miffed over rumours of planned redundancies, hate their shift boss and feel overlooked for promotions. Crew two, for one reason or another feel completely different, work enthusiastically as a team and like their jobs.

In one company that I have worked with, a software developer, one subsidiary was so full of clock-watchers that the car park was empty at one minute to nine and one minute past five exactly; 50 km away at another unit, you couldn't get in the car park at six in the morning and it was still full at midnight. In the second group there was a buzz of excitement and a string of 'walk the talk' managers – it physically showed. In fact, when the company got into some short-term difficulties they issued a group-wide memo cancelling Christmas parties. The head of the motivated business unit promptly paid for it out of his own pocket.

So, here's a tip. Next time you wonder how well an organization is performing, don't hire expensive consultants, just do the car park test. In one case I personally experienced, I couldn't get into the car park at three o'clock on a Friday afternoon for all the employees driving out of the exit *and* the entry in their eagerness to leave.

The art of being out of touch

Being good at the surprisingly prevalent core skill of demotivating your employees does not apply to everyone, but it is present in a lot of corporations who are paying lip service to the idea that people are important. What's more, research in Europe and the US consistently shows that employees think most of their top managers stink. As the McKinsey research mentioned in chapter one pointed out, most managers wouldn't recognize talent if they fell over it.

Further evidence that top managers are seriously out of touch with the minions toiling away below comes from a 13-country study by Gemini Consulting. Polling workers in ten European countries, the US, Russia and Japan, it concluded that 'employees really want, fundamentally similar things from their jobs, regardless of culture'. Sadly, what the employee wants, he or she is not getting. Gemini Consulting's chairman, Pierre Hessler says that, 'the study showed us that workers feel employers are not meeting core needs'. Gemini went on to suggest that, 'in an economy where knowledge, information and the quality of workers are vital to competitive advantage, this failure to meet employees' needs could represent a threat to competitiveness itself'. He continued, 'Those employers that re-examine traditional workplace models – especially in terms of time, opportunities and incentives – and build a truly two-way employment contract, will be the ones with the best chance to thrive today and in the future.'

Analyze the gaps

And what did employees from Kobe to Kiel, from Moscow to Miami, say were the missing pieces? 'Sizeable gaps between what workers say they want and what they say they are getting from current jobs. Among the largest gaps are in the areas of providing good pay or salary, the ability to balance work and personal life and the feeling that they are secure in the future – the attributes that workers said they value most.' In a similar study in Australia by outplacement firm DBM, '54 per cent of employees believe there is a lack of close alignment between employees' personal goals and the goals of the organization'. The organization

a lack of close alignment between employees' personal goals and the goals of the organization

Work Family Directions found that nine out of ten workers questioned singled out the ability to balance work with their private life as the key factor in determining their commitment to their employer. While another research project by New Ways to Work in the UK revealed that 50 per cent of the British workforce report coming home totally exhausted.

If that isn't bad enough, the Gemini study ends with the grim discovery that just '27 per cent of the sample of 10,339 feel that their employers are preparing them for a good future', a key concern as many cited job security as a necessary attribute to the job. DBM's study in Australia reported that '43 per cent were neither encouraged nor provided with the time and resources to develop their career plans'.

But there is evidence to show that helping your employees achieve their personal business goals pays off – particularly in securing talent. A survey by telecommunications giant, AT&T showed that 88 per cent of employees said that if the company went out of its way to accommodate their personal needs, they would go out of their way to support the company.

Why are we not learning from these statistics created by real, live workers? Add to that the fact that, as we saw in chapter one, many of the *Fortune* list of the best places to work in America, are offering some level of job security, but around the world only a quarter of companies are perceived as taking this into consideration, and you begin to see that there are some double standards and diverse ways of doing business.

And the real extent of the lack of care and concern by top managers is much higher. Remember, these surveys look at mainstream business, not the smaller enterprise, which often has far worse employment practices.

A similar study to the one by Gemini, but confined to the UK, was carried out in 1999 by Roffey Park Management Institute. Of 350 managers, 57 per cent said that they faced 'dilemmas in their careers, mainly due to poor management, a lack of recognition, lack of opportunities and little chance of promotion'. In the same survey 86 per cent of those polled said that their 'workload had increased over the last two years, necessitating longer working hours'.

Making sacrifices

Further results from the Roffey Park study, show that this paradox between wanting to hire in good talent and then treating it badly is very much alive and well. Fully 85 per cent of the Roffey Park poll felt that it was 'necessary to make sacrifices' to meet career goals and expectations of employers. Almost two-thirds said that these sacrifices 'had involved missing out on time with their children', while a third said that 'their physical health had been sacrificed for career success'. A further 20 per cent had 'sacrificed a relationship for a career' and others said that relationships had been put under considerable strain. A majority (62 per cent) of those questioned felt that 'it had been necessary to make these sacrifices primarily because the organizational culture had expected it'.

In the US sacrificing career for other priorities, like having a child, has given rise to a new word: 'sequencing'. Mothers-to-be who drop in and out of careers are said to be 'sequencing'. Such is the pressure – especially to keep up with emerging technology in the workplace – that the period away from work is getting shorter. Quoted in the *Wall Street Journal* in

May 1999, Ed Heresniak, a Boston-based management consultant observed that 'the metronome is clicking about four times faster than it used to click, product life cycles have shrunk. You can't truly focus on child rearing for 24 months and not get left in the dust.' Signs are that the same problem is getting to

> You can't truly focus on child rearing for 24 months and not get left in the dust.

Europe, home of mandatory maternity leave. Ambitious for their careers, more and more executive mothers are changing the diapers with one hand and tapping out e-mails on their lap-tops at home with the other.

The search for true work/life balance

Interestingly, those in the Roffey Park survey who said they had sacrificed their private lives for business said that they regretted some of that, but those that had sacrificed business life for their private lives weren't totally happy either – dwelling on what might have been. The conclusion that the report's authors came to was that few of us in business today have ever found a way to create a really satisfactory work/life balance.

But if we are to get to a point where we are able to give a positive response to the question, 'Is this place where I work, or this organization I work for, really worthy of my investment?' corporations are going to have to do things very differently. The truth is that some will and some won't. Therefore, some will win and some will lose.

Nick Winkfield heads the European operation of Wirthlin Worldwide, a global market research firm, and has spent years conducting and analyzing the results of employment surveys around the world. He has ceased long ago to be shocked by the disparity between what the employer perceives and what the employee expects. 'Survey after survey', he says, 'show that trust levels are worst between front line employees and top level executives. This is especially true in a world of constant change, mergers and acquisitions.'

> a chilling trend in the total collapse of loyalty and trust between employer and employee

Winkfield points out that a recent US survey shows a chilling trend in the total collapse of loyalty and trust between employer and employee. It is now so bad that some of us are unsure if it will ever come back.

The survey found that:

- 65 per cent of US workers say employers are less loyal to them than five years ago;
- 78 per cent of US middle managers say employers are less loyal to them than five years ago;
- 58 per cent of US employers say workers are less loyal to them than five years ago;
- 80 per cent of US employers say middle managers are less loyal to them than five years ago.

With the merger and acquisition mania just beginning to hot up and predictions of industrial downturns just around the corner you may well wonder. What is obvious from the figures above, is that trawling for talent is going to be hard work: tying down your talent and keeping it happy

80 per cent of the middle managers you are trying to attract and retain don't trust you

once you have found it is going to be harder still.

From this, it can be concluded that 80 per cent of the middle managers you are trying to attract and retain don't trust you, which means that their loyalty is fleeting at best.

What people worry about

And, in a world that is in a constant state of change, with organizational upheaval the norm, trust is harder to build anyway. Remember, as you face up to yet another reorganization, acquisition or takeover that people in *your* business, the senior and the junior, the old hands and the new arrivals, the enthusiastic and the time servers, all have the following in common to a greater or lesser degree.

- Fear of the unknown: 'what does all this mean?'
- Anxiety over the future: 'will I keep my job?'
- Nostalgia for the old days: 'it used to be a fun place to work'.
- Hostility to the new: 'it'll never work, you know'.

- Resistance to the new name, structure, manager: 'why did they have to bring him in here?'
- Resentment over loss of identity/status: 'I didn't work here for 20 years to be treated like this.'

Wirthlin's Nick Winkfield has compiled a list of the issues that middle managers (those that are left) worry about 'all day and every day, going to work, at work and coming home from work'. They are a stark reminder that if we are to have and hold talent we had better get to work – fast – on addressing many of these concerns.

In order of concern, middle managers (and you can include specialists in this list as well) worry about the following.

- Job survival (this is in first, second and third place).
- Financial security: 'will I be able to keep up the payments on my house, car, school fees?'
- Being re-engineered again.
- Coping with flat structures: no infrastructure, no support, e.g. in our company, 'empowerment means I'm doing all the jobs the people they fired used to do'.
- Keeping up to date with IT: another software programme to learn.
- Solving problems *not* looking for opportunities: no time to do anything but the basic job.
- Avoiding risk: don't make mistakes or do anything that will make you too visible.
- Their self-image as executives: not the same status or ego-booster as in the past, we don't even dress differently from the rest anymore, thanks to five day casual-wear rules.

Trust builders and trust busters

A study by the American Management Association (AMA) across the US in 1998 backs up this data. The AMA looked at what were the trust builders between employer and employee (what really got them motivated and produced a spark in the dying embers of loyalty) and what were the trust busters (the wet blanket on the fires of motivation). Here are the top four in each category.

Trust busters

Erode employee motivation by:

- acting inconsistently in what you say and do
- seeking personal gain above shared gain
- withholding information
- lying or telling half-truths.

Trust builders

Boost employee loyalty by:

- maintaining integrity
- openly communicating vision and values
- showing respect for fellow employees
- focusing on shared goals.

The 'no job losses' lie

Recognize any of the factors above? Anyone who has been through a merger or acquisition will know that acting inconsistently is par for the course. The phrase in the press release, 'there will be no job losses as a result of this merger of our two great companies' has to join those classics like 'your cheque's in the post' or 'our computer is down'. It has become a cliché and no one will believe it anymore.

During my research, I amassed hundreds and hundreds of press cuttings that show organization after organization making statements that could not possibly be true. A month later a second statement announced 5,000 redundancies and a month after that, a further 2,000. Then you discover that the top ten managers have pocketed $20 million dollars each in stock dividends. How can actions like this be expected to result in long-term loyalty?

But let us not forget that very often the people that make these announcements (corporate communications or human resources usually) don't know what the truth is either. They are being fed stories that shore up the stock price or deliberately keep competitors in the dark, or maybe get key personnel to stay just a few critical weeks or months longer.

There may be a battle for talent, but there is an ever bigger and much older battle – more heady than all the money – the battle for power. CEOs may have the odd concern to keep the best people, but after a few years at the helm they get bored. They have 'been there and done that' as the phrase goes. They need excitement, they need to prove themselves and they need their egos massaged. So they take off the gloves and go and beat up some competitor. The thinking process operates as follows.

- 'Let's make the shareholders an offer they just cannot refuse.'
- 'What about the people?'
- 'Oh we'll fix that, lets just get the merger over with first.'

When it comes to exercising corporate power, many, many times people are the last thing on a CEO's mind as the excitement of the acquisition rushes to a crescendo. When you think about those mergers that don't happen, like the much publicized Glaxo Wellcome/SmithKline Beecham debacle, it is all about egos and is nothing to do with people.

When soft and hard issues collide

Organizational consultant Mark Thomas, of Performance Dynamics notes, 'Mergers and acquisitions are superb examples of soft people and hard business issues colliding in a dramatic way. The reason for this, I think, is that when a deal is engineered the only people often present are the business leaders and huge numbers of financiers and corporate lawyers. None of these people have the detailed knowledge, interest or even incentive to work through the potential people issues. The result is often chaos, big cultural clashes, losses of business and losses of talent.'

Thomas makes a vital point. Some months ago I was in the Paris headquarters of a major French firm engaged in takeover warfare with a rival. Proudly, one of its senior strategists took me into the 'war room' where hundreds of corporate lawyers and financiers toiled, carrying out due diligence and other arcane practices of the dark world of hostile bids. These people have never met a product manager, nor seen a sales person. Their focus was on this great game. When you see hundreds of consultants like this in one room it makes you realize why takeovers cost so much in fees, there are literally millions of dollars of hourly fees being swallowed up in an ego-enabling enterprise.

The CEO's lack of compassion and interest in people-driven issues has even been turned into macabre business humour. The *Washington Post* featured a cartoon in May 1999 that showed a CEO type behind a giant desk addressing an underling with the caption, 'I told you when you joined that we were just one big family here, but as I said to my third wife . . .' The lesson is easy. A safe haven for a manager's talents today will turn into a storm-tossed ocean tomorrow: there are no hiding places, no cosy cubicles in today's corporations.

Let's say hello to human resources

Finding, nurturing and motivating talent has traditionally fallen to human resources (HR). And despite the fact that there has been a flood of corporate humour along the lines of 'people are too important to the organization to leave to HR to look after', they still seem to be the people who are expected to make it happen.

Or are they? What appears to be happening to HR is a kind of organizational metamorphosis, that some at least are going through.

As people have become more important – as knowledge workers have become more vociferous about their needs and expectations – we have seen the creation of a new breed of HR professional. Tightly focused, these people – and they are few and far between – have been able to take their ideas and abilities to the very top of the business, forcing people issues onto the strategic agenda and keeping them

being the owners of non-productive areas like payroll, training and compensation is a route to organizational oblivion

there. The very best share the corridor with the CEO, plus the heads of marketing, finance and IT: they really are accepted at the top table. Their contribution is invaluable, their advice eagerly anticipated, their future secure. To do all this, they have created a role as strategic advisers. They have been smart enough to realize long, long ago that being the owners of non-productive areas like payroll, training and compensation is a route to organizational oblivion.

Instead, they have marched to the tune of a very different drum; they know what the CEO needs. With little or no time to worry about the intricacies of finding, developing, rewarding and holding onto the best in the business, they can confidently leave the details and much of the strategy to this new organizational hero. He or she is no longer an HR professional; that isn't a cool term anymore. They have upped the stakes and grabbed a ladder further up the corporate food chain. They are well respected by their peers, very effective and well compensated.

Executives for the new corporate age

These are executives who have been self-created for the new corporate age. They carry little organizational baggage, they have an in-depth understanding of the business and they are able to fight in their corner. In summary, they are exactly what the corporation of tomorrow requires – a senior executive who knows the value of people, cares about their contribution, worries about their commitment and can sell those vital issues to the rest of top management. There is no common organizational label for these people yet, but you see them cropping up all over the place, IBM call their people mover and shaker 'VP of talent'. His name is Rick Martino and he says that his job is to 'think about people who aren't working for IBM and about people who already work here'. As an organization of 300,000, that hired 30,000 people last year out of some 800,000 applications, he has a real job to do.

IBM call their people mover and shaker 'VP of talent'

Interestingly enough, looking at new jobs, as IT becomes the dominant and real enabler of how businesses are run, look out for a top of the organization duo comprised of head of systems and head of people. And, if those two ever get together, with a morsel of marketing savvy, you will have the 21st Century CEO: technology, people and markets all in one.

What's holding back HR?

The change is happening. Companies are beginning to let people with HR thoughts into the top echelons, although with a new 'label'. However:

- it isn't happening that fast
- it isn't always HR professionals who are getting these super people-centric jobs.

Those are two main reasons for this.

- In some organizations there still seems to be a huge reluctance to let HR managers become involved in the real business of making money. As late as the end of 1998, I was in a large European company where they made a top management decision to hire a whole new group of people (200 plus software engineers). HR was not present at that decision, but they were given the order to go hire them. The order was made by phone.
- There is a new breed of manager in the hallways of corporate power. Often an MBA, they have been in line positions and they are bright enough and ambitious enough to realize that a lot of the kudos of tomorrow is going to come from being able to solve the people problems of businesses. They are the talent finders and the talent retainers, like IBM's Martino. They are immediately effective and they instinctively know how to make things work. We are seeing the evidence already. HR is becoming sidelined, it is back to opening the factory gates and collecting the sick notes, while this new, strategically focused, business-oriented, 21st Century manager is settling down at the right hand of the CEO.

There is a new breed of manager in the hallways of corporate power

HR doesn't deliver

Is this a fantasy? No way. Consider the evidence. HR as a profession – apart from a few great operators who deservedly fit into that new super organizational development (OD) category – has been on an out-of-control slide for years. Moans and groans about 'not being taken seriously' and 'not being allowed to sit at the top table' have gone unheeded by the rest of the profession. Thousands of words written in HR journals, hours of rhetoric on conferences that HR is really the chosen profession for the orga-nizational needs of the next Millennium have been totally ignored by the rest of the management firmament.

That is borne out by comments from Wim Noortman and Christian Goffin, principals of the search firm, Noortman & Goffin in Brussels, both former senior HR professionals (Noortman was head of HR for Europe, Africa, Middle East for Federal Express). Their view is that, 'HR pro-fessionals do not have the vision, nor capability to advise senior management, because they usually have not worked in line positions and have never been confronted with actual people management issues. HR people should work in the line and acquire business experience before taking on management development issues.'

And it gets worse. A study that I developed for Management Centre Europe (MCE) in 1998 on attitudes toward HR showed, that in terms of influence it had moved backwards from a similar study in 1979.

The study, *Behind the mask: a pan-European study of the atti-tudes and opinions of HR professionals and senior executives,* showed that non-HR professionals *and* HR professionals themselves have a low opinion of the function.

Asked what management disciplines were the most influential, both non-HR and HR executives plumped for marketing, the CEO's office and finance. Asked who was least influential, non-HR put HR at the bottom. HR managers were slightly kinder, they scored themselves just above logistics.

Back in 1979, in a similar survey, at least HR professionals had the confidence to put themselves in third position (in the UK and Sweden they voted themselves into second place).

So what has gone wrong? Why do HR professionals still not get the recognition they think they deserve? After all, if people power is the answer for the future, surely they should be out in the lead? The answer isn't difficult to find. In the MCE and similar surveys, line managers castigate HR professionals for continually misunderstanding and misinterpreting their needs. An innate ability to develop the wrong programme at the wrong time for the wrong reasons is a hallmark of HR activity. Having produced the wrong (often highly complex) programme, their inability to market it or communicate it to the rest of the company is legendary. Business life is moving just too fast to get it wrong.

The major criticism in the MCE survey, which polled 739 managers across Europe, was that HR does not understand the real needs of line managers and creates programmes that are so complex they are out of date before they could become effective. In today's world, annual appraisals are six months too late, salary surveys meaningless, and most hiring strategies useless. Banging the final nail in the coffin, line managers say that HR fails to communicate clearly to senior management (in the survey HR agreed that this, plus an inability to understand line manager's needs, *was* their problem).

Sticking new labels on old corporate baggage

HR keeps sticking labels on itself, in an attempt to resurrect or reinvent itself. Terms such as 'business contributor', 'employee enobler', 'quality fanatic' and 'change artist', are taken on board by personnel professionals and derided as self-important nothingness by hard-pressed line managers. Indeed, line managers scream for HR people to join them in the shell-strewn trenches of modern marketing warfare. The one phrase you here from line managers is, 'come and spend some time, and find out what I really need to do this job right'.

line managers scream for HR people to join them in the shell-strewn trenches of modern marketing warfare

Roy Williams, a management adviser to British Petroleum amongst others, spent years telling audiences of HR professionals to think about 'what table do you sit at? When you fly, do you get asked to sit with the CEO?' His attitude is, if you don't, then you are a second-class citizen and you need to push yourself to the top and get to eat at the top table. Not be showered with crumbs as they break the bread over your head. But when you get a result in a survey that HR 'creates schemes and plans that don't meet business reality', you have to begin to question the long-term nature of the role.

Glossy brochure rhetoric

Even Cranfield University and the *Financial Times* in their report, *Human Resource Excellence*, noted that 'the formal attempts to sell strategy may also be producing a form of glossy-brochure rhetoric, with resistance growing from employees who are suspicious of the attempts at marketing strategic goals to them as though they are customers without knowledge'.

All the same, the report does suggest that things just might be looking up. But my bet is that there will be a serious split between those who make it to the top tier and those who are left below supervising payroll, training and recruitment. Of course, the outsourcing phenomenon that is sweeping through most Western corporations means that areas like payroll, basic benefits, low-level recruiting and training are all being reassigned to external agencies anyway. This leaves HR people in a quandary: either move up or – in this unforgiving corporate world – move out.

Seeking line manager confidence

Having said all that, there are some HR professionals who do see – often with a righteous sense of frustration – that things could be better. Perhaps one of the problems we have in our corporations is that HR has seen the need to take great care of scarce talent for a long time and has been unable to get anyone to seriously heed the warnings. They are aware that they need to ratchet up their act to a new level and give, not just advice and counsel, but results.

Brad Thomas, a VP of Executive Resources at Citibank in New York understands only too well that for his organization to recruit and retain he needs to have the confidence of the line managers he has to support. 'We, in HR, have to demonstrate the value of what we can do', he says, 'Imagine that I am dealing with a prima donna derivative trader. His mentality is "how can you help me, when you don't know what I do?" We have to understand his job and gain his confidence.' Fellow VP, Peter Boucher agrees, 'It takes a great deal of skill to do that, we have to get across the important issues, we have to make them see that we can help them – you could say that we tell it like it is. It is either pain or gain.'

A huge selling job

Both Boucher and Thomas know that they have to gear up their selling skills to even greater heights. 'The function is going to be more and more valuable,' they say, 'so it is very important for line managers – especially senior line managers – to understand the people issues. We have to be able to fully convince top managers to be more flexible in how we employ and deal with people, otherwise we won't as an organization be able to move on and do all sorts of diverse things that will keep us competitive.'

Boucher and Thomas are, above all, pragmatists who recognize that HR hasn't been exactly at the top of everyone's thoughts in the past. 'Financial services, as a business has been a bit behind the development curve in HR', admits Thomas, 'we have tended to be reactive, rather than proactive. On that basis, we have a huge selling job still to do, to get the very real needs of our business over to managers who are concentrating 100 per cent on the business.' Boucher adds, 'We know that personal growth is the one thing that is going to keep people with us, they just want to go on doing bigger and more challenging things. We have a lot of these managers who have the experience of making a difference, and it is our job to keep a track of them and keep this happening for them – that's proactive HR in action.'

The Citibank approach of proactive HR is also the view of Gary Billings, Senior Vice President, Human Resources at Equitable, part of the global AXA financial services group. Billings, recently recruited from the advertising industry, sees the importance of 'truly adding value' by creating a dynamic HR operation, and being given the space to do that. He feels that HR has to be at the top table to make any inroads and have any influence. 'They have a high regard for where HR fits', he said, 'so when I was being recruited I made it clear that I was joining to fulfil a real role.'

Part of that role is to help the business develop its brand strategy through its people, an area where Billings' background in advertising and communications means he can make a real contribution. 'Part of my work here is not just to build a new HR infrastructure, but to act as an internal consultant and lead change management.'

This is exactly what the new generation of powerful, strategically focused human resource professionals are doing. Those that are able, that is. This is the role that they need and as long as they can produce real bottom line-linked results, this is where they should be, second guessing the CEO and adding people power to financial and marketing muscle. Of course, with this comes a problem. Anyone this good is an immediate target for eager recruiters, so how long they stay depends on the challenge they get and how that challenge is maintained.

HR strategy must be business strategy

Another long-standing HR professional who knows only too well that, 'HR strategy to be most effective has to be the business strategy', is Lance Wright, Mobil's human resources manager in Europe, Africa and the Middle East. Currently based in London, Wright is one of the corporation's longest serving and most senior Afro-American executives and has held down posts in Saudi Arabia, The Netherlands, Belgium and London. His view of what HR needs to achieve is uncompromising. 'I don't think that you can have an HR strategy, that isn't the business strategy', he says, 'that's where too many people get misdirected. It is simple: if in HR you are not following the business strategy it just won't work.'

An employee eco-system

Wright feels that organizational strategies, in a lot of cases, have to be better thought out and that we have all done a fair amount of damage to the image of business with our wanton downsizing. Now that industries are desperate for talent, he sees that we are reaping the rewards of what we have already sown.

'There is no free lunch in this world', observes Wright, 'you can't downsize and not expect it to be noticed by the relatives or friends of the victims. What we need to realize is when I say we are going to downsize, we understand that it has an impact, it sets off an employment eco-system. Downsizing doesn't just take place upstream, it affects the little fishes too.'

Wright's view, as we begin our often desperate search for new talent, is that having fired the mothers and fathers, we cannot expect the children – now of employable age – to line up for the same kind of treatment. His thought is that there is nothing much wrong with today's business graduate, just that they have 'a greater self confidence and an attitude of having the right to be challenged, stimulated, motivated and compensated'. All the same, Wright notes that we may live to regret our seeming insistence on hiring top performing graduates, 'Keep in mind', he warns, 'that we may have dug our own hole by only recruiting top MBAs who certainly have an attitude of how much they are worth and what they expect.' These are also the people who are only going to stick around as long as something is happening. They want action not words – promises won't hold them for long.

Having said that, Wright does have one concern. Very much aware that HR's role is changing, he feels it needs to sell itself as an area for career opportunity. 'I don't see evidence of people rushing out of Harvard Business School to join the HR ranks', he says. 'What we do need is some of those smart graduates going into the function.'

Merger mania or merger mess-up

Talk to human resource managers about mergers and acquisitions (M&As) and you get deep sighs, rolling of the eyes and plenty more. Anyone who's been through a merger knows that it isn't a fun experience, except for those spearheading the operation. The top CEOs and CFOs are in the throes of adrenaline-inducing decisions, for the rest, it is back to that fear of the unknown.

> 'I don't see evidence of people rushing out of Harvard Business School to join the HR ranks'

For the poor HR manager, it can be pure hell. Often with no more information than the receptionist on the front desk, HR can find themselves making statements that have little bearing on reality. As noted earlier, mergers are a fearful experience for most employees and companies still manage to get the whole process screwed up. Disrupted lives, departmental anarchy, broken trust, loss of valuable human assets and lost business are all part of the badly put-together merger.

Much of the initial damage of a merger comes from the plain fact that companies get bought or sold on the basis of numbers, not people. Most of the time there is a very good reason for that – secrecy. You can't have your HR people, or a bunch of external consultants, wandering around the plants and offices of your target company B asking how they feel about culture fit with company A.

As Silvio Conforti, an M&A specialist with UBS in Zurich, stresses, 'in theory, a human resource audit would be a good idea, but in practice this is not often possible in view of the need to maintain confidentiality. The task of doing this falls on the managers caught up in the transaction and often in the heat of the action the softer issues do not receive the highest priority.' And with CEO egos getting in the way of cold hard reality, it is incredible that there are not more disasters than we regularly read about. Says Conforti, 'Egos play a huge role in starting the M&A process, but they are crucial to it and will shape the final outcome, where there is always a winner and a loser. In my view, ego plays as big a role as rational consideration in determining the final form of the deal and the total integration process.' He adds, 'the most common pitfall is the "us" and "them" syndrome of the buyer, who cuts out the talent of the loser regardless of the strengths and qualities they may bring to the party.'

All mergers are acquisitions for somebody

One of the major problems is that the CEO and his takeover team is having such a jolly good time that they don't get around to thinking what the average manager or worker is thinking. They are having a fun roller-coaster ride that occupies all their waking moments.

Cary Cooper, a mergers specialist and prolific lecturer and author at the University of Manchester Business School, has a high degree of cynicism about mergers. 'We may talk about mergers, but in reality there is always one company that is being acquired – all mergers are acquisitions, there is always a dominant force.' When it comes to people issues, Cooper's cynicism goes into overdrive, 'almost unanimously they say there will be no job losses, but there always are to get rid of the overlaps. Actually it's unbelievable, but lies are told to stop the good people from leaving.' Cooper goes on with his advice on people issues, 'it's better to be honest, to manage the process and get people on your side. When they leave, they will probably go somewhere else in your industry and may not do business with you because they feel you treated them badly.' And what about the CEO ego factor? 'Oh yes, that's there too, of course. Usually, it is a CEO who has to resort to a merger because he isn't really bright enough to grow the organization organically, so he has to go out and buy something.'

> it's unbelievable, but lies are told to stop the good people from leaving

Ask questions

Experts in the human cost of mergers suggest that a lot of problems could be solved if the merger team stopped every day or so and put themselves in the shoes of those who aren't leading the charge. The questions that the 99.9 per cent left outside the funfair are going to ask include the following.

- What's happening?
- Why is it happening, do they know what they are doing?
- Will I have a job?
- Will I have to move?
- What is expected of me?
- Will I keep the same employment package?
- Will I be working for a new boss?

This is particularly true where you wake up one morning and hear on the radio that your business has just been acquired. The head of HR at software integrator EDS, Tony Ebbutt, notes that 'over 60 per cent of our employees didn't choose to join us, they were acquired or outsourced. They all bring their own cultures to the table and they are all very different. Often, you are acquiring young, hi-tech people with ideas of other rules and regulations that you don't necessarily want inside your company. That means it is the job of HR to repeatedly purge the system and try to get common approaches and common processes across the board.'

Four key insights into M&As

Roffey Park Management Institute produced a landmark study, *Mergers and Acquisitions: Getting the People Bit Right* at the close of 1998. Based on insights gained from a broad range of companies that have gone through the M&A process with different levels of success, they flagged four key insights that are worth highlighting. To them, I have attached a few of my own views and experiences.

Roles, behaviour and attitudes

The roles, behaviour and attitudes of managers have an important impact on the M&A process. They can make a fundamental difference to how well employees cope with the changeover and adjust to life in the new entity.

There is little doubt that this is a universal truth. Especially in times when even mediocre talent owns the market, the wrong messages can trigger a rapid migration of the people you would most want to keep. Or, as in the case of Renault in Vilvoorde, Belgium, the closure of the plant was announced on the radio and shift-workers heard of the losses as they were on their way to the plant. Years ago, I was witness to a smaller, yet similar incident in Luxembourg, when the press release announcing that British Airways was closing its local office there was telexed to the branch by mistake before anyone got there to explain.

Employee fears

Employees are often hit by waves of anxiety and need to be supported through the transition.

Sadly, that does not always happen. In one disastrous New York-based merger, already paranoid employees, who had heard rumours that lay-offs were imminent, discovered tiny red adhesive labels on open-plan office cubicles. They became panicked and assumed that the 'red dots' were a sign of the people who were being let go. Later, it was discovered that they were a guide to the company's software provider to show which desktop computers were to be upgraded.

Culture clashes lead to failure

Culture clashes between the joining organizations are inevitable and often become the main reason for failure.

When BMW acquired Rover Cars, lots of German engineers in immaculate white coats descended on the company's UK factories. The Germans walked around making notes and shaking their heads – thoroughly upsetting the UK workforce. But it wasn't arrogance, as it was assumed. They were showing their disapproval at the type of machinery the Rover engineers had had to work with during their joint venture with Honda. To make things better, BMW's top management issued a decree that no one could go to England without top management approval.

Importance of HR strategy

HR strategy is vitally important during all stages of M&As and needs to be addressed as early as possible.

Too often this is not the case. Such is the 'buzz' of doing the deal that the people issues are forgotten. It is at this point that newly acquired talent is likely to vote with its feet and leave. People often feel lost and not at all in control. It is useful to point out that top management, and even managers of business units might feel fine about the merger, because they are meeting counterparts in the other company. It is at the country and local level that it can take months, even years, for the impact of a merger to arrive. Living with that uncertainty is a sure way to alienate your people.

Learn to explain and motivate or they'll do it themselves

With all this activity and uncertainty, employees at all levels have the right to be confused and bemused – leaving it up to someone in the organization to make sure that their anxieties are carefully defused. And, in the battle to win the hearts and minds of graduates, there is another job to do – explain how business today is evolving. Jean Stephane, the president of pharmaceutical firm SmithKline Beecham, whose world headquarters are in Belgium, says that, 'we have to change our vision, the way we teach. We must explain to young people that society is changing, and what the roles of technology and business are.' He goes on, 'In a world where globalization is taking place, it's very important to explain these changes fully, so they're not afraid of what's happening. Changes are so rapid that people are destabilized and afraid to take risks. We must re-learn risk-taking and learn how to learn. The way we educate young people is vital.' Bravo Jean! Too bad, many of your fellow CEOs don't think that way. Certainly, explaining what is going on helps a lot (probably more so in Europe, where graduates seem to be a lot less worldly wise than in the US or even Asia).

You're in a seller's market

For in the battle to hire the best (see chapter 3) you had better realize that today's candidates are in a seller's market and they know more about your business and what it can do for them than some of your current staff. And if you make promises you can't keep, they won't stay around to hear you say sorry.

In this destabilized corporate world we occupy, where confusion is endemic, companies that want to hire the best have to understand that only by making it easier than their competitors for people to work will they stick around. Time after time in researching this book, I discovered – in Europe, in Asia and in North America – that the smart and savvy don't stick. They'll use your Internet connections to surf jobs and set up interviews with rival firms. They'll take a vacation, actually get hired by a competitor, go to the orientation programme. If they like it they stay. If they don't like it, they'll come back to you on Monday.

Even if they have no money – and a lot of bright kids in Asia fall into this category – and don't have access to electronic information, they'll learn anyway. One of my books, *Getting a GRIP on Tomorrow*, was part of a special display in a Singapore bookstore. It created a lot of interest, but few sales. A chat with the bookstore manager soon produced an answer:

'Yours is a two lunch book, Mr. Johnson.'
'What's a two lunch book, exactly?'
'That's a book that takes just two lunches to read, they mark the page and come back and finish it off next day.'

Motivating – a dying skill?

Their need for knowledge is great and those who need it, find ways to get it. The only problem with that is that many new entrants come into organizations only to discover that the rosy picture they had evaporates within the first 48 hours. Added to that, such is the pressure on people, that few determined-to-make-the-deadline supervisors or managers have time to stop and explain.

'Motivating is a dying skill', worries Gunnar Sandmark, a senior manager with telecommunication group Global One. 'Less and less companies are able to properly motivate, because managers have less and less time to focus on these issues,' he reflects. 'Everyone wants a quick fix – people want everything now or, better still, yesterday.' Sandmark, who, before his time at Global One, was with banking software group SWIFT and computer firm ICL, notes that studies he has done over the last decade with employees show that, in areas like strategic direction, communication, people development and customer service, the only one that has improved at all is customer service. The rest have remained static or got worse. 'It is this difference between what you read in the business press and what is actual, on-the-ground reality that causes much of the confusion in the rank and file,' says Sandmark.

So much confusion is out there that some see it as a chance to make money. According to Kennedy Information (KI), in the US, the market for HR consulting will be $5.8 billion by the end of 2000. KI's VP of Research, Tim Burgeois, says that, 'companies have paid too little attention to their workforces, now that they're squeezed they need help fast'. He adds, 'A growing need for HR consulting has arisen as companies struggle to find the people they need from the available pool of qualified employees.'

According to KI's research the top HR consulting firms to look out for are:

- Towers Perrin
- Mercer
- Andersen
- Hewitt
- Watson Wyatt.

All of these firms no doubt will be accepting CVs to fuel their need for talent to help out companies with a shortage of it.

Shell-shocked

One company that has tried to make some sense out of all this confusion is oil company Shell. Its US subsidiary ran an on-line poll that sought to discover Americans' core work and career goals. Its conclusion, to add to the talent debate is that, 'there are more than 120 million people working in America today, and no two have exactly the same point of view'.

Six worker types

Shell US came up with six different categories of worker all of which feature in your workforces to a greater or lesser extent. How many of these categories should be encouraged and how many eradicated is for you to decide. As Shell say, 'in each group you'll probably recognize a friend, family member, colleague – or perhaps even yourself'.

The Fulfilment Seeker (FS)

Working motto: 'It's not just a job – it's an adventure!'

A large number of FSers believe a good job is one that allows them to use their talents and make a difference, rather than one that provides a good income and benefits. Most would say they have a career as opposed to a job, and a substantial majority say they are team players rather than leaders. They are mostly white, married and highly satisfied with their jobs. Shell found teachers, nurses, public defenders, in a variety of 'rooms': classrooms, emergency rooms and courtrooms.

The High Achiever

Working motto:

'I've wanted to be a _____ since I was six years old'

To pass muster as a high achiever, plan on laying out a career path: a large majority say they have followed a career path since a young age. The planning apparently pays off – this is the highest income group (with nearly a quarter earning more than $75,000) and the group with the highest educational achievement. Most are leaders who take initiative and a majority are male and hold managerial positions. They manifest themselves as lawyers, surgeons and architects.

The Clock Puncher

Working motto: 'Take this job and shove it!'

Put on a happy face? Forget about that. Clock punchers are the least satisfied of any group, with nearly all of them saying they have a job rather than a career. A majority say they ended up in their jobs largely by chance, and nearly three-quarters say they would make different career choices if they could do it all over again, this is a group you really need to 'discover' in your business. Clock punchers are predominately female, have the lowest household income and are the least educated.

The Risk Taker

Working motto: 'Show me the money!'

Risk takers have something in common with bank robbers: they both go where the money is. Members of this group are far more willing than others to take risk for pure financial success. They are also the only group that likes to move from employer to employer in search of the best job. This group is young (45 per cent are under 35) and largely male. They are fairly well educated, but showing them the money is what motivates. These are software entrepreneurs and car salespeople.

The Ladder Climber

Working motto: 'Movin' on up . . .'

Ladder climbers aren't going anywhere . . . except up. These are company people who like the stability of staying with one employer for a long time. A substantial majority prefer a stable income over the chance of great financial success and consider themselves to be leaders rather than team players. Company loyalty still matters – more than half say they would move cities to stay with their current employer – find out in a hurry who these people are in your business! Most ladder-climbers are female and have significant incomes (48 per cent earn more than $50,000) even though they have modest educational backgrounds (just over a quarter are college graduates). The only way these corporate middle managers and skilled blue-collar people will change jobs is by getting a promotion.

The Paycheque Casher (PC)

Working motto: 'Workin' for a living'

Most PCers prefer jobs that provide good income and benefits over ones that allow them to use their talents and make a difference. Members of this group are young (46 per cent under 35), male and confused. Although, the majority say they will take risks for a chance at achieving great financial success, an even larger number want the security of staying with one employer for a long time. Most do not have a college degree, work in blue-collar or non-professional white-collar jobs and prefer working in a large company or agency. This group also has the largest group of minorities: 18 per cent African-American, 10 per cent Hispanic and 3 per cent Asian. These are factory workers and entry-level word-processors.

Be willing to work

The Shell poll also showed that over half of employed adults in the US expect to work for five or more employers in their working life, with a quarter expecting to toil for eight or more. Most revealing is Shell's finding that 'the youngest American workers already have had more employers (an average of five) than today's retirees had in a lifetime'.

And there is other news too, that employees on the hunt for talent had better heed. By a two-to-one margin Americans say that being 'willing to work hard is more important for success than having a college degree'. The poll also noted that 'nearly half of those polled said that their studies were not related at all to their current jobs'.

This finding was confirmed in my three round table discussions in Brussels, London and New York, where most of the participants – 37 in all – said that they were in jobs they had not studied for. But, another point that needs stressing is that the round table groups all said, 'when I stop learning I begin to feel insecure', underscoring the idea that those employers who don't provide constant learning are going to lose out.

What defines success?

Another issue that needs to be taken on board in these times of confusion is that – as the Shell poll shows – the people in our organizations are varied in the extreme and have different expectations and ambitions – some have no ambition at all.

Too often, I meet CEOs and other senior managers – all with strong success drives – who fail to understand that not everyone wants their kind of life. If we grow up on a diet of reading about success in newspapers and business magazines, it is easy to fall into the trap that everyone thinks

not everyone wants to be the CEO

that this is important. But not everyone wants to be the CEO, although, most employees are sure they could do the job a whole lot better! Most want respect, remuneration and survival: freedom from *the fear* is tops.

A fair day's work for a fair day's pay has never been more true. And if you can throw in some security so much the better.

Peter Felix, President of the Association of Executive Search Consultants in New York – a man who predicts that we have seen nothing yet in terms of talent wars and suggests we are headed for a shark-like 'feeding frenzy' in the wars to come – notes that many companies became very successful until now by having the ability 'to be incredibly good at managing mediocre people'. But today, 'that is not an option, unless we have the right people at the right time, we can hit the wall and destruct that much faster'.

Some of us know that already and have taken steps to secure our talent and to find new sources of human capital. Many of us are still wallowing in a sea of confusion and passing those uncertainties on to our human assets – creating concern and inevitable departures. A lot of

While it has never been tougher to be at the top, it is equally difficult at the bottom

acts need to stop rehearsing and go out on the stage and perform. Whether they get booed or cheered depends entirely on their abilities to read the signs that employees and would-be employees are sending to them.

Will technology save the IT talent trap?

The current focus on talent shortages in IT fuels a great debate. Will IT people continue to be in such huge demand as systems become, more and more, the key to operational success, or will technology leapfrog, or break through a barrier, that will change the way we think and use IT? Employment specialists use the example of the telephone, where it became clear at one stage in the 1930s that its increased use would mean that everyone in the US would need to be employed as a telephone operator if the demand continued. In that event, technology lessened the need for humans in the connection process. If this happens in IT in the next few years, it would mean there would be less dependence on talent to solve the problems and halt the shortage. However, such is the impact, and the huge areas of business that still are in the techno-stone-age (many parts of Europe, South America, Central and Eastern Europe and Asia) that demand would seem not to have hit its peak.

Points to ponder

- There are sizeable gaps between what workers say they want from their jobs and what they get. Companies who find the right recipe will be winners.

- There is huge pressure on working women who want to drop out for personal reasons – often they cannot get back into the technology race. Finding new ways to keep them on board and up to speed seems a logical move.

- The chilling trend of a total collapse of loyalty by employees needs to be addressed urgently by everyone. Like it or not we all have unhappy workers for one reason or another.

- Companies must find more honest ways to keep employees aware of post-merger developments. Saying 'there will be no job losses', doesn't fool anyone anymore.

- In a merger or acquisition those at the top playing power games need to stop every day or so and ask, 'what are the employees thinking about all this?' and address those concerns honestly.

- There's a new breed of people-centric person who has taken over where HR left off. Some call it the head of talent. Whatever the label they are a new force in helping the CEO concentrate on people issues.

- Human resource people must get a better understanding of the complex jobs people do if they are to provide the right support. Make sure your HR people know what business they are in – they must follow the business strategy.

- Unhappy employees will use your Internet to find jobs and their vacation time to interview and even try them out. Face it, we are in a different recruitment world today, peopled by intelligent, no-nonsense people.

- Don't forget, not everyone wants to be CEO or even vice president. Don't assume because you are ambitious that everyone shares your dreams, they have different ones of their own.

3 | The battle for the best

attracting exciting talent to your doorstep

Never put yourself in a position where you are irreplaceable. If you can't be replaced, you'll never be promoted.

Anon

Don't compromise yourself – you are all you've got.

Janis Joplin

Corporations the world over are busily upping the ante in the battle to grab the best talent they can: turning recruitment from a lazy Sunday afternoon fishing expedition, to a high-speed chase with big nets and harpoons. Shortages of leaders, shortages of technical talent, shortages of global expertise – all these trends are driving an ever more urgent need to catch, fillet and freeze the best fish before the competition. Failure to do it can spell business suicide.

Yet, despite the obvious need for top talent, it would still seem that business is intent on squandering what it has caught. Industry after industry is stuffed with unhappy, overworked and under-appreciated executives. As Bill Rothwell, a professor of workforce education at Penn State University, wryly comments 'Employers must get smart about managing their workforce. If they take the attitude that everyone is expendable, they'll get a chance to test that theory, because no one will work for them.' And if you look at the time and trouble that smart employers are prepared to put in and the kind of terms and conditions they are prepared to offer, you have to see that some companies that don't treat their people in the right way must eventually lose out.

Added to that, the amount of talent crossing over from one industry to another is unprecedented. Even a few years ago, an executive in the automobile, financial, retail or consumer goods industry more or less stayed there. Today, anyone can work anywhere and probably will. Newly arrived college recruits talk of having seven or eight jobs in their lives in four or five industries. It is a whole new world out there – how many of us are even remotely ready for it? Not only how many of us are ready for it, how many of us know how to take advantage of it to bolster our treasure chest of talent?

> the amount of talent crossing over from one industry to another is unprecedented

Best practices from other industries

'The smart companies don't want to recruit from the usual pool anymore', says Eric Gustafson, managing director of search firm Korn/Ferry in New York, 'they want to find people who can bring with them best practices from other industries. To use an ice-hockey analogy, they want people who know enough that they are able to skate to where the puck is going – to anticipate change before it happens.' Gustafson also sees a revolu-

> the CIO is the mailroom clerk of the information age – they know everything

tion on who will be in charge of a corporation's development. 'Smart chief information officers (CIOs) are going to be of great value in the future. Until now, most CIOs were kept at arm's length of the CEO, but this has now changed. Just think about it, the CIO is the mailroom clerk of the information age – they know everything.'

'There just aren't enough good people to go around inside a single industry anymore, so we will have to change and look on the outside', says Michael Michl, senior VP of human resources at MasterCard. Michl, an Austrian, who before entering the global card business was with IBM and Avon Products, has a very open view that is not always shared within the still-closed financial community. 'But that will change', he is certain. 'We will need to look outside for marketing, sales and technical expertise. Of course, human resources is human resources wherever you go, but I also think that today, a good CEO is a good CEO and the industry is almost secondary.'

Michl is also making certain that search firms that work for

MasterCard get the message about diversity too. 'We can't just poach people from American Express and vice versa anymore', he points out, 'and we insist that search firms provide a diverse group of candidates – we don't want to see just four white, male Americans.'

Find some new rocks to look under

Around the globe this same need to look under a new set of rocks and see what you can find is becoming a corporate mantra. Executives are not just job hopping like never before, they are hopping across industries, across national boundaries and across continents. 'Certainly there is not as much of this as you might think from reading the business press', notes Tom Acuff of search firm Neumann International, 'you read a lot about these moves just because they are different. But it is increasing, and yes, we are being asked to widen the scope of our searches, to think outside more traditional lines.'

Acuff's only gripe – borne out by others I talked to – is that, 'when it comes to making an offer they usually choose the easy option and hire a safe candidate – the man you flew from Tokyo to New York or from Sao Paulo to London, just made a plane trip for nothing'. (see A *clone, a clone, my kingdom for a clone!* on page 113)

Industry expertise can still count

But of course, in this new world of work, there are exceptions to every rule. You can't just go and buy talent solutions off the shelf. What makes an ideal solution for one company in one industry, will not work for another. While it appears that everyone – from CEOs to marketers and CFOs – is swapping industries, there are other businesses where you need a great deal of expertise in the industry and at the top.

Lance Wright, Europe, Africa, Middle East HR manager with Mobil points out that such is the need for technical expertise at the very top of an oil company that top jobs will almost always go to industry insiders. 'There are really two types of managers today,' says Wright, 'those with special skills that are transferable to other companies and industries, so they can job skip from an energy company to a retailer (this would apply to HR for example), and those who have very core competencies. Those are the ones who stay in an industry.'

Wright explains further, 'Working for a big corporation used to be very egalitarian,' he says, 'in theory anyone, from any discipline, had a shot at running the place one day. But as certain businesses – like the oil indus-try – have focused more and more on the core business, there end up being a few individuals that are truly core to the company.'

there are possibly only 'five or six people in the world' who could run a corporation like Mobil today

Noting that there are possi-bly only 'five or six people in the world' who could run a corporation like Mobil today, because of the sheer technical complexity in the search for oil and gas, Wright suggests that, 'it would be a very rare bird indeed in Mobil HR who would even think they can compete with a smart geophysicist for the top job'.

And this sort of thinking is borne out in other industries. In financial services there have been a series of high profile moves of top mar-keting talent from retailing and fast moving consumer goods companies (Heinz, Procter & Gamble). But Citicorp's Peter Boucher, a VP of Executive Resources observes, 'We hired a whole slew of consumer marketing talent. But the real challenge comes later. If these people had stayed in their pack-aged goods industry they would more than likely be in line to be general managers (GMs), but in financial services they have the difficulty that they don't really understand the technical side. Our job is to try and bridge the gap of technical learning, so that we can promote these people; because if we can't, they will leave.'

In other areas, this 'not born into the business' stigma is still – despite those talent shortages and needs to think differently – making it dif-ficult for new arrivals to make it into the senior ranks. While there may be some well-publicized industry hoppers (everyone uses Lou Gerstner's switch to IBM as *the* example), most on the lower rungs of the power ladder can have a frustrating time indeed. Many, I conclude, quickly or belatedly real-ize that their lack of long-term industry experience is going to count against them and they return to their old roots.

This is a point that needs keeping in mind the next time you brief your search consultant to 'consider everyone and every industry'. Sure they may solve a problem (most financial services people admit that they still haven't discovered what marketing is), but that could be something arranged on a contract basis. Hiring in retail talent to a bank, or IT talent to a fast moving consumer goods company, with the promise of vast future opportunities may not be the right route and can have unfortunate consequences. In the battle to attract talent, we have to think in less conventional ways to make sure we get the best out of it and that it creates sustainable advantages.

> have to think in less conventional ways to make sure we get the best out of it and that it creates sustainable advantages

Want a slice of what's hot this month?

Another trend is the 'love affair' syndrome, where an executive, or an industry is so hot that everyone wants a slice. As with the hiring of foreign elements into the body corporate in financial services, care should be taken in their consumption. Can executives brought up on a culture where you have no history to hold you back or preconceived ideas to confound you (the norm in Silicon Valley) actually survive in more conventional corporations? The much publicized move of Compaq Computer's number two Roel Pieper to the role of vice chairman of Philips under Cor Boonstra, didn't last too long. While all sorts of rumours were rife, could it be possible that transferring from a fast-paced, still-a-start-up culture in the US to a venerable giant in The Netherlands had something to do with it?

Then again, the love affair with US executives in general (particularly by UK based corporations) has not yet run its course, despite several disasters (both Michael O'Neill at Barclays Bank and Dick Brown at Cable & Wireless, the most recent high profile executives failed to live up to expectations – the first resigned on day one). Now Barclays is heading further north to Canada to bring aboard Matthew Barrett of Bank of Montreal on a $10 million package.

Other companies still see an American CEO as a potent weapon (at the time of writing both Reckitt & Coleman and Reed Elsevier had US searches in train), mainly because there is a belief that US executives have leading-edge experience that can give companies an advantage. Apart from the fact that their packages drive up local salary and bonus levels (*see* Chapter 6 on reward) and they are setting the scene for a single, global price for the job, there is nary a trace of evidence that they make any real difference.

On-line recruiting goes big-time

The Internet is well on its way to changing the recruiting world forever. In doing so, it is going to create a powerful new weapon for those who are determined to win the people wars.

When you consider that at the beginning of 1998 just 17 per cent of the global *Fortune 500* were actively recruiting on the Internet and one year later that figure was up to 45 per cent, you begin to get some idea of the revolution that is upon us. OK, for the present, it is mostly confined to the US and is just a fraction of the total of newspaper recruitment advertisements (about three per cent, say most industry watchers), but there is every indication that it will – quite rapidly – make the newspaper job columns redundant, kill off low-level recruiters and lay siege to all but the most focused, niche-playing search consultants.

So fast is the technology and the applications opportunities moving that anything written here has a good chance of being obsolete in weeks, rather than months.

> The Internet takes the whole concept of poaching people to a new and dangerous level.

Suffice to say, it is another area where smart firms have already taken advantage, while the slow-to-go are just getting to the start line and the rest (that include some very big industry names indeed) don't even know what's going on. The first thing to understand is that it takes the whole concept of poaching people to a new and dangerous level. Your people can be accessed at home, at work and more important, they can go job hunting, leading to job hopping without ever leaving their desks.

While some say this is still an area for college kids to find jobs, they couldn't be more wrong. A survey by JWT Specialized Communications in the US discovered that the average online job seeker is age 35, has an average income of $57,000 and works in the services sector: hardly a first-time job candidate.

A trawl through websites across the US reveals a picture that many seem not to have noticed, both job opportunities and job seekers are ever more transparent thanks to the World Wide Web. Consider these developments.

- Reports from business schools across the US and Europe note that students use laptops in class to surf job sites.

- Headhunters are getting scared, that's why Korn/Ferry teamed up with the *Wall Street Journal* and why others are set to follow.

- Hewlett-Packard has a system that processes CVs in different languages and deposits them in an English language, central database that all managers can access – the total number on file is claimed to be around 150,000.

- Cisco Systems says it now hires six out of every ten of its people on the Net and receives 80 per cent of its CVs that way. Also, because 90 per cent of job-seekers to their site log-on using their current employer's hardware, they have even created an 'Oh No! My Boss is Coming Button', which fills the screen with innocent graphics. According to Cisco recruiters, time to hire is down from 113 days to 45. In addition, Cisco's targeting of 'passive' job seekers goes further, they place ads on the Dilbert website, have booths at film festivals and other alternative events and have pioneered a free pizza service that sends food to halls of residence where students are studying for finals. A note inside says, 'Good Luck' plus the Cisco website address.

- Software house Inacom in Omaha runs an on-line game which is a blind for getting people to register with them who they can target as future employees.

- A little techno-savvy and you can get into so-called secure websites, and access employee details. As more and more companies build what they consider are secure Intranets and post complete employee details (even their photos) it is amazing how much data you can get with just a few keystrokes. In the US specialist seminar providers are offering courses on how to access poorly protected corporate Intranets and they are doing bumper business.

Moves like this would scare most HR professionals and top managers if they knew. The trouble is, in a lot of cases – they don't.

The news is that this is going to get much, much worse. And as the battle to hire and hold people hots up, a lot of the fighting is going to be electronic. Disgruntled, turned-off employees don't have go to interviews or even write CVs anymore. At the flip of finger, they can – using your hardware – send CVs around the globe. Interim job giant, Manpower, has already achieved this. Put your details of career, qualifications, industry and geographic preferences on their website and they'll e-mail you when a position is available.

Do foreign bodies work?

Certainly, if you are in a global business and need global managers it makes sense to go shopping wherever you can, but be sure you know who you want to load into your shopping cart. A hot manager from a hot industry might sound like a great idea, but can they really settle into the stuffy conservative atmosphere of a traditional industry?

Maybe, it is the job they are asked to do that counts and the amount of room they have to do it (where Roel Pieper – formerly of Compaq left Philips after a short boardroom tenure, another IT specialist, Robert Pickering, recruited to run Origin – Philips in-house software business – has succeeded. Observers suggest it is because he has been left to do his job and spends all his time travelling).

If you are a traditional retailer for example, and you want to set up an e-commerce outfit, you probably have two choices. Take a tried and trusted lieutenant – one of those people you need to 'use or lose' – and send them off to get it going, or hire in a hot manager from a firm that has experience, but has absolutely no reverence for the way you have done business in the past. Given the freedom to get on with the job, both could be good solutions, but the hot manager from outside – if left totally alone to build the business – is probably going to get there first and ring up profits sooner.

The other issue is location. A young manager in a Californian start-up who goes surfing or mountain biking every evening after a hard day at the VDU won't settle in a corporate glasshouse in Manhattan, London or Paris. If you want to grow a cool business, you have two choices: go to where the 'cool' businesses hang out, or buy your new-found talent a lot of air tickets.

Where's cool?

Of course who and what are perceived as 'cool' places to work depends very much on who you are and where you think you want to get to.

People who perceive Bill Gates as cool and offering an exciting work and career environment naturally beat a path to Seattle. Others who think that Citicorp is the place to be because John Reed is building a great global empire, shower it with résumés and Internet hits. Even the threat of mergers – and the fallout of job-cuts – is no barrier.

When Mobil and Exxon announced their forthcoming merger, applications went up rather than down as hopeful recruits regarded this as offering even more challenge than in the past. Once staid companies, like Prudential Insurance in New Jersey, are being transformed by a new top management that, in planning to demutualize the business, is generating lots of interest and applications from would-be employees who see it as a movin' and shakin' place to be.

Image is all

As the people wars hot up, making sure your external image stays polished is going to be critical. Start closing plants and laying off workers and you quickly slip off the hot talent A-list – as one-time cult status corporations like Body Shop, Levi Strauss and Laura Ashley are finding.

> Start closing plants and laying off workers and you quickly slip off the hot talent A-list.

Even supposedly fireproof brands such as Virgin can be affected. While Virgin Atlantic continues to garner industry prizes for superb quality of service, its ventures into rail privatization in the UK and cheap airline routes out of Belgium have met with considerably less success, consumer dissatisfaction and a consequent battering of its brand standard.

Lots of companies know that a good reputation will bring talent to your door, especially if you appear able to offer excitement and growth. While much of that depends on where you are located – and the attendant culture of your country or region – it is something that smart recruiters and CEOs must play on if they are to win the wars to come.

Everyone in IT has heard of Michael Dell, Bill Gates and Andy Grove, others are less visible, but the company's they command are the attractors. Few outside the industry have heard of Steve Case. But as head of AOL, he stitched together the alliance with Netscape and Sun Microsystems, making it a hot, hot ticket and a target for a lot of ambitious men and women.

Few people know the head of Nokia or Ericsson, certainly not as many as have heard of Galvin at Motorola. But in Finland and Sweden and around the world their companies are besieged for jobs. The name of Anders Knutsen doesn't ring a lot of bells, but as president and CEO of Bang & Olufsen (B&O), he presides over a company whose niche in the home electronics marketplace is well respected both for its design and for its technology and consequently attracts thousands of applications each year. Knutsen is a man given to humour. In a recent interview, when asked about the greatest challenge facing his company, he said, 'For our company the true challenge of the future is not the area of new technologies – or being able to keep up with the introduction of new features – it is the so-called dumbing down of TV programmes. Who wants to buy a high-quality TV to watch lousy programmes?'

The culture factor

Culture is, and will continue to be, a vital factor in who you choose and who chooses you. Eddie Bauer, the US clothing goods manufacturer knows that people come and work for them because of the reputation they have created as a fun, caring place to work. Other retail companies like GAP and Gymboree are the same. For example, at Gymboree they even have a Wednesday afternoon snack-time where the employees try out the merchandise and celebrate childhood.

> A tip to consider: when you find people who are culturally aligned to your business, hire them before someone else does – even if you haven't got a job for them. In the battle for talent you need to be as proactive as possible.
>
> Another issue that we need to be aware of, is that it is not just companies that are global, our individual tastes and habits have become more international too as the world is shrunk by modern communication – this leads to potential recruitment opportunities.

A rumour that Nike was to build a facility in Belgium led to a flood of applications from young Belgians who saw the sports equipment manufacturer as a 'cool' place to work. When BMW announced its plans to build a plant in the US, its Munich headquarters was inundated with job applications from US engineers.

Of course, culture plays a huge part in who ends up working where. Graduate from one of the exclusive *grandes écoles* in France and you will most likely end up in one of the top 200 firms (only about 5 per cent of business school graduates are hired into top French firms). To make it to the top of a German engineering firm would be unthinkable unless you were an engineer, probably German and most certainly male.

Tradition dies hard

Tradition dies hard in Europe, which is either its charm or its disease depending on your particular point of view. Don't forget that the work ethic differs from an early age. In the US everyone has a summer job during college. In Europe, this is less prevalent the further south you go. If you are from a good family you are not supposed to show that you need the money and this is evident in recruitment. While Disney will point to hordes of enthusiastic college kids filling Mickey Mouse and

> Getting French kids to smile at tourists isn't easy – we don't all belong to the 'have a nice day' culture

Donald Duck costumes in Florida and California, they and their rivals have a problem in Europe. Getting French kids to smile at tourists isn't easy – we don't all belong to the 'have a nice day' culture, which may be a good thing too.

Of course, occasionally we get it wrong. A series of rousing advertisements for Hyundai, the South Korean industrial conglomerate, managed to Anglicize the cult of the leader – not the way to attract burgeoning talent to your door. Huge advertisements extolled its '83-year young' chairman, who had 'over the past half-century found a way where others said it couldn't be done'. This included the glorious statement, 'this is the man who literally brought the sea to its knees'. Let me just counsel the rest of the corporate world, that modesty is a real virtue when trying to be admired.

Learning to use headhunters

The headhunting industry may be one of the great winners in the current battles for talent (firms are reporting fee income up 200 and 300 per cent in some regions), but they are still regarded with a mixture of love and loathing in many places – suggesting that they have still not been totally accepted into the business world. Certainly, they are viewed by many as the fox in the chicken house – unless, of course, they are bringing someone else's chickens tied and trussed to your corporate doorstep.

But some commentators say that the problem isn't just the headhunters. It is also the desperate corporations failing to develop the right kind of relationships that often hire less reputable firms – in the hopes of saving on the costs of a search. Talk to any major multinational corporation and they will have both good and bad stories to tell you about the search industry. But you will also find that most of them have developed a deep relationship with one or two firms (and one or two individuals in those firms) that they find produce excellent results. The whole idea that a CEO can discuss – in complete confidence and away from office politics – key people issues, with someone on the outside, but who knows their business intimately can be very useful. That's the reason IBM used a firm to find its new chief, and why even the ultra-conservative British Broadcasting Corporation did the same for its new Director General.

Where the search firm relationship seems to break down – particularly at the top – is when the firm gets really busy (like now) and passes valued clients onto others in the practice. That's when carefully nurtured relationships fall apart and, as individual headhunters can only fully service so many people, there is a stark choice to be made about who you fully and who you partially support.

The other issue that comes to the fore (more frequently as the market for hot talent tightens) is that CEOs seek out search professionals who really know their business. Most of the very successful headhunters I have known have all had deep insights into their clients' businesses, the industry in general and, in many cases, have been in line positions, where they have done the jobs of the people they are now searching for.

That track record applies to Tom Acuff, a managing partner of Neumann International, the Vienna-headquartered global search firm. An American by nationality, Acuff has an industrial engineering degree, and a career that encompasses the US Navy, investment banking, a vice president position in ITT (where he was head of advanced manufacturing technology) and global experience in the US, Asia and Europe. In fact, Acuff is the model for the new graduate recruits to business: lots of people, successfully doing jobs that they never studied for. I asked Acuff to give me his ideas of how to use a search firm in the best possible way. What did we, as corporations, all get wrong when we hired them; how should we choose them and how could we ensure we get the very best out of them for those huge fees they charge? Some of Acuff's responses are predictable – others less so.

Organizing to recruit the best talent

What we get wrong when we recruit a search firm

- Don't use the same firm for all your search requirements – industry sector, executive level and geography mean you need (as with any other consultants) to know (and use) who is best for the assignment.

- But, don't use either a great mix of different firms based on irrelevant issues (e.g. the golfing partner of your man in France, Germany, Taiwan).

- Don't get bogged down in price negotiations (when virtually all the good firms are in the same ballpark) which set the wrong tone from the outset. Ask what can they do for you, for your specific business needs.

- Don't use search when you don't need it. If you can catch the talent you need by advertising – just do it.

- Be careful as search assignments can often be handed out unilaterally by line managers eager to get to know some search firms for their own personal reasons.

- Don't hold back information and make sure you give the most detailed briefing possible. Spend the maximum amount of time with the consultant, it will save you time later.

- Don't sign up a firm based on its reputation or a word of mouth recommendation. Make sure you know just who is going to work on your assignment.

Top considerations in choosing a headhunter

- Check out – thoroughly – if the firm really is specialized in the search you require (position, industry and region).

- Use a firm that has (satisfactory) experience with you already, knows your business and is able to develop a close relationship based on mutual respect and understanding.

▶

- Make sure you know the current rate for the job for the class of work you require.

- Never take the ego route to using search ('we're using XYZ associates on a global search right now, it's been tough, but I've told them I need a result in ten days'). Be sensible. If you can hire through an advert, do it.

- Get to know the search consultant who will be working on your assignments and be sure you are comfortable with their competence level: no matter how busy you are, insist on meeting them, don't let HR do all the discussion and dealing.

How to get the best from your headhunter and the best candidates

- Always brief your search consultant in the greatest possible detail and be available to answer questions – fast. Don't have the attitude that it is the headhunter's obligation to do it all – the more you help, the better the end result.

- Insist on continuous progress reports (why should search people be treated any different from marketing, finance, engineering?) and ask to know the problems they are facing. Yes, it's just like doing business!

- React immediately when candidates are being presented. Too many clients come over all self-important and 'suddenly busy' when it is time to start the interview process. Remember in a tight executive labour market, these people won't hang around forever.

- Equally, get feedback to the search consultant, quickly and concisely. The faster they can re-tune or re-direct the search, the quicker they can make an offer and the more likely you are to get the candidate of your dreams.

- Finally, treat the headhunter like a customer or client – not like a service provider. You need to develop a healthy working relationship with them – it will pay off short, medium and long term.

A sustaining place to develop

'You get talent by reputation, but that reputation has to come by a commitment to excellence', says Keith Darcy, an Executive VP and director of HR at IBJ Whitehall, a Wall Street financial group. 'What we are seeking,' he adds, 'is a culture that builds a sustaining place that allows people to develop their potential. If you don't let people grow, you lose the sustainability to ensure their growth and with that your ability to attract the right talent.'

Darcy, and his president and CEO Dennis Buchert, have refocused their operation to try and get in the very best talent, 'the kind that is excited to work for us. The kind that doesn't see IBJ as a safe haven from the hard-driving, bigger Wall Street institutions,' he says.

Somewhere like Wall Street, and to a similar extent in the City in London and in Frankfurt, you have to select the people you want carefully – that enthusiasm is vital for building an excellent culture that can be sustained in the long-term. 'I see guys on the street here and they are dead,' explains Darcy. 'They may be making millions, but the pilot light is out!' And he also understands that in IBJ's quest for the right talent, senior management has to be able to show its commitment to the future by not standing aloof from the rest of the people. 'In this age of information we all have access to the same data, so management has to come out of its traditional ivory tower if it wants to earn respect and attract and hold onto the people it needs,' he says, 'that is why we are spending so much time trying to build a culture that is exciting and focuses on the people. In an age of speed, how do you hold a community of people together? You have to continuously reinforce the values, even if some seem to conflict with one another. And that has to be the task of everyone – including top management.'

Shared values

Darcy explains that at IBJ they have developed a totally new set of shared values, which he says are designed to ensure that they give the very best in support and personal development to the staff. While the values are in no way unique, they are supported by a couple of key statements that others may well learn from.

In setting out the values, a statement explains that, 'in support of our mission and vision, we must mutually commit to each other certain core values that are uncompromisingly shared across the entire organization'. In this, the words 'mutually' and 'uncompromisingly' stand out.

Then follow these eight values:

- candour and trustworthiness
- teamwork
- speed and responsiveness

- innovation and creativity
- uncompromising quality
- accountability for our actions
- respect for all individuals
- excellence in everything we do.

However, at the end of the values, there is a final paragraph that puts this into a human, very real, down-to-earth, end-of-the-Millennium context. 'We recognize our human limitations and the potential for values to conflict with one another. We will always seek the highest possible outcome when faced with difficult choices.' Perhaps when we are setting our strategies to secure talent we should look to this example as a workable vision. Get this right and live it everyday and you might begin to see a way of winning that war.

Focus on those who ensure your vision works

So, IBJ believes that to get the right sort of talent in the hothouse atmosphere of Wall Street it needs to be very focused not just on the vision, but on the people who will fulfil that vision. It is very aware that it doesn't want to just hire in anyone and see if it works out. It knows that sooner or later its reputation will grow and the best – and, most importantly, those that fit best – will begin to seek it out.

Who's doing what to attract? Some examples

So what are other companies doing to attract? What kind of reputations are they building, who are they aiming at and who responds? Here's how some of the world's top businesses are drawing their personal lines in the sand in the battle for the best.

Deloitte & Touche's, 'Technology Fast 500 CEO Survey', shows that the biggest and best things that hi-tech companies can offer are stock options; a unique work culture or good work environment (that fits everyone, by the way) and bonuses, benefits and boosting your ego development packages.

Conversely, few say that 'above high salaries' or 'flexible work arrangements' are part of their offer to attract the best talent available. In addition, in their focus on scooping up the best they can find, before it goes anywhere else, Deloitte & Touche's respondents say that the other 'carrots' they offer include:

- temporary to permanent positions
- internships (this is a great idea for any firm to consider)
- sabbaticals every five years
- the Monday morning free pizza meeting of all employees to share ideas
- employer-stocked kitchens that includes morning bagels
- free ski-days and field trips.

I hope that the US doesn't claim ski-days as its own invention, as the Austrians and Swiss have been offering office ski-days to their employees for at least 50 years. Employees even receive an extra day's holiday.

In Scotland, home of golf, many companies have employee golf-days, same idea, same amount of fun! Still in Scotland, the utility company

the Monday morning free pizza meeting of all employees to share ideas

Scottish Power has gone to great lengths to make its work environment one of the most attractive in the UK. It has installed learning rooms for employees' children stocked with PCs, free on-site dental and physiotherapy treatment and a gymnasium.

In a very un-American approach to attracting talent, the SAS Institute – a North Carolina software company – closes its doors at 16.30 (to drive home the point that the crèche closes at 17.00) to maintain its promise of creating a 35-hour working week. SAS, which specializes in data analysis software, has been able to do this in an industry where 80-hour

the SAS Institute closes its doors at 16.30

weeks are normal. It doesn't offer stock options, but it does offer a great quality of life that results in an annual staff turnover of just 3 per cent, compared to the industry average of 16 per cent.

Elsewhere, the news is out and would-be employees are flocking to get into organizations that offer such diverse perks as the following.

- Cheap car purchase: you call Ford or GM and say, 'We have 200 people who want to buy a car, what deal can you offer?'

- In-house video and computer shops: cheaper and more convenient than elsewhere.
- Valet services that will do dry-cleaning, washing, and other errands. Some even have a supermarket service that has groceries ready to pick up as you leave work.
- Cheap car, home and other insurance.
- Holiday bookings.

What's really new?

One of the most interesting things in all this will be how long these 'extras' last. Will a rough recession, as some predict to be due, change people's attitudes? Many of these perks that corporate America seems to be so pleased about as talent-getters have been around other parts of the world for years. Employer-stocked kitchens are a norm in most parts of Europe, vacation homes have been used as a perk in countries as diverse as Sweden, Belgium, Germany, Italy and Spain for decades (although often it was the unions rather than the employers that organized it). In countries like Poland huge worker hotels (most now closed) guaranteed a working family a vacation. Perhaps we have just moved all this onto a new generation in a new way. But can we – in a world of shareholder power – maintain it? Those that do, through thick and thin, will most probably win the long-term people wars as they create a new kind of loyalty based on consistency of action and clear purpose.

Another ruse to attract people to your firm is to have a reputation for doing a great job in a specific area. Candidates love that. They can add it to their collection of campaign medals and, by improving their skill set, make themselves all the more marketable. Michael Michl, VP of HR at MasterCard notes that his company's major sponsorship of sports like soccer, Formula One motor-racing and golf are attractors for marketers eager to prove themselves. 'Our brand name has become a major attractor because we are associated with so many exciting and prestige opportunities.' There is no doubt that this is true. The soccer World Cup gleans the biggest global TV audience (larger than the Olympics, sponsored by rival Visa), and takes four years to plan; so it is a highly prestigious event that punches the ticket of those involved in all the right places for the future. It gives them an enviable and marketable skill set.

Consequently, the learning point here is that the most vulnerable time is going to come in four year cycles – after every Olympics or World Cup as people realize they are marketable to other organizations. If you have a product or process cycle like that, be aware of it and take suitable steps to identify new talent or convince existing talent to stay.

Corporate turn-offs abound

No matter what defences you try to put in place, many companies are not doing a very good job in either attracting or holding onto their top performers. Outdated ideas, little in the way of benefits that meet changing lifestyle needs and an 'us' and 'them' attitude all add up to talent turn-offs.

Communication's director of Alcan, Marcel Daniëls believes that, unless many big companies change their recruitment policies quickly, 'they are going to have problems, because they cannot compete with the flexibility and excitement that others can generate'. Daniëls also warns against companies that create false expectations in the recruitment process. 'This just doesn't work. Most people today, go for a position only if it means that they can stick with their own career agenda. They want to be sure that reporting guidelines are clear, that they know who they have to work with.'

Brussels-based search consultants, Win Noortman and Christian Goffin, agree, 'Large companies are not doing enough to ensure an ongoing supply of talent,' they say. 'They either rely too much on what is available in the market or drown in bureaucratic systems of evaluating people.' They add, 'Not many companies are able to spot talent because they don't dare to take risks with young – not fully mature people.' Noortman and Goffin are also convinced that it is 'companies that offer working environments that do justice to health and family life,' that will be the winners, as people look for a more overall balance in their careers.

Advice about job-seekers

Mark Thomas, founder of consulting group Performance Dynamics and author of the book *Supercharge Your Management Role* has advice about job seekers, that should be carefully considered by any recruiters who want to ensure that they hire the very best talent available.

He points out, 'The last decade has shown beyond all doubt that loyalty to an organization is a dead concept. Organizations have always had to take tough decisions that have impacted on people in negative ways, but today, we have no lingering doubts – as an employee, you have to look after yourself. This changes the whole equation of how you attract, hire and retain talent.'

In this new environment, where the prospective employee is looking out for number one, corporate recruiters need to understand that several things have radically changed.

- Realize that the better the talent the more they will be fully aware of the market value of their skills and knowledge.
- Expect that they will have researched the market in depth and know what reward levels and employee packages are offered by your competition as well as your firm.
- Understand that they will be ever-alert to new opportunities and will have no fear of switching jobs every two years.
- Know that they will be looking for organizations that are offering more than just money. Talent wants to ensure it is developing its marketability for the day you don't want them.
- Don't expect them to settle for promises of pay reviews after six months. They know that the time to negotiate pay is at the point of hire. Similarly, don't be surprised if they want to negotiate time-off, sabbaticals, extra holidays, car, working hours, home working, etc.
- Look for them to dictate terms and conditions of how they work and to be very up-front with their dislikes.
- Realize that you can score big by offering them training and development on an ongoing basis.
- Expect them in return to apply themselves 110 per cent to their new roles.
- Understand that they will continue to network outside the organization, even with employees of your competitors. Don't look at this as a negative. This makes them useful as their knowledge is valuable to you.
- Don't expect them to have any concerns about letting down the company if they are thinking of leaving – they won't.
- Never forget, that as real knowledge workers, they have real power and they can use it – good or bad.

For companies aspiring to recruit talent, Thomas recommends that they look long and hard at the following:

- What exactly are you offering? Remember that good pay and conditions are nowadays just an entry ticket. Most knowledge workers are looking for an exciting work environment, so company leaders need to ask themselves if they have – or are they capable of – creating that. Too many companies still offer dull, boring and meaningless environments.

- Recognize that it is not just about pay and rewards: the London financial markets employ, with the possible exception of Wall Street, the most highly paid knowledge workers in the world, yet the levels of employee loyalty are almost non-existent. Loyalty, in many parts of this market, is solely based on the carrot of the next bonus. It is also a sector that sees many people quit after a relatively short period, despite the high rewards, because of dissatisfaction and associated work pressures. The consultancy industry is another sector that rewards extremely well but suffers from high staff disenchantment and turnover. The result is that many people use these and other 'show-me-the-money' sectors as short-term career accelerators. They move in for pay and experience and move out once their objectives have been achieved.

- Create something unique and distinctive: companies that offer an exciting and interesting place to work, plus good rewards are most likely to win the race to employ the best talent. Review the working environment in your firm and what you ask your people to do. Are you realizing people's talent and energies or subjecting them to a mindless regime that limits their potential?

- Recognize that people have a life outside of work. The need to balance public and private life is becoming a prerequisite to employ talented people. There is a huge amount of dissatisfaction amongst knowledge workers that there is too much rhetoric by employers on the subject and not enough action. Employers who recognize this dissatisfaction and do something about it will win.

- Monitor the behaviours of those who currently lead and manage: the problem in many organizations is that the pressures of business are such that the people who are promoted to positions of power are anything but role models for a balanced lifestyle. Too often it is the person who gives most in terms of time and blind ambition who is promoted. This results in a vicious circle where anything less than total commitment to the company is seen as a sign of weakness and becomes career limiting. Managers need to be carefully counselled in this area and challenged on the effects of their behaviour. An alternative perspective would be that continued and excessive working is a sign of inefficiency, ineffectiveness and addiction.

- Invest in people: organizations that expect to hire and hold the best people will have to show that they are prepared to develop people and take a strong and lasting interest in their progression. Training and learning opportunities that offer individual growth are prerequisites for attracting today's knowledge workers. The effective use of challenging projects and job assignments is paramount.

- Do we need to change our employment packages? In the IT world, products are conceived, made and marketed in six month life-cycles, yet the vast majority of HR processes and reward packages are based on an out-of-date assumption that they will last for two or three years. Shouldn't companies expecting to hold onto top-performing talent consider revising their systems in line with today's market reality?

A clone, a clone, my kingdom for a clone!

There may be a global talent shortage, but is it really making companies think differently about who they hire? Not likely. Of the hundreds of companies I have spoken to in the past three years, few have made any real attempts to seriously change the type of people they recruit. Sadly, in most cases, it is a barely disguised clone of themselves or their colleagues. Pioneering international organizations apart – like Citicorp who have set out to have a truly global line-up, and succeeded – most companies still hire in their own image. Pick up any handful of annual reports of the *Fortune 500* and you will see little difference in a decade. That picture on the inside back cover of the operating officers is frighteningly the same: male, white, all in blue suits and sober ties. Sure when a position opens up they brief headhunters to scour the world for the very best talent but, when it comes to a final decision, they just hire what I have come to call 'a different kind of Bob'. The rationale is that, 'he's safe, he'll fit into our culture. We could take a chance, but why bother?' It's the same around the world. Will the talent shortage change this? Yes, eventually. But at the top it is unlikely to be very soon. For all our global desires we are remarkably parochial in our actions.

Taking back talent

Another point that has been stressed by many people interviewed is that the old way of shutting the door on people who left is definitely rather like cutting off your nose to spite your face in these tight times for talent. Few companies today will not take back their prodigal talent with open arms. And while they won't be killing the fatted calf to

> # Few companies today will not take back their prodigal talent with open arms.

celebrate, they won't tell you how lucky you are to have your job back either. As several interviewees noted 'they have usually been lured away on promises that did not materialize – or were, quite frankly, lied to – and they come back and work all the better because they realize that the grass is not always greener in the next field. These people can be great assets, particularly if they discovered that the promised environment didn't work out – they become re-converted boosters for how good your business really is.'

Smile and you're hired!

In Japan, some foreign firms, e.g. McDonald's, put such a premium on smiling faces that they discriminate against poker faces in the hiring process. The dean of the company's Japanese training institute, Yurchiro Koise says that, 'in interviews, job applicants are asked to describe their most pleasant experience, and managers evaluate whether their faces reflect the pleasure they are discussing'. Training for McDonald's (there are more than 3,000 restaurants in Japan), includes spying on the competition to evaluate both the frequency and the quality of their employees' smiles.

What about Generation X?

Laying down some new rules for how you are going to recruit and retain has never been more important and one of the key areas for this is what has become labelled 'Generation X'. Ask five people what Generation X is and you'll get five different answers. The only part people will agree on is that they are young (it seems that European and US age ranges differ widely in perception if not original reality). However, I was very conscious that the group from around 25–35 were the range that many of the enlightened management professionals I had talked to felt really needed to be treated in new ways in the workplace. Their contention was that this was the group that expected things to be different. And as they were holding all the new skills that modern business required, our failure to accommodate those needs would create serious problems for our organizations.

It is increasingly clear that this group has a new idea of what the world of work should look like and what it is and is not prepared to do. What seems to be at issue is the ability or the willingness of the older generation to create the environment that these young, dynamic knowledge workers want to toil in.

Ken Brotherston, managing partner with headhunters Korn/Ferry in London is somewhat bemused by the fact that business seems unable to deal with these Gen-Xers, 'I can't understand it at all,' he says, 'after all, business fired their fathers and mothers and all they are doing is ensuring they don't meet the same fate.' He adds, 'What we need to work on as managers is how do we reach these people and what sort of relationship do we have to build with them. Therefore, I think we should try and understand them much better than we seem prepared to do right now.'

What do they want?

What this 25–35 year-old group wants (and it doesn't matter whether it is in the US, Europe or Asia) is instant gratification, an exciting work environment and the opportunity to keep on learning. They know they won't have a job with the same company for long and they want to be fully prepared. Right now, the very best and brightest seem to be heading for the consulting companies and the major multinationals.

In Europe, the 1998 European Graduate Survey, conducted by Stockholm-based Universum, listed the top 15 ideal employers of business, engineering and science students.

- McKinsey
- Boston Consulting
- Andersen Consulting
- Procter & Gamble
- Coca-Cola
- BMW
- Nestlé
- Hewlett-Packard

- Microsoft
- JP Morgan
- Unilever
- Siemens
- Goldman Sachs
- IBM
- Shell

A similar 1998 study of US graduates listed the top 15 ideal places to work.

- McKinsey
- Goldman Sachs
- Boston Consulting
- Bain & Company
- Morgan Stanley
- JP Morgan
- Booz-Allen & Hamilton
- Merrill Lynch

- Hewlett-Packard
- Intel
- Walt Disney
- Coca-Cola
- Anderson Consulting
- Nike
- AT Kearney

Pressure for companies to respond

Noting that European recruitment tactics to search out and sign up these bright young things were getting more and more like those of the US, Yann Blandy, VP of Universum in Sweden noted that, 'as the competition to attract and recruit talented employees heats up, the pressure is on employers to anticipate and respond to graduates' needs. Companies are meeting the recruitment challenge with sophisticated and creative methods to identify, attract and sign top graduates.' According to Blandy's research, the Dutch were amongst the most advanced in Europe, 'I have seen everything, from rock concerts organized

One company conducts the final interview in a car showroom; if the candidate is hired, he or she drives away with a new car as well as a new job.

to attract engineering students, to recruiters visiting students at home to discuss opportunities. One company conducts the final interview in a car showroom; if the candidate is hired, he or she drives away with a new car as well as a new job.'

Failure to take notice of these new recruiting initiatives and reward strategies will be fatal. The best will go to the best deal. What's more they'll tell their friends.

Where graduates go and what they want

Major multinationals and consulting companies are the favourite places for MBAs to head for, certainly to get their first experiences. A survey by Wetfeet.com, a San Francisco on-line career advisory service, of 300 companies, found that the largest number of business school graduates in the US were recruited in 1998 by:

Andersen Consulting	(500)
General Electric	(425)
PricewaterhouseCoopers	(400)
McKinsey	(350)
Booz Allen & Hamilton	(260)
Ford	(250)
Ernst & Young	(200)
Boston Consulting	(187)
Deloitte Consulting	(183).

According to another study by Universum, 80 per cent of MBA graduates say they want to go to an employer who will be a reference throughout their career. However, as with other studies, this shows that they are a footloose lot, with 31 per cent saying they would stay just two to five years and only 20 per cent prepared to stay more than five years.

And what do these youthful hot properties expect from their employer?

good references	(78%)
good pay	(64%)
interesting products	(62%)
varied activities	(59%)

immediate responsibilities	(58%)
a dynamic organization	(53%)
strong corporate identity	(52%)
international operations	(52%)
friendly supervisors	(45%)
training	(39%).

As you can see, hands-on experience is paramount and the type of organization and its ability to parley that into future jobs is of the utmost importance. All of us attempting to do business with this group had better heed its needs. Also, it is not a bad idea to know what MBA graduates are getting on their first jobs. Here are the average rates for the top 11 schools:

Stanford (US)	$105,000
IMD (Switzerland)	$95,000
Intl. University of Japan	$87,000
Harvard (US)	$80,000
Wharton (US)	$79,000
MIT (US)	$78,000
Fuqua, Duke University (US)	$71,000
Kellogg (US)	$70,000
IESE (Spain)	$67,000
INSEAD (France)	$67,000
Melbourne (Australia)	$62,000

Talent crashes along with economy

Talent wars don't always work out in the long term and this story may be worth more than a passing glance, predicting, perhaps, what could happen in other regions or business disciplines in the future. Five years ago, as the race to get into Russia moved into top gear, multinationals were parachuting in top earners to get a foothold in this giant market: remember all the gung-ho headlines?

Talent wars don't always work out in the long term

What happened to a lot of those early arrivals was that they got lured by more money (that's about the only way you can lure people in Russia) to a rival firm. From then on, compensation levels just kept spiralling upward. A reasonably effective

▶

manager could go from an initial package of $150,000 to $300,000, to $600,000 in just a few years. Trouble now is two-fold. One, the economy is in the toilet – and looks set to stay that way. Two, they have got tired of life in Moscow and want to come home. However, they now sport $500,000 life-styles and can't get rehired in the West – their only talent differential is they know how to do business in Russia, which is no longer such a hot skill to possess.

Attracting graduates to your business

OK these are the very best, but it gives a guide to what is beginning to happen, in their bids to get top graduating talent into their businesses the costs are beginning to spiral. This has to have a knock-on effect further down the food chain. But getting graduates to be attracted to the idea of joining your company – like anything else – takes quite a lot of dedication and single-minded purpose.

Outplacement and recruitment company DBM, where one of the founders has written a useful guide, *The Complete Guide to Campus Interviewing*, suggest the following ongoing activities really pay off:

- advertising year-round in the college newspaper
- visiting faculty members and sharing industry developments, providing technological reports, and books or papers by company employees
- making offers of financial assistance to needy students
- offering faculty members employment during the summer
- offering internships to students during summer vacations
- inviting faculty to new plants or research centres
- donating obsolete technical equipment or office equipment to the school.

DMB adds, 'companies that always seem to get the "cream of the crop" usually have established excellent relations with the faculty'.

Non-negotiable issues

Further up the scale, those that already have jobs have absolutely no loyalty either. To get them to move to your business, you have to convince them that you are open to their needs and their ideas. Failure to do so can only lead to a bad hiring experience on both sides.

Hanneke Frese, a senior HR professional with Zurich Financial Services after several years with Citicorp in New York, comments 'A lot of these people have seen their parents being made redundant and they say, "why would I let that happen to me?" So their search for a balance in

you have to convince them that you are open to their needs and their ideas. Failure to do so can only lead to a bad hiring experience on both sides

their life is absolutely non-negotiable. They are not lazy, as some people have suggested, they just have different values.'

Those different values can be confusing at times. While a huge number of surveys talk of the younger generation being adventurous and wanting to work abroad, just as many don't. While companies, in their quest to be truly global, need more and more people willing to work one or two years in an overseas market, they are often having trouble filling those needs.

The other thing that needs careful watching when recruiting this younger group, according to Hanneke Frese, is monitoring how well you are meeting the expectations you created when you hired them. 'You gave people high expectations, but by year three or four some of them may not come about. Equally, the mentor you gave them may have left or been transferred.'

Global One's Gunnar Sandmark agrees, 'it is back to this ability to motivate people, if you don't keep track of how well you are developing them, you do risk losing them – which seems a pity when you have invested so much in them.'

Even the advertising changes

Even advertisements to attract this fickle generation are different. For example, business application software supplier SAP, whose meteoric rise from Germany's Black Forest to a major hi-tech player has been built on youthful enthusiasm, heads one of its recruitment adverts, 'Why Choose Between Learning and Working? Now you can do both at SAP!' This message strikes right at the heart of the expectations of today's knowledge workers – it's right at the top of the list of what they want.

Start-up phone company, Phones4U in the UK heads its

Talent in a T-shirt

Apart from those entrepreneurs in the software industry and the hot guys in the movie business, where's the smart money in Silicon Valley? Why in T-shirts of course. It seems that every time a company, division, business unit or group starts a new project they head down the road to Mike's T-shirt shack, or wherever and print up a bunch of white T-shirts with their new assignment proudly spelt out on the front. I call these the turn-of-the-century equivalent of battle flags. They are a simple, yet evocative rallying cry, they enforce loyalty and they mark people out as part of a group – however briefly. What happens is that techno-nerds prize these T-shirts as a visual memory of their careers (some office walls boast upwards of 200 T-shirts, indicating a hardened industry veteran, even if he's only 30). Anyone looking for talent that can do stuff, need only to count the shirts, or hang out at Mike's T-shirt shack to see what's new that's going down.

recruitment adverts with quotes: 'It's all about coaching others to excel'; 'everyone has their own way of making it work'; 'fast-paced doesn't cover it, but the rewards are fantastic'. The final copy line asks 'I wonder how you'd do it?' Once more, this appeals to the new type of business person. One that knows what he or she wants, has the confidence to ask for it and to make it happen. But please, they expect a private life too.

Is Europe catching up?

Although there is plenty of evidence to say that Europe seems to be catching up in the ability to recognize and utilize the new generation of workers, there is still a very old guard that disapproves of change.

Although there have been some high profile appointments of precocious thirty-somethings to run major pieces of business in France, Italy and Germany,

> Although there have been some high profile appointments of precocious thirty-somethings to run major pieces of business their uniqueness is more in the fact they are few and far between rather than in their abilities.

their uniqueness is more in the fact they are few and far between rather than in their abilities.

For example in France, a research report commissioned by the youth magazine, *Phosphore*, reported that, 'flexible, dynamic and creative… but also too cool, is the way employers in France describe the under-25 age group'. The 50 firms polled described the under-25s as not immediately operational and criticized their priorities in balancing their professional and private lives.

A further study in France, by Manpower, showed that youth and the establishment are at odds with each other. Seventy-seven per cent of companies believe that their qualities of prestige and stability appeal to youth more than the opportunities for self-expression or career development. Conversely, youth views the early part of a career as a time to acquire experience they currently lack.

Levels of cynicism

In round tables I ran in London, Brussels and New York (which were frank exchanges of views in the extreme), everyone who attended was using their current employment for everything they could get out of it. More important perhaps was that few had any plans – once they had learned all they could – to stick around and make a career with their employer. Indeed, most had no plans to stay in the business area they were in.

The level of mistrust and downright hostility to the business establishment was incredible. Most talked of a total lack of support and morals amongst those they worked for and believed that flexibility had a long way to go. What was also obvious was that few were concerned about losing their jobs (several had already been through the process) because they knew their value and were super-confident of getting another.

> The level of mistrust and downright hostility to the business establishment was incredible.

Levels of cynicism were highest in the financial services industry (where many had never seen a top manager since they joined), consulting, the law and advertising. Young lawyers talked of partners who had absolutely no idea of current market conditions, who 'occupied little fantasy worlds of their own'. Young consultants knew they were 'useful bodies, today, a burden tomorrow'. Another young banker, who said he was disgusted by the antics of his employer, said he hoped that during his career he could 'find a better way to deal with people, because this was not managing talent at all – it was using them until they were no longer required'.

Perhaps the most important lesson in all this, is that anyone who does try harder with this group and can convince them that life doesn't have to be like that will strike a very rich chord indeed.

A cautionary tale of the future

One man's experience

The following interview shows the views of a 26 year old graduate and what he thinks business needs to do to keep him and his peer group motivated and on your team. Patrick McCaughey has had university and work experience in his native Ireland, in Belgium, the Netherlands and Hungary (I have to declare my interest and admit that he worked for my firm in Brussels for two summers). He is typical of today's knowledge worker and, for anyone wanting to win the talent battles of tomorrow, his views count.

Q. *Is it harder to retain talented people today?*
A. There may be no hope of keeping people, as there is a great reluctance to find yourself at age 40 in the same company as you were when you joined the job market – even if you are the CEO. What people my age want is short, well-paid contracts. For that reason there may well have to be a continual turnover of people, who know little about the internal workings, but come in, do the job and then get out; while at the core there will be a group of loyal members who can see to and maintain the structure of the company. The question is not how to attract and retain talented people, but rather to know which are the people who are the 'loyal keepers' and which are the transient and contract workers. Because these two groups want different things you also have to be able to offer different packages to both.

Q.. *What are the key factors that will attract high calibre people to a business?*
A. The most important part of any young person's ambition is now *not* money, but rather personal job satisfaction, this is what prospective employers most need to remember. The opportunity to work either

the way you want, or at least to have the potential to direct some aspect of policy is very important. Of course, money is a real incentive and no one would dismiss that, but the potential to be judged on your performance, not relatively, but individually is what would drive me. By the way, the other issue is the location of work – is it exciting and attractive?

Q. *What would you say is the single most important factor in creating loyalty?*

A. A belief that you have a personal stake (whatever that might be) in the business. That your contribution is one that is fully recognized and appreciated: that you are an asset to the company. All the other things can be had anywhere: there is always a company that will pay you more, or offer other material benefits. But if you believe that you personally can make a difference – and be allowed to – then you'll stay.

Q. *Do companies need programmes to identify and develop talented people?*

A. Yes. They should form a group who seek and develop different categories of employees. They should be divided into three main groups.

- Those that headhunt and find already successful general managers and other knowledge workers.
- Those that retrain existing lower level workers who offer any potential and generally seek external talent as well (eg employees who have completed training with a big firm and may want to change: it may be the only time these people come onto the market).
- Those that target and recruit young graduates. Not only those from business schools – where the standard of business knowledge is high but business acumen and ability is low – but throughout colleges: particularly the previously untapped resources of humanities. The people who lead are in humanities, those in business schools are the ones who do the work!

Q. *Do you think that organizations are committed to looking outside their traditional recruitment area to attract talent?*

A. Of course not! They are too lazy for that! Those who say anything else, just don't know the people who are slipping through their fingers. They need to find the potential CEOs who are not offering themselves; huge amounts of preparation needs to be made to improve the market for women. Looking for leaders in non-traditional areas is hugely important and there must be a decision taken by leading groups to target the rich potential of humanities graduates and other 'non-business' areas.

Q. *Finally, if you could have a completely free hand, what is the one thing you would do to ensure that the organization you headed was able to attract, develop and retain the very best business professionals?*

A. Create a situation where there are clear and easy lines of communication to and from top management which highlights the ability and potential that exists in the company for real and definite promotion and a say in what the company does. Furthermore, I would create a department which is designed specifically for targeting and recruiting people from a wide range of areas in society, instead of relying on the 'usual suspects'.

Women – a waste of talent continues

McCaughey's views bear thinking about and, for those who want to win, taking some action on. What it probably needs is for smart corporations to hire the McCaughey's of this world to create and operate that in-house talent-targeting taskforce he described.

And one of the things that a group like that could do would be to make sure that women are being used to their full potential – because, as I already explained, they are clearly not.

In the UK, although the number of women in executive positions has more than doubled in the last decade (almost one executive in five is now a women), this is not mirrored in top management, where in 1998 only 3.6 per cent of all company directors were women – *down* from 4.5 per cent in 1997. In the US, it is also getting worse. In 1987, there were 11 women directors in *Fortune 500* companies, by 1997, there were just eight.

What organizations need to do is look to examples like Procter & Gamble, where a third of brand managers and half of all marketing managers are women.

But will that ever happen? Jacques Bouwens, managing partner of search firm Russell Reynolds in Amsterdam, points out that he is working on an assignment to replace a CEO at a $1 billion, 10,000 people company. 'It's sad to say, but there is no way we would put up a woman, they just wouldn't believe she could do the job.' Even in enlightened, sophisticated corporate players like Citibank, that pride themselves on cultural and ethnic diversity, women at the top don't get much visibility. Of the 101 countries they operate in, women head up just four of those. This reluctance by even

> 'It's sad to say, but there is no way we would put up a woman, they just wouldn't believe she could do the job.'

enlightened firms could well mean that they will suffer a drought of loyal employees who can do those top jobs in years to come, as failure to bite the bullet now – linked to increased executive poaching – will reduce the available talent pool.

Then again, others will just get tired of trying. Says organizational psychologist, Elisabeth Marx, 'A lot are going to fight their way to a senior level and get blocked for one reason or another and say, "I don't need, this – I'm out of here". Really it is such a waste.'

The spouse thing

The other issue that raises its head when it comes to women managers is that of the spouse thing. When one gets asked to move, what happens? Evidence I have collected in the US and Europe shows two things seem to happen. In more and more cases – particularly early in careers – there is a new trend to take it in turns. I get moved to Buffalo, you

> the day the big job comes along it is usually the man's career that wins

come. You get moved to London, I come. This it seems can work, until the day when the big job comes along. Then it would appear that a final career choice has to be made and it is usually the man's career that wins (maybe that's why there are so few women in the boardrooms of Europe and the US).

'The whole spousal issue is a problem', says Alan Jones, VP and head of human resources at Citibank, Global Corporate Banking in New York. 'One of the difficulties is that intelligent, high-achieving people tend to pair off, so the old days of one person's career to consider have definitely gone.' While being very flexible, 'we are open to people taking it in turns to move'. Jones notes that 'children and education systems also play a part, so I think we still have a lot to do here and have to be more thoughtful about how we tackle these issues'. Jones, however, points out that sooner or later, if you move up the hierarchy you get to a point, 'Where both of you can't work, there is just too much to do.'

At that point, Russell Reynolds' Jacques Bouwens says he knows what happens, 'the wife stays home. For any guy running a large operation, it is the wife who creates and provides the support system, the total infrastructure.' Yes, it is true – even in the year 2000.

The rejection package

One of my favourite stories is told by Jim Harris, author of the book *Finding and Keeping Great Employees*. Explaining how Ben and Jerry's the famous ice-cream maker turns job applicants into customers, he tells of how he applied to their 'Yo, We Want You to be Our CEO' contest – along with 20,000 other ice-cream fanatics. Harris didn't get an interview but he got something else instead. Enclosed in his 'rejection' package was a full size 'Official Rejection Letter', suitable for framing and picturing Ben (Cohen) and Jerry (Greenfield). The caption read 'We almost wanted you, Jim Harris, to be our CEO.' It added that, 'it warms our hearts – and blows our minds – that someone of your high caliber would even consider a career with us. Your talents and potential convinced us that a much higher calling awaits you. You're just too valuable to the world to be peddling ice cream. Be happy, go lucky.' Included was coupon for a free pint of ice cream.

Only in America perhaps, but it points to that method of knowing who your people and potential people can be. Even if you can't use someone today, don't close the door on tomorrow. In this new world where potential employees call the shots, you need to keep them happy. Upset them and you upset others they will talk to – family, friends and neighbours. Many of us won't be able to afford to be dismissive of people. By the way does your firm make a policy of writing kind rejection letters?

Seeking the global player

Ensuring a supply of up-and-coming talent, that wants to be truly international, is also an issue that Jones has to tackle. 'We worry that our future leadership won't be mobile enough, so we have deliberately gone out to find people who are bi-lingual or tri-lingual from the very best schools worldwide.' Based on a constant intake (there are currently 45 in the pro-gramme), Citibank has put together a programme that tests them and also stuffs them full of knowledge. They spend the first month at New York head-quarters, then five months in a country, then another month in New York, then five more months in a country, until the 18-month process is over. While not all make it, the success level is high and breeds a fierce loyalty and a tight knit future international cadre that is able to operate almost any-where. And, as Jones observes, 'If you are heading one of our emerging markets, you probably get to play golf with the prime minister and you can have a profound effect on some local economy – for the ambitious that can be a real turn on.'

Location, location, location

The other vital issue in the attraction of talent is not who you are but where you are located. Companies are beginning to realize that talent migrates to the kind of place it wants to work. In fact it always has, we just didn't observe it that closely. Especially for the young end of the work-force, who know that the life/work **talent migrates to the kind of place it wants to work** balance isn't going to be found in a backwater, they want access to places where they can enjoy their leisure hours, whether they are in a big city or out in the country.

Some examples

Here's a round-up of what smart companies are doing to ensure that talent has no problems ringing their doorbells.

- Hong Kong-based airline Cathay Pacific moved its data headquarters to Sydney, Australia, citing availability of IT skills.
- Phone-maker Ericsson says it will leave Sweden, 'as our people in R&D would rather relocate to the US or the UK'.
- PC maker Gateway moved headquarters from Sioux City to San Diego to attract managers and engineers who won't move to South Dakota.
- The only way Sweden's Electrolux could get a new head for its data pro-cessing operation was to agree to locate it in London.

- Agricultural machinery manufacture John Deere says it has problems hiring at its Moline, Illinois centre.
- Electronics giant Philips has moved its headquarters from remote Eindhoven to Amsterdam where it says it can attract more international managers. It also has two major world headquarters in San José, California to access hi-tech talent.
- Cruise operator Cunard moved headquarters from New York to Miami, the centre of the global cruise industry.
- Federal Express had problems attracting young professionals to headquarters in Memphis, so has moved its IS operations to Dallas, Colorado Springs and Orlando, giving potential recruits a choice of location.

Excellent infrastructure wins out

Around the globe, companies are paying less and less heed to countries and concentrating on moving to locations where there is an established talent pool. Excellent infrastructure, international schools and a secure lifestyle are key factors, as are local costs and taxes.

Consequently, areas like London, Paris and Frankfurt become critical business hubs, as do San Francisco, Los Angeles and New York. These cities and the areas around them are set to grow as they continue to attract more and more people who want to work in an exciting, hot-house environment and have access to the lifestyle they expect.

companies are paying less and less heed to countries and concentrating on moving to locations where there is an established talent pool

The other issue is that, if you are not in one of the trendy areas that talent seems to gravitate toward, you may find it not only difficult to hire the best people, but simply impossible.

At that stage, companies are beginning to get very inventive and are using top-of-the-line technology to make it possible for new hires to work in a virtual world. If senior managers are spending large amounts of time travelling to see clients, where they locate is largely irrelevant as long as they come to headquarters once or twice a month. For service providers and members of task-forces the ability to access an airport or an e-mail is often the critical factor.

These sorts of developments are also creating more and more executive commuters who work in one city or country during the week and go home for weekends. British bankers head out of Frankfurt, multinational marketers leave Brussels and drive, take the train or fly home to Paris, Bonn, Amsterdam and London (all less than two hours away). This is

more and more executive commuters work in one city or country during the week and head home for weekends

bringing unprecedented flexibility to recruitment and a focus on these areas as true 21st Century regions of business talent.

Take care with job-hoppers

Job-hopping may not be frowned on anymore – working at five jobs in ten years isn't the turn-off it used to be. But be careful. When candidates come flocking ask yourself this, 'Is my offer really a whole lot better than where the person is working now?' If the answer is not a resounding 'yes' then seriously question whether you want to hire this person. The chance that they are moving before the decision is made for them is high, or they may just be mediocre performers. As one recruitment expert put it, 'in many cases, 12 years of experience translates into one year of bad experience repeated 12 times, you could just be taking part in the re-circulation of mediocrity – not everyone is a high performer you know'.

Taking care of people is taking care of business

People matter, and if you want to attract them to your door, you need to let them know that they do. Here's how some companies deal with attraction and retention.

Zurich Financial Services

Zurich Financial Services (ZFS) is a fast-developing group headquartered in Zurich, Switzerland but with a truly global business focus. Created around a series of high-profile mergers in the last few years, it is now a major player in the financial services industry and has the task of making itself more attractive to top talent. As part of that process, it has created a dynamic people management policy that is built around four key pillars:

- selection
- development
- performance management
- compensation.

ZFS chairman Rolf Hüppi says that, 'only those who clearly know their objectives, who are genuinely motivated and feel their potential has been recognized and encouraged, can demonstrate top performance'. It is very aware that, as a newly created, global group, it can't afford to deal just in mere words – there must be action. The ZFS view is, 'if we are to succeed in becoming a people-based organization it is vital that we agree on the foundation for world-class people management. To do this we need to sponsor a common understanding and a logical approach throughout the group. Our focus will be on getting the fundamentals right – and getting them right quickly.'

The story that ZFS wants to sell – externally to attract top talent, as much as inside to retain it – is how do we put the principles of the policy into practice. In their case by being very direct and 'walking the talk' around the whole business.

Much of that is based on the following actions:

- make selection skills a promotion and compensation criterion
- hire internal candidates
- recognize development as a leadership priority
- encourage leaders to spend 20–30 per cent of their time on people-management-related activities; especially developing their people
- encourage individuals to take the initiative for their own development
- identify high potential executives as successors for key positions
- provide accelerated growth opportunities
- coach to improve performance
- use performance measures that drive business results and customer satisfaction.

But ZFS make it clear that unless you *do it* rather than *talk about it*, it will never work.

DERA: creating a market niche

In the UK, DERA is the former Ministry of Defence operation that found itself privatized. By no means a leader in compensation, it discovered that it was able to create its own niche in the marketplace simply by being known as a place where great research was happening. Although many of its sites in Southern England are surrounded by hi-tech competitors who offer far more money, people knock on the door because they know it is a place with great research credentials and a long-term commitment that is accepted and believed.

Ann Chivers, head of human resources at DERA also places great store for the future in its graduate programme. 'We have a scholarship scheme where we match our students up with a "buddy" (a scientist) and they work closely with them at vacations. Most of them get so enthused they later join us.' She adds, 'We found that once they know the kind of work they can do, they want to join us. We see this very much as our competitive advantage as salaries are poor compared to the competition.'

ICO: talent to feed a global plan

ICO is a global mobile personal communications company founded in 1995. Once fully operational, it will enable anyone, anywhere to use a phone through earth stations and a dozen satellites. It's greatest challenge has been to attract top talent to feed its global plan, although at the end of 1999 it had a more pressing challenge in raising additional capital.

Philip Guy, global resourcing manager at ICO explains how they attract talent, 'The market for management talent is tighter than ever, especially in any business related to telecommunications. This is a buoyant, fast-growing sector, with a shortage of good people at the right level of age and experience. We need experience and we need to pick from the English-speaking pool.' Guy continues, 'Take the cellular phone industry. It is unusual to find candidates in the 40–45 age range with the right experience – they simply are not available. The reason is clear: cellular is in its infancy – only mature industries have an excess of talent floating around. The squeeze for us is worst in such functions as engineering, infrastructure, commercial and IT; pressures are less in the broader more industry-transportable disciplines like HR, legal, finance and communications.'

It's all about content

So what attracts people to ICO? Guy explains. 'We offer the right content. In this kind of industry, people in demand can afford to look around for the most fascinating project and so it helps that we can sell ourselves as creative, innovative, leading-edge. We have quite a sexy project, in fact it's hard to beat what we have: satellites being launched into space, a new global phone network that will operate anywhere under any conditions. Best of all we are inventing a new industry, a new market. Everything we do starts from a blank sheet of paper. That's a powerful draw for the right kind of person. It's the uniqueness and the challenge of the project that attracts.' Guy adds, 'In addition, the work environment – including the calibre of the people already on board – is a big factor in attracting talent. In our selection process, a candidate might meet four or five people. Often they will come back to HR and say, "Wow! I've met some really impressive people today," that works wonders.'

Although a very flat organization, ICO provides what Guy describes as, 'fabulous opportunities for personal development. Not a day goes by,' he enthuses, 'that you don't learn something significant – this means personal growth at a fast pace.' And with currently 43 nationalities on board they say that another key attraction is their 'internationalism'.

Portugal's point of view: Autosil

It's a long way from the world of global telecommunications to a car battery manufacturer in Lisbon, Portugal. Or is it? In the battle for talent, both have to use the market as best they can to get on board the people they need.

Pedro Sena da Silva, chairman of the board of Autosil, one of Europe's leading automotive battery manufacturers notes that, 'even in Portugal the battle for talent is taking on a new face'. Da Silva, explains that even in a country where 98 per cent of medium-sized industry is family owned, anyone who wants to attract the best talent is having to seriously rethink and give professional managers a piece of the action. 'If you don't begin – as an owner – to share with your managers, you are not going to survive long-term. Sooner or later, they will leave you,' he says.

Da Silva, whose grandfather started the firm, which now works for most of the major car manufacturers in the world, plans to take the company public within three years and make sure that his top people get equity. That will include his marketing director, who – unlike most directors in a still-macho nation – is female. Autosil has bought companies in France and Spain in recent years, 'a David eating a Goliath' and he has seen that often women are far better at international operations than men. 'One thing I discovered was that men are very traditional and very national. When they read newspapers or magazines they read what happens in their country: when they support a soccer team it's the same. So the French stay French the Portuguese, Portuguese. With women it is different. A women's magazine has the same things in it, so they are more aware and more able to share ideas. They are much more open than the men.'

So how does he attract the talent he needs? 'I think it is much easier in Portugal,' da Silva says with a grin. 'First we are known as a good employer – remember everyone knows everybody in Lisbon. Second, I know where all the people I would want to see eat lunch, so I go there and talk to them – maybe that is why we have so few headhunters in Portugal, we know where all the talent eats lunch!' I support this view. Flying with a well-known Portuguese management consultant from Lisbon to the northern town of Porto one morning, I discovered he knew at least 75 per cent of the people on the plane.

It can be concluded that, wherever you are in the world, attracting the right people is a tough, tough business and it's getting tougher all the time. Creative solutions abound, you and your business are simply the prisoner of the systems you have created that can restrict how far you can – or are willing to throw your net. Go on, be bold, try something new before the competition gets there first.

Going talent shopping

And then again, sometimes you just pay. There are moments when you have no alternative but to go shopping with your cheque-book.

The advice from those who have done this in the past is, make sure you know what you are going shopping for, have a list and a budget and try and keep to it. Body shopping – especially at the high end –

> There are moments when you have no alternative but to go shopping with your cheque-book.

Call centres fight for scarce talent

One area where the talent battles are already raging at full force is in the call centre industry – a business that has mushroomed in recent years as technology and the need for greater customer services have converged. Lyndon Evans, director of marketing in Europe for Manpower, a major call centre staffing provider, forecasts that in 2000, 1 per cent of the working population of Europe will be employed in call centres – they are facing critical shortages of staff that are restricting their growth.

In countries like Scotland, Ireland and throughout the Benelux states, a well-educated, articulate workforce has been available for telesales or as customer service providers. However, such has been the demand that there are no people left that qualify. Major corporations like IBM, with its huge European call centre in Scotland, have struggled to get the people they need. Worse still, the call centre is getting the reputation of being the modern day equivalent of a sweat-shop or Victorian workhouse.

But while turnovers are high, smart employers are creating the best environments they can, putting in gyms, swimming pools and massage parlours to ease the aches, pains and strains of days spent on the phone. As one of the major outsource operators of call centres, Manpower has even developed a unique rota system that allows those facing burn-out in a sales-oriented call centre to move to less demanding roles.

Lyndon Evans explains, 'in some areas we manage different centres for different clients. While some are pure telesales, which brings a lot of pressure, others are handling enquiries (like insurance claims or utility information) which is very much a reactive role. What we do, if we see people are coming under strain, is recycle them to a calmer environment. This means that they can continue to work and if they want to go back to the more proactive call centre job at a later date they can.' This way, Manpower is able to hold on to scarce, well-trained talent and keep it motivated. It does wonders for reducing turnover.

should really be a last resort. But such are the surprises of the marketplace that many top HR professionals say that it is becoming a frequent event. So much so, they say, that it is now being seen as a key skill to be able to offer your next employer.

Sudden departures are difficult to deal with, especially if they are key executives, so any HR manager who is good at his or her job in today's volatile marketplace should know how to get replacements – even if they are only temporary – fast.

This is shown in a possibly apocryphal story of Bill Gates and Microsoft (we couldn't confirm it, but it sounds good anyway!). The story goes that Bill Gates wanted a very senior software engineer at IBM. So much was he enamoured of this tower of talent that he offered him 25 per cent more money to join Microsoft. The engineer told his boss and IBM matched the bid. Next, Gates offered 50 per cent more – again IBM matched the bid. Then, Gates changed the rules. He offered the man's wife $1,000,000 of Microsoft stock. IBM had no systems, no procedures to make a counter offer – they just weren't equipped to deal with a totally new tactic.

It doesn't matter if this story is totally true or not, it serves a purpose. It shows that a smart operator who wants something, can always think of new ways to get it. IBM was still in its box of offering counter bids to something it could deal with. When the rules were changed, when the aggressor became super-flexible, it couldn't play anymore.

Watch out! There's a spy about

Companies in hard-pressed industries are now running scared that the headhunters' calls are more than just wanting to steal bodies from your business – they want the secrets as well. In fact, in some cases it seems they didn't really want the people at all, the information will suit them just fine.

Loosely labelled the 'Lopez syndrome' after the General Motors executive who went AWOL with a bunch of files and a string of his people, executives are getting concerned that hostile hiring is being combined with espionage. In fact certain companies have discovered that you don't have to hire people to discover a competitor's secrets – one or two interviews may well do the trick.

Some companies have been known to send employees on job interviews to obtain information. Sun Microsystems in Silicon Valley believes it is a victim – of 87,000 candidates interviewed in 1996, more than 200 submitted a false identity. Worse still, there was a rumour that one US corporation created a phony headhunting firm in London with the sole object of interviewing candidates from a competitor.

The rise of the Internet poses more security problems, with it being easy to post a fictitious advertisement and wait for the replies and the information to come flooding in. Employers beware.

Breaking the rules

Another story (again no one knows if it is true, but I heard several versions within days of being in Shanghai), shows that anyone who is prepared to break the rules can cause havoc.

An American manager is sent to Shanghai to run a business. He arrives in the city to find a company but no workers. What to do? He walks up to the reception area of the hotel where he is staying and says, 'who here speaks English?' Hands go up, behind reception, all over the lobby. 'OK, I'll give everyone who works here double what you are getting, if you follow me.' Two minutes later, the story goes, 'the hotel had lost 25 per cent of its staff'.

What all this proves is that, in organizing to win the people wars, you can never stand still, never afford be complacent. You must use all the ammunition you can find to not just hire, but make it clear that you want to attract the best and brightest. Want ads and recruiters just won't do it on their own, you have to be a lot more innovative than that. You need a website that attracts people – the kind of people you want – like moths to a flame. You need to be represented where your target talent wants to be, you need to be at colleges and recruitment fairs and aware of what is available in the local community. Don't do all these things – or don't do them consistently and well – and you may as well surrender. There's a whole series of opposing armies out there marching to the sound of a new, very different drummer. If you can't match the fast paced beat they have adopted, your talent is going to cross over and go to war with an army that it knows can win.

E-commerce equals employment flexibility

One of the great talent fiascoes of 1999 was the rush to hire e-commerce experts. Stories abound of CEOs – learning that e-commerce was the hot new trend – demanding that specialists be brought on board pronto. Mid-level executives were dispatched to set up e-commerce operations, HR was told to hire e-commerce talent. The trouble was, no one knew enough to hire the right people, no one really thought through what they wanted. Meanwhile, the price of e-commerce people (or rather people who claimed to be e-commerce experts) began to soar. The more CEOs wanted them, the higher the price went. And it didn't stop in the US either. European Geschaftsfurhers and President Directeur's joined in. And, with few real e-commerce experts (technical people with a lot of marketing knowledge as well) around, the prices just kept climbing.

And other issues came up, as my visit to Citigroup in New York showed. Like others, they were determined to get a march on the marketplace and get an e-commerce operation off the ground as soon as possible. The only problem is that the techies that make it work don't really want to hang out in some canyon of steel in Manhattan. And – no detraction from Citigroup's excellent reputation for management – they didn't, in their techno-junky world, think that Citigroup was a cool place to be. The result? Citigroup have had to build a facility (it is called 'e-city' to separate it from the bank's name and sound trendy) that can compete favourably for the talents of these people with the hottest outfits in Silicon Valley and Seattle. As one Citigroup HR executive said, 'We have to create a culture amongst these people that meets their needs. This type of business is a world away from a derivative trader, but unless we are flexible we cannot do these things and we just won't be able to access this talent.'

The lesson to learn is that it is not just having the muscle and the money; in today's marketplace you have to be flexible (that word again) and know how to appeal to those you want to hire – because you need them more than they need you. Really, it is a positioning exercise, which you have to get right.

Points to ponder

- It's just not enough to have the muscle and the money anymore – to attract the new talent you need, you have to be cool too. Be prepared to reposition your firm – even move parts of it geographically to where the talent lies.

- Expect potential employees to tell you what they want in terms and conditions – today's job candidate is forthright and needs to be treated in new ways.

- Companies that report most satisfaction with headhunters have built deep, long-lasting relationships with them – have you done this?

- On-line recruiting is set to be a huge revolution. What have you done about this? Too many firms are missing out on opportunities to snare hot talent in this way.

- The amount of talent crossing over once-closed industry boundaries is breathtaking – your competitor today can be any corporation.

- Hire the best you can from other industries, but remember that business specific experts have their place too.

- The time's come to make sure your CIO is part of top management strategy making – if not, they'll either leave or you'll be unable to compete in this high-tech world.

- Reputation is all. You cannot afford to let yours slip, it will seriously damage your recruitment chances.

- You must have the machinery in place to let people grow – constantly. Failure to closely monitor employees' enthusiasm and contentment is unforgivable – they'll leave you.

- Think outside that box that you call employee compensation – others are, with discounted travel, cars and holidays, valet services for dry cleaning and groceries and learning centres for employees' children.

- Thoroughly review the working environment in your company and what you ask your people to do. Are you realizing people's talent and enthusiasm or creating a regime that stifles their potential?

- Be careful of giving people high expectations when you hire them and then failing to live up to those promises further down the road – this is a major turn-off.

- It's all about content. Get that right, job, future, reward and you'll be fine. Just make sure you have the systems to keep all those balls in the air at once.

- As a last resort, know how to go shopping with your cheque-book, and make sure your HR people have this as a key skill – the ability to fill critical positions quickly. In fact, make it part of their job descriptions.

4 | Holding the talent line tight

We can't all be heroes because somebody has to sit on the curb and clap as the parade goes by.

Will Rogers

If the house is on fire, forget the china, silver and wedding album – grab the Rolodex

Harvey MacKay

At IBJ Whitehall Financial Group on Wall Street they call it 'project dandelion', at Zurich Financial Services (ZFS) a very clinical Swiss-sounding 'people management policy' – yet they are both about the same thing, all too serious methods for getting real values, rather than rhetoric, at the top of the people agenda.

What IBJ and ZFS have rapidly learned in the battle for talent is that hiring it is one thing, keeping it is another thing altogether. 'We call it project dandelion for a good reason', says IBJ's VP of HR Keith Darcy. 'It reminds us that we have got to get total top

in the battle for talent, hiring it is one thing, keeping it is another thing altogether

management commitment to our programme of engaging all of our people. If we don't have top management on board – every day – it just won't happen. If you just step on a dandelion it will just grow back and you have changed nothing. Our aim is to get to the root cause and make the changes there.' Similarly with ZFS, its view is that you must – especially in a situation where you have mergers and acquisitions taking place – have more than just a message, you have to have actions that continually underscore your commitment to people.

'A vision of growth is what is going to keep people', enthuses Brad Thomas, a VP of Executive Resources at Citibank in New York. 'Today people want to do bigger and more challenging things. It is when they slow down that they begin to look around.'

Citibank take potential losses so seriously that they have hired in a specialist from General Electric to help them create systems to track people and make sure they stay happy and focused. Alan Jones, head of HR for Citibank's global corporate banking points out, 'Our task is to kill the departure rate – although it isn't that bad – and we are gearing up to better manage that.' Why do Citibank people leave? 'Most likely because they can't get past the boss,' says Jones, 'or they feel they will get a bigger stretch somewhere else.' Both Jones and Thomas know that Citibank is a

others, who are a lot less rigorous in their development of talent, view hitting on and snaring a Citibank employee as a real battle honour

major target for others, who are a lot less rigorous in their development of talent, view hitting on and snaring a Citibank employee as a real battle honour. 'Just because of our reputation,' says Jones, 'they often see the employee as a lot bigger in stature than we do. Look in Asia, virtually every Asian bank is full of ex-Citibank people.'

Jones, who says that he has, 'never seen anyone who's any good quit if they are kept on a diet of a steep learning curve and real challenges,' knows that his firm has its work cut out. With operations in over 100 countries, keeping track of the happiness factor of your high performers can be tough in the extreme.

Stretch your people

But if you don't do that you risk losing them, especially if their attention is diverted to something that looks like a much bigger challenge over the hill. As most interviewees testify, the grass always looks greener, so it is vitally important that you not only track progress and put in challenges, but you stretch your people as much as you can.

'Use them or lose them' may be a trite phrase, but it is an increasingly valuable one to remember. Imagine, if you will, spending five or six years developing a cadre of high-performers who, just because of the firm's reluctance to give them 'the big job' are picked off like targets in a shooting gallery.

As several senior managers pointed out, your concerns about giving them a top job, won't be matched by the

> it is up to the company to take on the risk. You have to do that – especially in today's marketplace

competition seeking to hire them. Therefore, as Patricia Seeman, an organizational development adviser with Zurich Financial Services, points out, 'it is up to the company to take on the risk. You have to do that – especially in today's marketplace.'

Expectation fails to match reality

Of course, all the planning in the world won't make up for happy accidents and it seems that a lot of employee motivation (and the reason they stick around) is due to the fact that often poor management has meant truly exciting – if unpredictable times – when employees can excel.

However, this unfortunately usually ties into working excessive hours, which is an issue that recurs as a definite demotivator. A 1999 study by the UK's Roffey Park Management Institute noted that, '95 per cent of our study considered that they have developed in the past year, largely through informal means as well as training . . . this was not necessarily brought about by skilful management interventions or by succession planning, but by organizational growth and structural change in many cases'. But the study found that top management involvement – vital to instilling a vibrant culture into a business – is still not taking place.

As Roffey Park's, Linda Holbeche, explains, there is still a great deal to do. 'Employers need to provide clear and unequivocal support for better balance, rather than appearing to endorse the principle of work/life balance but doing nothing to make reality match aspiration. Management appears not to be "walking the talk". In fact, our survey showed that 76 per cent of respondents suggested that organizational practices are very much out of synch with espoused value statements.'

This is borne out by the daily experiences of top HR professionals. At telecommunications company Global One (the joint venture of

Sprint, France Telecom and Deutsche Telecom) project manager turnover at one time reached a heady 35 per cent. Global One's Gunnar Sandmark explained, 'no project man-

no manager is going to stay in a business if he doesn't think it is really solid

ager (or any other manager for that matter) is going to stay in a business if he does-n't think it is really solid. Exit interviews told us that it had nothing to do with money, it was lack of direction and support. OK they got more money anyway when they left, but that wasn't the issue.'

Own the issues

Roffey Park's Holbeche believes that top management must take on a great deal more responsibility and ownership of issues that concern employees – if they do not, they cannot be surprised when people leave. 'From our study, reward systems were considered particularly contradictory,' she reports, ' with few incentives or sanctions to encourage management to model the values. There was a definite call for a culture change to be led by senior management.'

'This appears to be important in not only providing a climate for high performance, but also because of the perceived affect on employee morale of inappropriate behaviours.' She adds, 'Several respondents reported that where senior managers did model organizational values, individual commitment to the organization increased. On the other hand, the disconnection between management rhetoric and practice appears to be a strong reason for people wishing to leave.' Holbeche ends, 'Management needs to set a clear priority on introducing effective policies and practices which are more than just window dressing.'

I hate the boss

If the British think that differences between top management and the rest of the workforce are still causing problems, the Germans are much more forthright – they simply dislike their bosses. The Geva Institute in Munich reports that 88 per cent of workers think that their bosses are 'disagreeable or incompetent' and '20 per cent admitted they hate their bosses. Conversely, half of the managers surveyed said that they felt 'rejected by their subordinates,' who, 'at times rebelled or attempted to be revengeful'.

What Germans hate most about their bosses

- Use improper criticism   85%
- Stifle employees   79%
- Are unpredictable   74%
- Fail to recognize staff contribution   72%
- Are unfair   69%
- Refuse to communicate   67%
- Are dishonest   65%
- Lack a sense of loyalty   54%

Ninety-seven per cent of the 770 respondents suggested that 'social skills and good communications are essential in the workplace'.

Brace yourself for the 4Bs

From all the conversations about retaining talent, it is clear that none of us can afford to go on managing our people the way we have in the past. But it is more than that. It is coming to an acceptance, an understanding that we need to use every piece of armoury that is available – and that includes hiring in 'mercenary' organizations to help us get focused on the pieces of our business that we do best. Keith Darcy of IBJ Whitehall Financial Group in New York, possibly put it most simply when he said his view was to urge managers to concentrate their energies on the four Bs:

- buy
- build
- bounce
- borrow.

Buy in what you don't have in-house; build up what you do best; bounce out the things you do badly to others who do them well; and borrow ideas from external experts and alliances.

Shorter tenures at the top

Whether top management's wholehearted involvement in 'walking the talk' ever happens is open to question, as they have no plans to be around for a long time anyway. A worldwide study by the Association of Executive Search Consultants (AESC) in 1998, found that 'over seven in ten corporate leaders expect shorter tenures for most CEOs over the next ten years'. The main reasons cited for the difficulty in retaining corporate leaders were:

- diminished personal commitment (two-thirds said that most CEOs in the future will have only a short-term personal commitment to the company)
- extreme demands of the job, driven mostly by intense pressure for immediate results from shareholders, that has reached 'fever-pitch' (almost all labelled this as a 'major factor' in high CEO turnover – see also list in Chapter 1, about top issues for CEOs)
- fierce competition for the best, 'the markedly competitive battle for effective CEOs typically results in large compensation packages being offered to lure the best candidates and increases the desire to job jump' (seven in ten corporate leaders – particularly 'up-and-comers', say this is a major factor in high corporate turnover).

And in case you are thinking, 'what about non-compete agreements?' Forget it, they don't work, and that's official. Seventy-six per cent of CEOs say so, and so do 77 per cent of CEO wannabes.

Challenge beats money

Meanwhile, below the heady heights of CEOs, Roffey Park's 1999 study of business issues also highlighted – once again – that the main reason for staying in a job was challenge, which won out over money (greedy CEOs take note!).

Other similar motivators that they recorded in their research were, variety, autonomy and good relationships. These are exactly the stay-put factors that I encountered in the three round-table sessions with young managers, where the social aspect of the job was a vital element. Many of the managers put work colleagues as the prime reason for staying in a job – far ahead of money or future opportunity. Indeed at 25–30 age level, few were worried about promotion – and it certainly wouldn't have pushed any of their motivational buttons. Most felt that they would do this job and then move on to something else. Again this was particularly prevalent in the financial services industry, where people had plans as diverse as: 'open an art gallery'; 'buy a bar'; 'start an e-commerce operation;' and 'run my own alternative investment club'.

When we come to think of retention, it is important that we don't treat every group and every generation the same way. A strategy for holding onto a top salesperson, will be very different from that of keeping a 30-year-old IT specialist – their wants and needs are so very different.

Opinions count

Another opportunity that top management should face up to is that people at all levels of the organization like to feel that their opinions matter. Many of our interviewees noted that letting people have their say and knowing that they can influence decisions are vital in creating a retention culture. As one senior manager pointed out, 'it isn't always the big things that count with the majority, it is a lot of little things that add up to make one workplace a whole lot better than another'. As a management consultant – who spends time trying to get top managers to understand the importance of building exciting workplaces – said, 'management should have a huge advantage – most people don't want to change. We humans like predictability. So they must be doing some really stupid things if people walk out. Maybe they could get away with it even five years ago when the economy wasn't in such good shape, but with today's knowledge workers forget it.'

Living for the business

Let us not forget, however, that there will always be some people who totally and completely enjoy working. So much so that it *is* the dominant factor of a large part of their lives. Those people will never change and I suspect, despite all the talk, that they will still be – in the majority of cases – the people who make it to CEO or senior partner. The life/work balance equation is important to the majority, but it isn't to the minority who see 60-hour workweeks as normal and fun.

Take two people in a consulting firm, for example. One works at every opportunity and then looks for more. They always seem to be there, they are eager to take on the most onerous challenge. The other is different. Equally intelligent, they see that the life/work equation is important to them (for all sorts of reasons), so they negotiate and get a deal where they can work two days a week from home, get extra vacation time, maybe even a four day week. Five years down the line, who makes partner?

There you have it. You can say, 'well not everyone wants to be a partner'. That's true. But if we make a decision on more life and less work, we have to be able to accept that fact as well. Right now that is part of the debate that's not been resolved – people seem to want their cake and the partnership too. And that is just not going to happen.

In meeting the 21st Century needs of the workforce we must also be aware that our top deal-makers, salespeople and chief executives will always 'live for the business'. So will all those entrepreneurs we rely on to create new, exciting jobs. Yes, I believe we have to make changes, but I am also a realist.

A real value shift

As organizational psychologist Elisabeth Marx of consultants Norman Broadbent observes, 'Of course expectations have changed in the 90s, the personal component of people's lives is stronger and stronger. There has been a real value shift, but most organizations have failed to properly notice it. Lots of people are now clamouring for flexible work styles and sabbaticals.' She goes on, 'But those that want that lifestyle will have to realize that they can't have it both ways. Some people will still happily work 70 hours a week; so if others want less they will have to expect less.' And she concludes with the question, 'the challenge is, will there be room for organizations to have those two very different kinds of people inside them?'

What we need to be able to do is realize that we are not all the same anymore, and to get the best out of scarce talent. Some will want to work extremely hard and others won't. Do we let people go because they only want to work for three days a week or do we find ways to usefully use their talent? Times change, flexibility has to be part of an organization's approach to people management. Fail in that, fail to control the climate of the business and you will lose.

The downside of group rates

The art of holding onto talent isn't always just concerned with individual managers or specialists. In many businesses (financial services, consulting and hi-tech are good examples), whole teams come under threat. While there may be a lot of short-term gain in stealing a team from a competitor to give you an advantage – watch out. Many corporations say that they are strongly against bringing in teams as, if and when they leave, you are left very vulnerable indeed. It is particularly worthwhile to guard against a new senior manager arriving and then – over a period of time – bringing into the firm people he has worked with in the past. Often this creates clashes of culture that are hard to resolve and puts the retention of others in question. Worse still, if the newly hired manager leaves, his newly recruited team will slowly (or perhaps very quickly!) leave as well. Where a team leader shows up on your doorstep, saying he can deliver his entire group, make sure you do any deal with your eyes wide open. Yes, such leaders may be able to deliver what they promise short-term, but don't expect these people to stay – they are fully operational mercenaries, loyal to no one but themselves. As soon as they have achieved what they set out to do, or get a better offer, they will leave.

Whose finger's on the climate control?

Back in 1984, Harold Geneen, the legendary head of ITT wrote, 'Good management executives, with a proven track records, are a rare breed. They can get high pay and long limousines almost anywhere they choose to go. Those who remained with us did so because they were happy in the ITT environment, where we all worked hard, were continually challenged, were amply rewarded and could continue to grow. They stayed, too, out of a sense of well-being and loyalty.'

Geneen built an amazing industrial conglomerate based on watching the numbers, but he watched people too. This is what he had to say about people. 'Once the right men are in place, a company's working environment becomes the most important, ongoing element in the success or failure of the enterprise. The climate control is in the hands of the chief executive. He sets the temperature and quality of the air of the place.'

That is exactly what CEOs and their top management teams must do if they are to ensure a stable climate. They need to make sure that the temperature and the air quality meet the needs of the workers of today.

Ideas to have and to hold

Companies around the world are facing up to the need for flexibility as a key retention strategy in a variety of ways. Here are some ideas that may help you better hold on to your people. Implement all of them and you'd have the nightmare of zero turnover – remember, no one wants to achieve that.

Sonae

To many, Portugal doesn't sound like the epi-center of the business universe, but once attracted to the country, even ambitious foreign executives are likely to stay. Diversified conglomerate Sonae (which has a portfolio from supermarkets and shopping malls to wood products and mobile phones), employs 22,000 people and has an operating board of eleven that includes five under 40. Its chairman, Belmiro Mendes de Azevedo, says that, 'Portugal is the European Florida,' and that 'once Northern European executives and their families get used to the lifestyle in the country (its headquarters is in the northern city of Porto), they never want to leave. They can live in a huge house by the sea and play golf every evening,' he says.

Granada and BT

In the UK, television provider Granada boosted retention by putting its engineers onto flexible work contracts that better suited customers and employees. Now able to work more from their homes, through the use of new technology, they are better able to utilize their time. Installation engineers at British Telecommunications have also moved in the same direction. Hand-held computers download details of the following day's work plan, allowing them to avoid commuting to a central location.

Service-Ware

How flexible firms across the US can be was illustrated when the latest *Star Wars* movie débuted in May 1999. Some companies gave employees half a day off to see the movie, others – recognizing an opportunity for people to have fun – organized a dress-as-your-favourite *Star Wars* character day. In another move, hi-tech firm Service-Ware in Philadelphia ran newspaper ads saying that job candidates would get free movie tickets – they received 100 applications for 10 openings.

The eclipse phenomenon

Where America gives time off for Hollywood blockbusters, Europe does it for the real thing. The August 1999 total eclipse saw thousands of companies across the UK, France, Germany, Austria and Turkey give employees a day off to observe the unique phenomenon.

Hoechst

Often it is just reminding people what they have that counts. Chemical giant, Hoechst Celanese went out of its way to explain the benefit packages that employees took for granted and discovered that employees were 40 per cent more likely to be retained when they were aware of the value.

Origin

Similarly, Origin, the software arm of Philips Electronics, was having a hard time holding programmers and project leaders until they realized that their package was much better than the 'cash only' offers of their competitors. Although some still jumped for the money, they found that more mature managers – the ones they wanted to retain – tended to stay.

Silicon Valley

The importance of knowing who wants what and at what stage in their career is important. Studies by Silicon Valley employers show that employee churn lessens as they pass age 35. Real life responsibilities like marriage, kids and mortgage take hold making people less likely to move and take a chance. Employers need to know this and be aware of the different levels of retention risk.

Marks and Spencer

Asking what employees want, isn't a bad idea either. British retailer, Marks & Spencer did this in Hong Kong and found that employees wanted share options, training and development. The company has already responded by paying for 70 per cent of education fees.

Training

Offers of training are an excellent way to keep your staff in Asia – but beware. Make sure you attach strings, of the legal variety. Increase the skill set of your employees and they become even more valuable, so link training to an agreed (legally contracted) work period (two years is the norm in places like China).

Hewlett-Packard

Hewlett-Packard is proof that money is not the prime motivator. In 1998, after poor earnings, it asked its top 2,000 staff to take a 5 per cent pay cut. Seen to be 'walking the talk' and making a visible contribution, the decision boosted employee morale.

Philips

At electronics giant Philips, retaining talented researchers at its main operation in out-of-the-way Eindhoven in The Netherlands isn't the problem many would think. 'Our research reputation is second-to-none', says their chief technology officer Marino Carasso, 'plus our people get to work on blue-sky research of their own'. Philips is famous for breakthrough electronic technologies like the CD player and the VCR, and is highly supportive of its research staff in pursuing their own ideas and funds their work. But they are also aware that there are more exciting environments, 'which is why we have a lab in California too, notes Carasso.

3Com

Santa Clara, California-based 3Com has given up worrying about working hours entirely, moving from the objective of work/life balance to what it calls 'work/life integration'. 3Com says that set working hours are ridiculous when people often work much longer due to the projects they are involved in. So employees choose their own terms of employment and the benefits that go with them. Technology drives the whole operation from the work to the reward system.

Xerox

Xerox claims that in the parts of its organization where it has piloted work/life programmes productivity has improved by as much as 30 per cent.

In their book *Sacred Cows Make the Best Burgers*, management commentators Robert Kreigel and David Brandt report that, 'when we ask people in our programs what inspires them at work they tell us:

- to be part of something great
- to do something I've never done before
- to do something I didn't think I could
- to do something meaningful for people, the community, the world, the environment
- to learn something new and interesting.'

As they say, 'notice that not one of these motives is about money or base self-interest. They are all about going beyond self-imposed limits and in some cases beyond the self entirely'. I hope employers are listening.

Ben and Jerry's

Everyone has heard of the success of ice cream producer Ben & Jerry's, where a lot of small things come together to create an organization where retention levels stay high. Part of that came from the creation of the Ben & Jerry's 'joy gang' that was given the task of finding ways to put fun into work. One huge success was an 'Elvis Day', another serving surprise breakfasts.

Burston Marsteller

Public relations firm Burson Marsteller, in Manhattan, has an electric golf cart, kitted up like an ice-cream truck, that the chairman uses to tour the corridors giving out free ice cream. His avowed intention is two-fold, 'making people smile' and 'getting them out of their offices to talk instead of sending e-mail to each other'.

Microsoft

No matter how successful you are, it is never too late to worry about what the future holds. While the myth still holds that knowledge workers are beating down the doors of Microsoft to get inside, people do leave. According to the company's own research, reasons are that work/life balance again, plus the rigorous intellectual competition and – wait for it – concerns that the company is becoming too bureaucratic as it gets ever bigger. This is a concern that will affect many start-ups, even those a lot less successful than Microsoft and need to be addressed carefully. What one pocket of talent perceives as a great place to work is a turn-off for another, and this can happen – it would seen – almost overnight. This shows that as a company ages, who it wants to retain and who it wants to attract will change – possibly dramatically.

Midland Bank

Britain's Midland Bank (now HSBC) raised its retention rate for women on maternity leave from 30 to 80 per cent by allowing them to work more flexibly on their return.

A lifestyle example

Retention takes on different forms. The US magazine *Girlfriends*, regularly lists the ten best lesbian places to work. In case anyone thinks I am being frivolous, this is an interesting listing of corporations where women get to the top and where the life/work balance is being taken very seriously indeed. The top ten are as follows.

- **Chase Manhattan**: 61 per cent female; 46 per cent upper managers. A big presence in the Houston, Texas gay community, and sponsor a local gay youth group.
- **Monsanto**: 38 per cent female; 27 per cent upper managers. Chemical

company (at the heart of the genetically modified food debate) offers such perks as fitness centres, mother's rooms and business casual dress every day. Also they don't track employee sick days.

- **Fannie Mae**: 54 per cent female; 32 per cent upper managers. Prides itself on treating its employees well – housing assistance, full tuition support and free on-site health assessments.
- **American Express**: 68 per cent female; 53 per cent upper managers. The company with the highest percentage of female employees and managers. Regularly recruits at Gay Pride events.
- **Coors**: 24 per cent female; 29 per cent upper managers. The Colorado brewery goes beyond being merely gay friendly, by actively recruiting lesbian and gay employees and funding gay events across the US.
- **Eastman Kodak**: 37 per cent female; 27 per cent upper managers. *Girlfriends* notes that 'it has shed its reputation as a stuffy, old-fashioned corporation and judging from its active gay and lesbian employee group and the "out" lesbians in upper management, it has become a place that lesbians can feel comfortable calling home'.
- **Aetna**: 76 per cent female. This Connecticut company encourages flexible schedules for its workers including telecommuting, compressing workweeks and reducing hours to part time.
- **Bank Boston**: 66 per cent female; 31 per cent upper managers. During the company's Gay and Lesbian Awareness Week, a huge rainbow flag flew outside company headquarters.
- **Chevron**: 23 per cent female. The first oil company to incorporate sexual orientation in non-discrimination and non-harassment policies.
- **NCR**: 30 per cent female; 10 per cent upper managers. The company's gay and lesbian employee group sponsored its own professional development conference in 1998.

More examples of getting it right

- Want to work less? Go to Sweden. Government rules on night-shift workers means that they now work less than 30 hours a week and get paid same as 40-hour-a-week day-shift workers.
- Still in Sweden, Ford's purchase of car manufacturer Volvo has caused ripples in the Olympic-sized pool the HQ workforce use. Swedes worry that their pool, along with the tennis courts, tanning beds and athletic track, physiotherapy centre and saunas may not survive the Detroit takeover. Local

press stories say that Volvo paid over $600,000 a year to maintain the centre. However, although a union-backed idea, the centre paid off. Absenteeism fell from a heady 10 per cent in the late 1980s to less than 4 per cent.

- At market research company, AC Nielsen, they have found a great way to make sure managers keep the employees happy. 'Twenty-five per cent of the incentive bonuses of our senior people are based on how satisfied the employees are', says Richard Savage, their head of HR for Europe, Africa and the Middle East. A case of no smiles, no money.

- The sandwich chain, Pret à Manger, goes one better than AC Nielsen. If you are promoted they give you a cash bonus, but you are not allowed to keep it – you have to give it away to your staff. The assumption – in this youth-driven company – is that you are now alright (you've been promoted), so it is time to help those who got you there. Founder of the company, Julian Metcalf believes that 'people will have gone out of their way to help you and you should give something back to them'. A great – and unconventional way – to build a company culture.

- At the other end of the spectrum, the London financial markets usually offer those that are making them millions the standard perk, 'if you work after eight at night we pay for your taxi home'. Many have been known to take the money and stay out all night instead.

- At Californian software company Oracle, they have developed a welcome pack that they give to every new recruit. More than just a handbook, it includes videos, a catalogue of its clothing, stationery, discount cards and lots more. Its objective is to make certain that 'from day one, they'll have at their fingertips the materials they need to get acclimatized and productive – fast'. And they've made a fun package out of an often boring necessity.

- German industrial giant Siemens is hell bent on creating a new image for itself – especially in its ability to retain top performers. To achieve that, it completely altered its age-old management selection process and created a system that reflected the importance of social skills and the ability to moti-vate people, creatively. When management launched an internal 'innovation competition' an amazing 6,000 employees entered – half of them outside Germany.

- DERA was part of the UK's Ministry of Defence and is now privatized. Although it pays considerably below market rates, retention is high (less than 4 per cent attrition). The reason is that it gives its people what they want:

  – the ability to work on exciting projects

– time-off to speak on international conferences
– encouragement to take lead roles on professional organizations all over the world
– the creation of a 'fellowship' programme for long stays that allows for time off to do blue-sky research.

Formerly part of the Royal Aeronautical Establishment, when it's lack of activity gave it the nickname 'sleepy valley', it is again proof that, not only is salary not everything, it doesn't come close.

● At Volkswagen they built a tight-knit cadre of high potentials from all over the globe and get them to spend time working together on problem-solving projects. The belief is that this builds long-lasting relationships and a strong sense of belonging to the business.

● Deloitte & Touche rates number eight, and the only consulting firm, on the *Fortune* best place to work in America, largely based on its innovative pro-gramme to retain female workers. As a result of its efforts 88 per cent of female and 81 per cent of male recruits cite people/office environment as one of their most important reasons for joining the firm.

● Consultants Peat Marwick also created programmes to be more flexible to retain its valued employees. Programmes included work-at-home and part-time, especially for professional women who wanted to cut back on their hours.

Supporting the spouse

The dichotomy of an increased need for global managers to take up foreign assignments and the unwillingness of working couples to sacrifice one or another's career for a foreign posting, is leading to even more out of the box, let's-be-flexible thinking. Managers are having to face up to the fact that the old days of the executive (a man) who you could post off abroad with the spouse (his wife) have gone. There are few non-working wives these days, and with the twin spectres of schooling for children and care for elderly par-ents, getting people to move can be difficult in the extreme. On that basis it requires careful thought and planning to get it right.

The following examples show how companies thought beyond the conventional in order to get much needed talent where they want it.

● SWIFT (Society for Worldwide Interbank Financial Transfer) wanted to move a software engineer to the US. The engineer's wife, holding a low level, but for her very worthwhile job in social services, didn't want to go. The company, thinking outside the conventional, found a degree course at the local university and enrolled her on it, paying the tuition fees. Result? Happy wife, happy company. Their take on this was, 'we aren't recruiting the husband, we are recruiting the wife'.

● Defence group DERA in the UK has a unique method of getting people to move – they put the spouse on sabbatical (if they are also employed by the company) for up to three years. At that time, if the partner goes back to the old location, the spouse will get his or her job back. If it needs a hard-to-get specialist it will also try its hardest to find the spouse work in the new local area.

● In Paris, a group of US corporations have clubbed together to create a job market for trailing spouses. Once it is known that a new transfer is coming in, the details of the spouse are sent out to the different companies showing their qualifications. Whilst work permits can be a problem, this kind of proactive approach helps a great deal.

● Market research firm AC Nielsen need to move an English woman executive from Russia to the Netherlands. The husband comes too and they fix him up with (and pay for) outplacement assistance to make sure he finds a job.

Expatriation horror

The need to have executives in overseas locations has never been greater. However, study after study makes it clear that few companies are really much good at managing the expatriate process. While it would seem that a stint outside the home country is almost a prerequisite for advancement, it also appears to be one of the best ways to lose scarce talent.

So badly is talent treated – especially once the assignment is over and they are repatriated – that many leave their companies within two years of

> it would seem that a stint outside the home country is almost a prerequisite for advancement, it also appears to be one of the best ways to lose scarce talent

The joys of the telecommute

Telecommuting, or teleworking, is apparently taking off big-time around the world – and boosting retention rates with those who seek a better work/life balance. With technology ever improving and phone charges ever falling, it has become easier and easier to allow staff that you really want to retain to be much more flexible in their 'office' location (currently telecommuting is growing at between 10–15 per cent in the US). While many old-fashioned managers think that out of sight employees are out of mind and out of control, there is growing evidence that this form of work (for those who like it) really does boost both productivity and retention rates. However, here are a few warnings for would-be employers setting up a telework operation.

- Don't ever force people to take up telework if they don't want to – they'll leave you sooner or later.
- Make sure that they are kept in the 'office loop' on a daily basis, otherwise they get panicked, or bored, or both.
- Make sure they come into the office on a regular basis and are seen as very much part of the team.
- Make sure that those who still commute don't think that telecommuters have a better deal or are being treated as 'special'. Office employees need to understand and appreciate the need for workforce flexibility.

their return. Taking on an overseas assignment can be fraught with problems, from the reluctance of a spouse to give up a career, to concerns that the expatriate will be outside of the power structure and not know what is going on. Many CEOs and HR professionals admit that, with mergers and acquisitions, restructuring and other corporate change endemic in our business, managers are more and more reluctant to leave the comfort of corporate headquarters. Swapping a spot in head office, where you can keep up with rumours and politics on a daily basis, for a desk in a foreign subsidiary, where you have little regular contact, can seem like a poor career move. On top of that, many corporate attempts to provide a management mentor – or champion – back at HQ have come to little as often the mentor gets reassigned or quits. Few companies have the systems to replace them when this happens.

Indeed, it is a rare organization – despite all the discussion and literature on the subject – that has much in the way of a plan when it comes

Indeed, it is a rare organization that has much in the way of a plan when it comes to overseas assignments

to overseas assignments: people get sent for very wrong reasons. Worse than that, when they return, there is little planning on what they should do next. The result? Many get underutilized or sidelined and eventually take off for other opportunities. 'Don't send the person who wants to go on a foreign assignment,' warns one HR professional, 'send the person who should go – the one that can get the job done.'

Demotivating the repatriates

A study by Prudential Relocation reported that 'HR executives said that workers based overseas feel "out of mind" and only 22 per cent believed that companies rewarded these type of assignments with career advancement.' The study suggested four proactive ways for expatriates to let their presence be known:

- keep the home office aware of successes
- insist on a mentoring programme on your return
- make sure the assignment is linked to your long-term career plan
- ask for networking opportunities with colleagues during your home leave.

One of the biggest problems confronting most expatriate managers is the huge degree of autonomy they get – often running their own mini-version of the corporation back home. I can remember sitting with a young US engineer in China, who pointed out to me, 'at headquarters my peers have to get five signatures to get a new photocopy machine, here I'm negotiating with the government!'

Experience like that is both career broadening and fun, so it's not surprising then that disillusionment can quickly set in when you get back to the centre of things. You are no longer a big fish in a smallish pond, you have to conform again. In fact disillusionment can be very high.

A report in the *Financial Times* noted that, 'of US managers, 26 per cent were actively looking for work in other companies after returning from overseas and 74 per cent expected to move on within a year'. This is tragic. A report *Managing and Motivating the International Executive* by

HR consultants DBM points out, 'When this occurs, the enormous invest-ment in the employee is lost. Even if the employee remains in the organization, his or her motivation and commitment could be significantly impaired.' The report goes on, 'From the perspective of the organization's global management development efforts, the loss of the very employees who have gained first hand international experience is a critical setback. The dis-satisfaction with the career management of repatriates sends out a damaging message to other potential expatriates.' DBM's advice? 'International assign-ments must be integrated into the organization's HR planning process. In addition to tracking where international assignees can contribute most to the organization in their next assignment, expatriates must be communicated with in a way that – while not promising them a specific next job, does inform them of what is expected in order to prepare for further career enhancement.'

Merger paralysis

DBM don't say it, but there is one flaw in all of this – merger mania is raging around the globe. And what merger's create – especially for the expatriate – is paralysis. In preparation for this book, I spoke to several dis-enchanted expatriates who had believed themselves to be on the corporate fast track (had been told they were on the cor-porate fast track in many cases) only to discover that, after the

> after the merger, the line from HQ went dead – they were out of sight and out of mind

merger, the line from HQ went dead – they were out of sight and out of mind. As several said, 'If a headhunter rings, I'll jump ship.' What a way to deal with retaining top talent.

Advice on the returning expatriate

Elisabeth Marx is a psychologist, a director of Norman Broadbent, a worldwide executive search company and the author of *Breaking Through Culture Shock*. Her views on the travails of the return-ing expatriate provide a crucial insight that companies would do well to heed.

'Returning home is not that simple for many international managers,' she says, 'their own country has changed, their organization has changed, their friends and family may have changed, and most importantly they have changed too.' Noting that many of the managers she has worked with reported difficulties with repatriation, Marx has found six points that need to be worked on:

- loss of lifestyle
- no appropriate job available
- loss of autonomy
- being made redundant
- handling politics at head office
- having to deal with uncertainty.

Marx notes that, 'managers frequently get slotted into jobs on return that are too low a level and they consequently experience immense frustration'. Some don't even bother to come home at all. As a region, Asia is crying out for can-do managers. Many, on hearing that they were being pulled back to Europe or the US, made a decision to 'go native' and get a job. This is another risk that companies take when they send people overseas and don't stay fully in touch with them. They risk losing the ability to retain them because they simply don't know what their needs and expectations are anymore.

> managers frequently get slotted into jobs on return that are too low a level and they consequently experience immense frustration

Motivate diverse groups

While researching *Building and Retaining Global Talent: Towards 2002* for the Economist Intelligence Unit in 1998, it became clear that the old-style expatriate, sent overseas with wife in tow, was not just an anachronism, but had been replaced with a whole series of new-style expatriates that meet the changed needs of today's corporations. If you are seeking to retain talent, you need to be aware that you have to motivate and manage diverse groups, whose needs are very different.

- Go-it-aloners: managers who, because their spouse refuses to budge from home base, are quite happy to spend two or three years abroad on their own (if they get plenty of home leave).

- In-betweenies: executives who are willing to go – often for extended periods, if the company will guarantee a job or suitable occupation for the spouse. Companies are also aware that today's family will probably consult the kids too before they may the 'buy' decision, and are factoring that in as well.

- Trailing husbands: An increasing number of these are taking place (including those that are based on the 'it's my turn this time' rule), with companies being quick to try and find suitable employment. But with skills shortages a global phenomenon, most Westerners have little difficulty in finding a job if they want to. Then again others go back to school and still others concentrate on lowering their golf handicap!

- The over-50s: This group (if the spouse will travel, and most times he or she will as the kids are up and gone) are a huge – underutilized – asset. They have encyclopedic knowledge of the business, are respected in many cultures (in the Middle East and Asia in particular) and are great in start-ups where a firm, reliable hand is paramount. Often the right package can boost retirement benefits and act as a superb motivator.

- The solo manager: Model A. Often on short-term assignment, the solo manager is parachuted in – usually to work with a task force. Living out of hotels and furnished accommodation they will be overseas for three or four months at a time. Global corporations increasingly see these people as the most flexible and most economical assets to have around. How they manage them is something else again – and their retention rate is finite.

- The solo manager: Model B. Picked because he or she is still single and has no real roots. There is an increasing tendency to use these sort of people as they are ultimately the most flexible. Danger-levels are reached when they get attached abroad and don't want to return – ever.

Who do you want to hold onto?

Having said all that, we need to remember that no organization wants to keep everyone. As a majority of interviewees pointed out, 'there are some people who just don't fit into the organization and need to be professionally managed out'. Very often in today's fast-paced world, change in an organization catches up with people who just can't cope. Failure to deal with this can cause retention problems with those you want to keep.

'You have to be very selective when you put that list of who you want to retain together,' warns Gunnar Sandmark of Global One. 'You might say, 'there's no way we can lose this guy for the next 24 months, but after that it probably won't matter that much.' He goes on, 'then there are those that you really want to hold onto long-term.'

As Patrick McCaughey pointed out earlier (see page 100), there are at least two streams of people operating here (in fact there are more permutations than that), those you want to keep as core operators (that define the culture and direction of your organization); and those you need for a period to do very focused, specific tasks. The others don't come into the retention loop so much, as they are the short-term contracted, consultants and organizations that you outsource to. However, beware. When consultants get busy and the firm you outsource to gets a lot of new work, make sure that your agreements and contracts with them ensure that you keep their talent (the ones you want to retain) working on your business. All too often this does not happen. For example, I have met a lot of very unhappy clients of headhunters – who in this climate of executive shortage are very busy indeed – who have had searches conducted by second tier staff who are not nearly so quick or effective.

Bidding doesn't work

Once you know who you want to retain, how hard do you fight for them?

According to Richard Savage of AC Nielsen, 'it depends'. He points out that, 'If someone comes to you and says I have an offer for 25 per cent more money and a real challenge, do you try and match the bid? My view is that, one; sooner or later they will leave you (usually within the year) as they have tasted the outside and their head is never completely with you; two, be mercenary about it. If you really need that person until you can get someone else in, then yes, match the bid and call your headhunter immediately to start finding a replacement.'

Veteran strategic people experts like Savage know only too well that you cannot expect to retain people – especially in present market conditions – but all of them say that it is up to you to expect that and be ready (not

be ready (not surprised) when the resignation letter arrives

surprised) when the resignation letter arrives. HR professionals (or whatever we are going to call them) and general managers today must know where to get new people from inside or outside the organization if they are to stay competitive.

As one New York HR professional recounted, 'If we lose our CFO today, and I can't have a new one filling the desk on Monday, there's a good chance I won't be here either. My job is to retain talent, and if I can't do that it is to replace it with the very best I can find, very quickly indeed. Believe me, in today's market, my performance is judged on that as much as anything else.'

They're weird, but are they wonderful with it?

Where do you draw the line in the battle to recruit and retain talent? No matter how good at their job, how they excel at their specialization, is there a point when you think they would be better off giving your competitors a bad hair day? Researching this book, I came across a company that has a development centre where most of the employees (they are all over 50) regularly come to work in shorts and Wellington boots in the middle of winter; another where the chief scientist is so scared of traffic that he ropes his entire family together (he has six children) to cross the road; a high tech company where one employee, asked to put up his photo on the Who's Who Intranet site willingly complied, only for his employers to discover that when you click on the photo his head explodes!

Winners, losers and cruisers

When it comes to retaining talent – as we have already briefly looked at above – all of us have to be sure who we really want to keep. Probably the best way to do that, and the simplest, is divide up your workforce into categories (e.g. top 50, top 500, top 1,500, key specialists and so on) and then apply a simple test of just how much you really want to retain each of them. At the same time, it is vital that you have some sort of formalized succession system that is realistic and doesn't just put names into boxes in the hope that they will be available if something happens.

Too often I hear stories where a manager left and the so-called successor had either, left earlier, been transferred or was unwilling to take on the job (to the surprise and chagrin of the rest of the organization). Hard-pressed line managers, asked to give details of their successor often spend little time on it (unless motivated or forced to do so) and quickly

Hard-pressed line managers quickly write down the name of their current favourite

write down the name of their current favourite. Unless you are doing this every three months, things can become quickly out of date in this fast changing marketplace. Smart companies seeking to retain talent are looking more and more beyond simple succession plans and doing full people audits and lengthy exit interviews (*see* page 146).

Three types of people

However, I have divided the organization into three types of people – and they are to be found at all levels. Whatever else you don't do in getting ready for the talent wars to come, it is vital that you at

Winners, Losers and Cruisers: every organization has a plentiful supply of each category

least recognize these three groups in your business. I call them Winners, Losers and Cruisers: and every organization has a plentiful supply of each category. The challenge is to know where they are and just how to deal with them.

Winners

Most of them are mavericks, but you need them and so does everyone else, so you need a plan to hold onto them. These are the workaholics, the over-achievers, the super-salespeople. They may frustrate you, they may not conform, but they will grow your business. Winners are entrepreneurial spirits who challenge themselves, the status quo and everything else around them. If you cannot continuously challenge them, they will move on. However, also consider how long you need them for. Are they core to your long-term business, or just the key to short-term growth?

Losers

These are the people you most assuredly don't need. Even in this current climate, losers hold back the business and hold back other people as well. These are disillusioned employees with low morale who hate change and spend vast amounts of time demotivating everyone around them. You owe it to the rest of the company to tactfully and professionally manage them out of the company. Failure to do this, can have a potentially damaging knock-on effect as good employees look for other opportunities on the outside. Every company has more losers than it is willing to admit to (often people feel sorry for them and cover up their limitations). The feeling of most managers I spoke to was that the time for covering up for people was rapidly passing. In the people wars – when retention becomes a strategic goal – there can be no place for losers to hide.

Cruisers

So busy are we praising the winners and trying to motivate the losers, that we often forget that vitally important category – the cruisers. These are the people who could leave your organization tomorrow but they don't particularly want to. These are the people who like the social aspects as much as the challenges, they stay with you because they like the team or group they work with. These are the people who have that work/life balance more or less in sync. These are the horses of the organization. They will pull and pull, year in year out. They just need a leader to take them in the right direction. Of course the cruisers – by their very nature – don't like change, so they have to be dealt with carefully and candidly. Do that and the horses will pull happily for your side for along, long time. They can do 5 per cent better tomorrow with a better leader who can engage them fully.

Retention strategies – more than just a luxury

Retaining employees is going to become super-critical in the years to come as our pool of talent, that can meet future needs, fails to grow large enough to maintain any kind of surplus in the system. That's when the people wars will begin in earnest. At that point, retention strategies won't just be nice things to have, they'll be an integral part of how a company performs.

Demotivating your employees over some trivial issue is going to be tantamount to organizational suicide – they just won't take it, and they won't have to. Recruitment tactics are going to get uglier and more desperate and the cleverest and the most ruthless will survive and win. If we consider that some companies are already using tactics that many of us have yet to really experience (especially in targeting Internet users), then we must improve the way we tackle this soon-to-be-crisis issue. Much of our success in winning the people wars is going to be based on our own innovative abilities to come up with new ways to hold our people. If the price of peace is eternal vigilance, then the war will be won by those who exhibit that total paranoia, that Intel's founder Andy Grove suggests is his reason for success and subsequently the key word in his autobiography.

People audits

Finding out if and, more importantly, where talent exists in your organisation can be an essential first step before you rush out to buy more high-performing individuals. Too often, people are hidden in an organisation doing the wrong job and not doing it very well when they could be of much greater benefit to the company and much happier in another function, division or even region – where you are much less likely to lose them. This is especially true in cases of mergers and acquisitions, where the acquiring company cannot be sure where the talent lies in the company it is procuring. Even in a merger situation, where there is usually a dominant partner – who could be seen to be acquiring the other, if not officially – it must be ensured that employees fit the corporate culture of the newly merged organization. One sure way to do this is through a people or management audit; a thorough investigation of the senior management of an organization.

International executive search consultancy Neumann International describes a management audit as 'an external consulting-based approach of the top human resource issues faced by corporations to determine and execute the alignment of their human resources with the corporate strategy evolution'. It goes on, 'management audit has developed as a legitimate and positive tool contributing to the management of this continuous and ongoing phenomenon. By developing adequate alignment between the corporate strategy and corporate human resources, a management audit helps the senior executives avoid hectic and chaotic moves and to create a continuum.'

Serge Lamielle, of Neumann's Paris office, who heads up their management audit practice explains: 'If you look at the existing organizational chart of a company, particularly a company you are acquiring, you don't know what's really going on.' Through a people audit process – that involves extensive staff interviews – Neumann is able to assess 'how the organizational chart functions in reality, whether people are in a position where they are truly able to perform according to their own skills or whether they are in the wrong position or even the wrong organization'. It highlights the informal networks that exist in every large organization and allows the company to leverage these to full advantage.

Such an audit also allows a discussion with shareholders and shows the true situation an organization is in and the holes it has – in terms of talent. It then allows you to build a target organization with existing management.

Lamielle's colleague, Thierry Raickmann, explains 'We start when the organizational structure is not yet fully defined and functions have not yet been completely determined.' Neumann has identified three key phases as a part of its management audit process. First, the identification of a list of participants for the audit, which, depending on its view of the merger or acquisition, can have a significant impact on the results of the audit. In addition, base documentation and research is also amassed on the background of both parties involved.

The second step of the audit is individual interviews with two Neumann consultants – this avoids any bias and allows an international element to be brought in which is especially important in the case of a cross-border deal. As Raickmann recalls, during the recent acquisition by a large European financial services organisation of a smaller concern, in which Neumann was involved, 'during each interview we were able to have one interviewer with the same mother tongue as the interviewee as well as a consultant of the same nationality as the dominant player, which means that every case is balanced. Similarly, in the case of the acquisition of a Bulgarian insurance company, in every interview one consultant was Bulgarian and the other from a western European country, which again meant there was a balance in terms of Western European experience being brought in.'

The results of these interviews are then crossed with the internal information initially provided, that Neumann refers to as the 'brainstorming' phase.

In addition, as the interviews are carried out by external consultants, there are no preconceived ideas about any of the individuals or bias from internal management. As Raickmann enthuses 'top HR people understand this and they know that this is one of the reasons it is such an interesting product'.

The fourth phase of the audit is the analysis and recommendation to senior management on two levels; global and strategic advice; and recommendations about the placing of senior managers in the new organizational structure. And finally, every participant in the audit process receives individual feedback.

Basically, a management audit allows a target organizational chart to be built incorporating top talent in the appropriate places. As Neumann's Lamielle explains this significantly reduces the risk of failure of their merger venture. In his experience, although there may well be some individuals who do not fit into this new structure, 'the majority of management is reused. And sometimes you discover talent that has been hidden in the organization and forgotten about. This,' he continued, 'is particularly true in the case of women managers.'

Once a new organizational structure has been developed the search consultancy works closely with HR to help implement it as effectively and efficiently as possible.

Points to ponder

- Be careful about hiring teams – or new senior executives who bring their own people with them over time. If they leave, you are vulnerable.

- Think long and hard about people audits, not just for mergers and acquisitions, but to really know where your people are and what they want in the future.

- Similarly, don't trust succession planning, the speed of change puts it out of date – *fast*. Create a system that meets with reality, not some executive wish list.

- Be bold in your promotion strategy. Failure to move high performers means they will make the decision for you – outside the company.

- How real is your message to employees? If it is just window dressing, don't be surprised if the top talent buys at a store down the street.

- Realize that there is no single answer or action that can make people want to stay with you. Doing a lot of little things better than the rest is a sure-fire winner.

- Be prepared to deal with people who have different views of work. They can get what they want – and be loyal – if you stay flexible enough.

- Few companies can boast a great track record in sending people overseas. Almost anything you do to improve this area will be time well spent.

- Don't be surprised when the resignation letter from one of your most valued employees arrives – be ready. Know where to get a replacement in a hurry.

5 | Don't follow the rest – play by your own rules

Learn to love change. Feel comfortable with your own creative intuition. Make compassion, care, harmony and trust the foundation stones of business. Fall in love with new ideas.

Anita Roddick, Body Shop founder

We play by the lion-tamer school of management here. We keep them well fed and never let them know that all we've got is a chair and a whip.

Anon

If ever there was a time in the history of corporations not to follow what the competition is doing, this is it. Slavish, copy-cat behaviour is not going to get you the talent line-up you need to win the people wars.

If ever there was a time in the history of corporations not to follow what the competition is doing, this is it.

The main reason is that hiring and holding the talent you need doesn't come in a pre-packaged box with a set of easy-to-follow instructions – it requires a very careful assessment of your situation today and what it needs to be tomorrow. In the past, products or services have governed how we do our business. In the future, it will be what talent we have available to do the work that will make the difference.

More proactivity please

In the process of researching this book, a very senior manager said to me, 'one piece of advice you should give, is that anyone who is working for a company where the top management don't care about people should make urgent plans to find another job.' He's right. Unless top management put a great deal more care and attention than hitherto in people, they are going to find a dearth of talent.

'Most CEOs aren't people people at all,' complains organizational psychologist Elisabeth Marx of consultants Norman Broadbent. 'They are recruited for how they fit at the top level. In fact there has been little progress in this direction in the past 20 years.' But Marx predicts that things may be changing soon, 'Today, companies are still too reactive when it comes to people issues and not nearly enough proactive. However, I think this might change now that we are seeing the departure of high profile senior managers. This is beginning to force top management to look at proper succession planning – that they have ignored in the past – and also formalize ways to give top talent more interesting careers.'

Marx's other point is that, 'the only way you can switch on a board of directors or top management team to HR issues is to talk money'. She continues, 'You need to be able to show the cost of losing people, of recruitment, of lost business.'

> the only way you can switch on a board of directors or top management team to HR issues is to talk money

No realistic assessment

This could be hard to do for many top managers, who are seriously out of touch with the reality of the marketplace when it comes to human resource issues. 'They don't make a realistic assessment of the firm and its image', criticizes Keith Willey of management consultants Siddall & Company. 'They need to realize that it is different today than the one that attracted the top team. They need to be able to compare themselves to the competition and find out what they have to offer as unique selling points.'

That top management is seriously out of touch with the marketplace is illustrated by a 1999 survey of over 200 company directors by the Aziz Corporation in the UK which showed 70 per cent of companies, 'thought that perks were a more effective means of motivating staff than training and professional development'. Some even suggested that they thought membership of a health club was valued higher than professional development.

As the firm's chairman, Khalid Aziz commented, 'These results highlight the short-sightedness of employers and employees alike in their views concerning the comparative merits of benefits and training.' He continues, 'The advantages of perks are clear – the employee receives a tangible financial incentive, which requires little effort on the part of the employer. However, as these benefits often become taken for granted, only having a temporary impact on motivation, it is questionable whether they actually deliver long-term benefits of increased staff productivity and reduced turnover.'

A widening gap

Aziz's concern that companies are not taking on board the importance of people is echoed by Chip Bell at Performance Research Associates in Dallas, Texas. His view is that flexible, aware companies won't have to worry too much about talent shortages because people will beat a path to their door. 'Talent attracts talent,' says Bell, 'but this means that the gap between the have's and the have not's is going to get wider.' He adds, 'Among companies like Sun Microsystems, Dell, Amazon.com and Southwest Airlines there will be plenty of talent, but not in those organizations that still value control over creativity, that are managed – not led – by administrative babysitters.' He concludes, 'The key word is not top, or executive – the key word is "talent".'

there will be plenty of talent, but not in those organizations that still value control over creativity, that are managed – not led – by administrative babysitters

Those in organizational denial still have to learn the lesson; they haven't yet worked out that the world has changed.

Hanneke Frese of Zurich Financial Services notes 'The values have changed, but a lot of people at the top don't know that. You get a lot of very rich 50-year-old managers who are totally out of touch and extremely complacent.

with everyone going for a similar profile, the winners will be those who are able to differentiate themselves

Will the IT talent famine ever end?

The short answer to this is a resounding 'no'! An analysis of research and survey work around the globe, plus discussions with commentators, consultants and analysts yields some interesting universal truths that corporations should be aware of as they prepare to face this most intense of talent wars; a war that many predict can last for the first decade of the new Millennium – until 2010 – or even further to the middle of the century.

- The talent for software development is required to be even more talented than before, such is the complexity of today's systems and our insatiable expectations. This means that the quota of good people available is not growing to any significant degree in most advanced economies.

- Countries like India are getting more expensive by the day and threatening to price themselves out of the market if costs and salaries continue at the same pace. Analysts say that there is no immediate rising star region to replace India with thousands of cheap, talented programmers.

- Being a software engineer is not a 'cool' or 'sexy' job. Its image is poor and it is still largely looked down on by other professionals. Added to that – despite the monetary rewards – much of it is boring and repetitive in the extreme, but demands perfection in its execution.

- The current shortage will not be helped by the imminent retirement of the first generation of programmers who were followed by a recruitment gap, as the importance of programmers declined in the 1980s.

- IT seems to set its own 'recruitment boundaries', taking in virtually no women or minorities – it remains heavily dominated by white males.

A solution to the shortage seems to be based on changing the image of the profession, redefining and redesigning (where possible) the work to give it more interest and – most importantly – attracting new categories of workers into the field as a matter of urgency.

This really needs to change if we are to be able to recruit, especially young talent – we need to fully understand their values.' And, as Frese points out, 'with everyone going for a similar profile, the winners will be those who are able to differentiate themselves.'

Fatal flaw

Failure to change how you think about people will be just as fatal a flaw as anything plunging sales or crashing markets could wreak on your business.

Indeed, the chairman of the board of partners of Andersen Consulting, Terry Neill says that 'today's most valuable employees are agile, quick thinkers – speedboats, not oil tankers – very different from the analytical, procedural left-brain thinkers who got ahead in traditional organizations'. Noting that there is a real sense of urgency to all this, Neill urges that, 'companies need to demonstrate their commitment with more

> today's most valuable employees are agile, quick thinkers – speedboats, not oil tankers

flexible human resource programmes that can be tailored to individuals. You need to understand that you will never own these employees,' he says, 'and they will not be subservient to you. Job satisfaction is what they most need.' Andersen Consulting's chief adds a key thought, 'Ideally, HR will act as a talent scout, constantly seeking people both internally and externally who have the right aptitudes, then fostering them with fulfilling job opportunities.'

Neill also predicts some of those changes that we will have to undergo if we are to make an impact in the talent war. 'In the information age, smart, competent, motivated people are the scarce resource and the key to competitive advantage. Organizations that want to stay ahead must recognize the value of human capital and make the most of it. They must attract and retain rare talent, developing it in support of strategy three to five years ahead. Completely new processes may be necessary: for example, reverse apprenticeships, whereby senior employees can learn about technology from their younger colleagues.'

Issuing a warning that any CEO needs to heed, Neill ends,

'human capital, unlike most traditional assets, is inherently versatile and grows in proportion to the investment made in it. At any time, it can be reviewed, redeployed, redirected, reassigned or re-skilled. The companies that recognize this, and act on it, will have the greatest competitive advantage in the next Millennium.'

Not the job, the person

Even in countries like Belgium, where businesses are often slow to change, there is recognition that something is going to have to happen if we are to get the value out of our existing talent and attract others to our organizations.

Sonia van Ballaert of PricewaterhouseCoopers acknowledges that 'it is important for everyone to realize that the value today is not in the job, but the person.'

This message is also recognized in Portugal. Jorge Jardim Gonçalves, chairman and CEO of Banco-Commercial Portuguĕs, the nation's leading bank, says, 'corporate image and reputation are vital factors in attracting talent and this certainly includes the reputation of its leaders'.

Performance Dynamics' Mark Thomas says that he has even witnessed the first flurries of concern. 'I do detect that some enlightened CEOs are trying to put back a greater sense of spirit in their organizations and that a new focus on knowledge management and intellectual capital is helping us get people issues on the table,' he says. Thomas adds to this, 'There is increasing recognition that knowledge is the future engine of value, so, for sure, the best companies are working very hard on these issues and, I think, a new generation of leaders is slowly emerging who see the people side of the business equation very clearly.' But, like many others, Thomas is not totally convinced. 'I remain sceptical as to whether there is some kind of big breakthrough. Indeed, if you reviewed some corporate leaders' behaviour you would have to conclude that selfish greed and ego is where their ultimate focus lies.'

Most of these people are deadly dull too! They may have a mile-long CV, but they are still dull and very, very non-creative. The ability to inspire Terry Neill's 'speedboats' won't be part of their skill set. Perhaps we are going to see great shake-outs in corporations as shareholders see that incumbent CEOs are getting it wrong and – although making short-term profit – look unlikely or unable to deliver in the medium term.

History lessons

Lesson one

'. . . the following management techniques were being consciously applied: a workers' training programme; an executive development programme; payment by results based on work study; advanced division of labour.'

That's part of the description of working life at the Soho Foundry of James Watt Jr and Mathew Boulton in the UK in 1795. So advanced was this first engineering factory in its focus on people that it was described as, 'possessing an organization on the management side which was not excelled even by the technical skill of the craftsmen it produced'. How many of us can say that today?

Lesson two

The book *The Vital Difference,* by Fred Harmon and Gary Jacobs was published in 1985, they observed, 'in company after company, we were struck by the intensity of the atmosphere we found. It was not just the energy of the countless individuals, but a solid mass of radiant power that seemed to pervade the entire organization, supporting and energizing its individual members at least as much as it was supported and energized by them.'

Harmon and Jacobs continue, 'At Intel, we found the energy disciplined and tense. At Apple (this was 1985, remember), it was buoyant, youthful enthusiasm. At General Mills, there was a dynamic exuberance. At Merck, it felt like the controlled power of a well-oiled machine. At Coca-Cola, it had vibrancy and charm. At Delta, it was the intense warmth of a close-knit family. At Northwestern Mutual, it was a smooth quiet hum, yet very active and alert.'

What they hit on was that every company is different, but every company is a sum of its parts – and those parts are people. Some of those organizations listed may have gone on to have very different futures, but their focus on people at that time was palpable and it drove them forward and attracted people to them. Just how long is it going to take for a large number of CEOs to realize that?

Shifting ambitions

For some, ambitions may not change in time. As psychologist Elisabeth Marx, regrets, 'Top management is not switched on to the motivational needs of their organizations. What they need to do is re-examine their firms from a people

> they need to re-examine their firms from a people point of view, up, down and sideways

point of view, up, down and sideways, then they'll come to realize the need to be more flexible, to understand that the ambition of those they employ and would like to employ has shifted.'

Much of this comes down to the image you project to the outside world. Today, any company that isn't getting a large number of requests for jobs should question what it is doing wrong. Even if it isn't doing anything wrong, external perception could be different from the truth.

During my research, I found several companies who track how many applications they get and measure these against different types of initiatives. Also, many now do a lot more than just add up the number of hits they get on their websites, they want to know who and why as well. Getting on top 100 or top 500 lists of the biggest corporations or the best places to work can also help, although of course, many exciting start-ups don't even begin to qualify. Others, who just get on with being good employers and don't do anything spectacular or have an exciting, trendy product or service, just keep plugging along. It is these employers who are possibly the ones that have understood – in their own quiet way, how to win the business battle. They do think differently, they are more flexible, they just don't tell too many people about it – certainly you don't imagine *Business Week* or *Fortune* getting excited.

Building a reputation quietly

TIAACREF

Most people, for example, have never heard of the TIAACREF (Teachers' Insurance and Annuity Association, College Retirement Equities Fund). It isn't on any best places to work list that I know of, but it has employee turnover of less than 6 per cent and is known in the insurance industry as a feisty little innovator.

Managing the managers from hell

One of the most frequent comments when talking to executives about the issue of talent is that there are plenty of managers, but very few leaders. 'Let's not confuse the issue here,' said one, 'managers get their teams to do something and that is about all we can hope for. None of them care at all about leadership – that's just management-speak – and they don't care about that at all.' From a mass of anecdotal evidence, industries like financial services have a lot of managers who don't even manage. 'They just ensure you are making enough money to keep your job,' said one disillusioned trader at a round-table discussion. Another opined, 'my team leader doesn't know what the word "manage" means; we have never had any guidance, the only way we get any training is to go ourselves and ask the personnel department. If we push enough, they reluctantly let us have two days off for development.'

Financial services is certainly one of the industries where the soft skills are often missing. The story is gleefully recounted of the eager new human resources vice president who introduced the concept of 360 degree feedback to the bank's equity managers; they immediately began to sell it thinking it was a new financial instrument.

But if these kinds of people sound like monsters, most people I talked to pointed elsewhere for the managers that can't be managed. New media organizations, advertising and film companies all report that creative types, including managers, directors and vice presidents, are a thousand miles away from anything that remotely looks, talks or acts like a manager. And, whatever you do, don't ask them to interact with anyone because they won't.

Some years ago, I compiled a list of all the bad things you could expect in trying to get these people to work. Reviewing it I discovered a very interesting point. They are exactly the same as totally demotivated employees.

- They need constant praise and reassurance: they are certain that the world, the company, or the client is conspiring against them.
- Timekeeping – 'what's that?'
- Criticism is not permissible.
- Positive actions are always perceived in a cynical light.
- Their attitude is that you are working to make their life better, not the other way around.

Come to think of it, I've met a lot of Generation Xers like that too.

From its headquarters on Third Avenue, New York, TIAACREF has built a reputation for more than just making money. With no excessive but adequate salaries, it attracts and holds the kind of people that know the organization stands for more than just profit at any price.

'Our roots as a not-for-profit organization that began by offering pensions for high school and college teachers, are important,' says Bill Shanahan, VP of human resources. 'Our challenge is to hold onto our basic beliefs as we evolve and grow. For this reason, we are very specific in who we want to recruit, we want people who have the same values, who fit and identify with who we are.'

we want people who have the same values, who fit and identify with who we are

Shanahan notes that TIAACRFEF has never made *Fortune's* list of the 100 best place to work, but he did note that '37 on the list were displaced by 37 others, so maybe much of that is being the "flavour" benefit of the year. Our goal,' he says, 'is to keep our culture and take it forward. We try to transition change, so we are reluctant to make people change overnight and we make a major effort to show and explain as well.'

Maybe TIAACREF will never be on any hot recruiters list, but they have understood the secret of creating an exciting work environment (they regularly launch new products and attack new markets), are open (communication is a top priority) and believe in the people they hire (they are highly selective and believe this pays off in longer retention).

Often the quiet approach can be better, it doesn't draw too much attention to your carefully stockpiled pool of talent

The lesson to learn here, is that you don't have to have the visibility of a hot Silicon Valley stock to be doing good things. Often the quiet approach can be better, it doesn't draw too much attention to your carefully stockpiled pool of talent.

Siemens

Another company that has an excellent image in its home market, where it always rates in the top five places to work (and is the number 12 choice in Europe for business graduates), has no presence at all in one of its biggest growth areas – the US. Based in Munich, Siemens is seen as the quintessential German engineering company; solid, staid and slow. That is far from reality. In the late 1990s, Siemens metamorphosed into a truly global company, 'where over 50 per cent of our turnover comes from IT', says Günther Goth, corporate VP of HR. 'The trouble is that not enough people on the outside know this,' he says, 'particularly as we don't have an MBA culture and don't know how to integrate these people. The result is that they don't put us on their shopping list.'

For a globally operating company like Siemens, having access to the best and brightest IT talent is vital. But there's not a great deal of point in going shopping in Palo Alto unless you are going to get name recognition. Knowing full well of the talent wars to come, look out for a very visible Siemens emerging out of the shadows of obscurity.

So let's get some new leaders

As we have seen earlier, a lot of what the future holds for our businesses will depend on who's running them. Someone with good people focus and the ability to inspire, will not only retain a lot more people but attract them too. And the game is changing quickly as well. A study by the Association of Executive Search Consultants (AESC), *Chief Executives in the New Europe*, showed that CEOs themselves forecast a change in the priorities their successors would need to concentrate on. According to the study, the current top three issues for CEOs were:

- managing change
- vision
- adaptability in new situations.

For the next generation of CEOs these were set to change order of priority to:

- adaptability in new situations

- international strategic awareness
- managing change.

This realignment of focus shows that rapidly emerging issues are going to become a prime consideration, as is fighting the global battle on a daily basis. But, without the proper people skills and the proper people in place, no CEO can do that effectively.

Identifying the best new leaders

So, if we need leaders with a different skill set, how are we going to find them? How do we know when we go out looking for the top man or woman that they are the best for the job? Global executive search firm, Korn/Ferry reckon they know a thing or two about finding effective CEOs. So much so that they have drawn up a list of 20 questions that you can put to any top management candidate to judge how fit they are to run an organization in the new Millennium. Remember, we are looking for people today who can make that difference and help to build an exciting corporation that becomes a talent trap. As they say, 'At Korn/Ferry, we've found that these questions reveal where a candidate stands in leadership ability, communication skills, building and empowering teams, motivating people, ensuring results, negotiating agreements and handling conflict.'

If you are – or aspire to be – a CEO, why don't you try to answer them and see how you rate.

The Korn/Ferry assessment

Leadership ability

Q. *How do you define leadership?*
A. For starters, the response will show whether the person has given much thought to this topic – no small matter for someone who aspires to a high position in a company. In addition, the response will indicate whether the individual is a consensus builder and team leader – essential traits in today's world – or an autocrat with a much more outmoded style.

Q. *What are some samples of change that you instigated in your organization?*

A. The changes don't have to be big or dramatic; often, the best leaders make many small, incremental changes, saving the organization major trauma by anticipating the larger changes that would otherwise be required. Whether the changes are large or small, the key question is how those changes fit into the larger strategic vision.

Q. *How were the changes successful?*

A. How do the candidates define and measure success? Do the individuals set high, but realistic goals, or do they unrealistically shoot for the moon? The first course can lead to confidence in tackling of additional challenges, while the second can lead to defeatism and inaction.

Q. *What did you do right or wrong in implementing these changes?*

A. This will indicate a willingness to review results objectively and to accept responsibility for mistakes as well as triumphs. Listen for clues that the candidate can admit shortcomings and move on without becoming bogged down in self-recrimination. In touting successes, you'll want to hear that the candidate credits others where it is due.

Q. *What did you learn personally as a result of making the changes?*

A. People who have not analyzed and learned from past actions are unlikely to be effective leaders over the long haul. Learning from experience is a hallmark of true leadership.

Q. *What might you do differently if a similar situation arose again?*

A. Drawing lessons from experience will have maximum value only in so far as they are used to help chart future paths. It is a positive indicator if the candidates can outline how they would proceed if the situation were replayed.

Q. *How did you secure support from key constituents when unpopular decisions had to be made?*

A. Since aversion to change is widespread in most organizations, the response will indicate how effectively individuals are able to 'sell' change – including enrolling other leaders in a new direction for the organization. After all, high on the list of effective leadership traits is the ability to persuade others to share a vision.

Q. *How did you build the support needed throughout the organization?*

A. Savvy leaders navigate the white-water rapids of organizational hierarchy and politics. Candidates need to be forceful enough to get the job done without alienating many of the different constituencies that exist in organizations. The ideal response to this question should indicate that the candidates can motivate both the lower-level staff members and fellow executives.

Q. *What methods did you use to minimize disruption to the organization as the changes were implemented?*

A. With the breakneck speed of today's business environment, leaders don't have the luxury of putting a company's operations on hold while tinkering. Change must happen 'on the fly' – and it is up to the leaders to reduce disruptions to a bare minimum.

Communication skills

Q. *How do you communicate with your staff and the community?*

A. Leaders must have a vision – but for that vision to count they have to be able to communicate it to others. Ask the candidates to draft a one-page description of their vision for your organization. This will enable you to see whether they can express ideas, clearly, logically and convincingly.

Building and empowering teams

Q. *What strategies have you employed to enlist commitment to your personal vision and your organization's goals? Discuss your hits and misses.*

A. Communicating a vision is an essential first step, but taking concrete additional steps to enlist people's commitment to it is necessary as well. Consider how (and how well) the candidates have managed to do that.

Q. *To the extent your strategies have worked, why do you think they have been successful?*

A. This question helps reveal perceptions about human nature and group dynamics. Again, it comes back to the candidates' ability to 'sell' on many different levels.

Q. *Would your board (or the person you report to) agree with your answer?*

A. Leadership is vital as is the ability to take direction and carry out a superior's vision. 'Lone Rangers' are effective on the high plateaus but can wreak havoc in the boardroom. Listen for nuances and underlying attitudes in the answer to this question.

Q. *What process would you use to solve the following problem?*

A. Candidates should be given a hypothetical problem to solve – one that might be encountered in an organization and industry similar to yours. This exercise will help you determine whether the individual would take a team approach to developing solutions, empowering others in the process, or use an autocratic command-and-control approach.

Motivating people and ensuring results

Q. *Having established your objectives, what motivational techniques will you choose to ensure that they are met?*

A. The ability of leaders to motivate cannot be underestimated. The candidates should be able to articulate the tested motivational techniques they would use to move the plan forward.

Q. *How will you measure your progress in reaching your objectives?*

A. It is essential that leaders gauge how well a plan is working out every step of the way, in order to be able to institute mid-course corrections if necessary. Otherwise, they can propel a company into a lemming-like change right over a cliff.

Q. *What will be the follow-up procedures?*

A. Once a plan has been carried out, it is important to look closely at how things went to determine if there are any loose ends to tie up, and to see how to proceed in the future. Will the candidates take a hit-or-miss approach to accomplishing this or create an effective mechanism that will make sure it gets done?

Negotiating agreement and handling conflict

Q. *Does your negotiation style emphasize competition, collaboration, compromise, accommodation or avoidance? If you employ a combination of these, which do you use most often and why?*

A. While most individuals will use all of these techniques as circumstances dictate, few will admit to being highly competitive or avoiding responsibility. The style they turn to most often, will be a better indicator of their leadership style.

Q. *Please give examples of situations in which you might have used one style instead of another. Why would you have picked that style?*
A. This question will provide a reality check for candidates' responses to the previous question. It will also help to show candidates' flexibility in adapting their styles to a given situation.

Q. *What conflicts have you recently faced in your organization? What role did you play in resolving them?*
A. The response will provide one last reading on leadership ability and management style.

Don't hire in your own image

One of the dangers with recruiting is the tendency for people to hire in their own image or that of their work colleagues. It is very tempting to opt for the candidate that seems a close personal fit with you and the rest of top management. But if you want different thinking and to shake up those complacent ideas, you need new, aggressive input.

Senior VP of HR at Equitable Life Assurance, Gary Billings, notes, 'Today, we need a diverse workforce, so you can't just hire in your own image.' He should know, he was recruited into this financial services business from the advertising industry with the intention that his views and skills would make a difference.

Billings points out that Equitable now have a performance management programme that rewards diversity 'if the manager gets it right', and to this end they 'make sure that managers, when they are recruiting, see a diverse slate of candidates, including women'.

Herb Greenberg, president of consultants, Caliper, says that, 'If you hire an entire staff of people just like you, you're bound to create a situation of imbalance – a staff with the same set of abilities and all the same faults leaves a lopsided organization. The key is to build an organization with balanced attributes.' Greenberg advises managers that, 'if you're a manager who's looking for an assistant, ask yourself whether you like an applicant

Southwest Airlines freedom charter

Dallas-based Southwest Airlines is known for its excessively happy employees and delighted customers. The company is a classic example of how making your employees happy means that they will take care of the customers. Zany tactics, like telling jokes in-flight, pay off in a firm where fun comes first, second and third. What might be not so well known is the airline's employee charter, which is a serious bill of rights wrapped up in a candy bar. How many other companies would dare adopt it?

'We believe that all people of Southwest Airlines have unalienable rights to life, liberty and the pursuit of happiness with a passion and reckless abandon never anticipated by the founding fathers. We hereby dedicate our hearts and minds to create:

- Freedom to earn through shared efforts to free the people of the United States of America to roam about the country making new friends, eating excessive holiday dinners, participating in sporting events beyond their physical capacities and connecting with people and experiences that make the world bigger and brighter.

- Freedom to learn how to change software, tires, diapers, investments, elections, our minds and other important stuff that allows us to do the best work of our careers and take on personal challenges that mere mortals would never attempt. (And, yes, we will try this at home.)

- Financial freedom to buy cars, homes, stereos, college educations, comfortable retirement accommodations, insurances and really great pizza with lots of extra cheese (but no anchovies).

- Freedom to live, take road trips, coach Little League, hang out with our kids, go to school, be weekend warriors of the courts and fields, do the culture thing, take sabbaticals and give back to our communities.

- Freedom to be healthy, happy, eat tofu, yogurt and those little nuts that taste like tree bark, join great health plans, visit awesome doctors and protect our family's health and well-being.

- Freedom to roam about the country celebrating the value of travel in our lives by using travel to learn, strengthen relationships, renew our souls, connect with loved ones, see the world and yes... to seek out great shopping.

- Freedom to have fun, be ourselves, and spread laughter, humour and the Southwest spirit of freedom (but no airline food) across the good old US of A.'

The difference is that everyone believes in it and lives it every day.

because they are like you or because they have the technical skills necessary to do the job and respond well to your management style. If you end up with an assistant who is too much like yourself, you will be duplicating your strengths rather than strengthening your limitations.'

Most of us are so busy these days that we scarcely lift our heads from our keyboards (except to scuttle to meetings). As Russell Reynolds' Jacques Bouwens says, 'Our ability to network in most Western societies has actually diminished – once it came naturally, now it is a formal process that we allot time to.' In the age of the global corporation, we spend time on planes and in hotel rooms, whereas, in a less hectic business world, we had time for colleagues and even competitors. 'Senior managers don't make it to trade shows and seminars anymore,' says Bouwens, 'they just don't have the time.' But maybe we should find the time and maybe it would pay off.

Grab a bite and some talent too!

I particularly like this true story from Portugal, which shows that in our ability to attract the best and brightest we may have forgotten a lot of what we once knew and used to great effect. Portugal has a small population (10 million) and quite a big agrarian economy, so the management group of its industrial base is far from large. Pedro Sena da Silva is chairman of Groupe Autosil, a leading European car battery manufacturer outside Lisbon. Da Silva explains that in Portugal there is a tendency to keep in touch with employees, 'even if they go and work for the competition. For example, we had a very bright young manager, who we would have liked to keep on, but he got a great offer and I could see no way that we could hold him back.'

What da Silva was able to do, in Portugal's tiny management community was to keep track of his protégé. 'I would see him at industry events and so on,' he said, 'so I knew the kind of progress he was making.' Then Groupe Autosil embarked on a series of heady takeovers of competitors in Spain and France, practically trebling its size. 'I knew one of the people who could help us, and I knew where he would be – because if he was in town he had lunch at the same place every day.' Da Silva reserved a table and propositioned the executive. 'If I hadn't stayed in touch it would have been a lot more difficult,' da Silva says, 'this way it makes it all the more personal.'

Maybe in the hectic paced world we inhabit, we should spend more time thinking about keeping up those personal networks, not just for ourselves, but for our organizations as well. As Lisbon-based management consultant, René Cordeiro points out, 'the reason that there are few head-hunters in Portugal is because we know everyone and we know their strengths and weaknesses because they are very much on show'. For most of us in London, Paris or New York, we are even losing touch with the people in our own industry, that's why we have to resort to professional help. Maybe one of the new ways we should be judging CEOs and the rest of top management is by how much time they spend and how good they are at tracking talent and getting their hands on it when they need to.

Of course, being busy executives, most of us are apt to find alternative ways to keep track of and size up talent.

Search firms are now making lucrative dollars, pounds and euros out of checking out the talent for companies looking to poach executives or even take over the whole company. Offering post-merger human capital reviews (*see* pages 146–148), has been common for some time, but firms like Egon Zehnder and Spencer Stuart will develop confidential reports on talent targets that assess their strengths and weaknesses.

Others see this as the wrong way to go. Korn/Ferry have moved out of virtually all their add-on businesses in recent years, citing a desire to concentrate on what they do best – place people. As one partner pointed out, there is another reason, 'Why would any sane company pay good money to a headhunter to go out and assess the value of people. You are paying them to do their own research. Worse still, you buy a company and then ask them to do a people audit to assess the level of talent. Isn't that rather like paying the fox to go and visit the chicken house?'

And still you have to make sure that you are hiring the right people. At Prudential Insurance in Newark, New Jersey, Deborah Gingher, VP of Policy and Strategy is worried that you can get the wrong person, when you thought you were hiring for all the right reasons. 'Try hiring a 48-year-old who has held ten jobs and says that they now want to settle down,' she says, 'you either get someone who is not telling the truth and will be on their way inside two years or they really do want to settle as they are looking for an easy home until retirement!'

This type of being careful who you hire is prompting firms, even in staid management environments like Germany, to look at new ways of getting talent on board. Christian Pape, founder of Pape Contract Consultants in Munich – who numbers names like Motorola, Siemens, Sony and Oracle amongst his clients – says, 'The old-style manager, who can only fit into a conservative German environment just isn't needed anymore. These people need managers who have new experiences and are open to outside stimulation.'

Who meets the talent?

When you are trying to recruit new talent into the business, do you let them meet future work colleagues or not? The jury seems to be out on this one.

Eric Gustafson, managing director of Korn/Ferry in New York reckons it can be a 'huge turn-off, unless you are very careful who they meet'. He adds, 'Too often, no one thinks about it at all and they just leave candidates with executives who may or may not be boosters for the organization.' Noting that, 'it can really backfire,' Gustafson says that 'it can do more harm than good, especially if you ask people to interview the candidate. 'Few people have any well honed interview skills and it can really turn a candidate off,' he warns.

That view is opposed by Philip Guy, global resourcing manger of telecommunications provider ICO. 'The work environment – including the calibre of the people already on board – is a big factor in attracting talent. In our selection process, a candidate might meet four or five people. Often they will come back to us and say, "Wow! I've met some really impressive people today." That works wonders.' Keith Willey, a partner in consultants, Siddall & Company, concurs, 'I think people are attracted by meeting your best people. Involve them in the front line of the hiring process – not a grey person from the personnel department.'

Hey oldie! I need you

The really big winners so far in the people wars – and looking set to remain that way – are the over 50s. Once considered too old to know anything, they were fired in their droves as company after company found it the easiest way to downsize (offer a really cool separation package to everyone over their half-century). Now, with the talent crunch accelerating, oldies are back as flavour of the month.

Note human resource consultants, Watson Wyatt, 'The labour force in the US of people between 25–44 will shrink until at least 2006, so for most employers the tight market has just begun.' Watson Wyatt believe that the key to surviving this demographic tidal-wave is to plan early. 'If employers want to maintain a swell-staffed workforce and there aren't enough entrants to the labour pool, they may have to find a way to employ veteran workers. This is an unavoidable problem, the only question is to what degree each company will be affected.'

Another human resource consulting firm, Hewitt, says that its research clearly shows that, 'unless companies are willing and able to offer their greying senior staffers flexible work options, their competitors will'. They go on, 'smart employers, will look for creative mechanisms to attract and retain talented elders'. But Hewitt points out that many companies still haven't heeded the road signs warning of a need for a change of direction ahead. 'Many companies are still fixated on the downsizing craze,' they report. 'There is still a proliferation of early retirement "windows" that try and seduce employees to retire as early as possible.' And Hewitt raises the ultimate question, are companies, by not heeding the signs and still trying to package the over 50s out, 'subsidizing their own corporate brain drain?'

Of course, keeping older managers on the workforce has to be carefully managed. Too many clogging up the top of the organization wouldn't be a good idea. So, some way has to be found to ensure that younger managers can get to the top to keep the business vital and full of new ideas. While the employment experts are still working on that, it seems that part-time and special job categories for older workers will come to the fore as an easy-to-operate process.

Did we get it wrong?

The chairman of UK-based Cadbury Schweppes, Dominic Cadbury, has this to say about the usefulness of the ageing workforce, 'I believe many employers might have got it wrong. There is more to people planning than headcount – quality and skills matter too. Those people could well be walking out of the door with skills the business can least afford to lose. There is nothing wrong with aspiring to become a lean organization, but what remains will need a heart and a soul, a brain and a sense of purpose. The alternative is a wasted anorexic structure.' The lesson to learn from this is that not every oldie is redundant in skills and usefulness, in some cases they have only just begun. Employers who discover this truth early, will give themselves a huge advantage as the talent shortage really begins to bite.

Hire me a manager

You lose your marketing director one Friday afternoon. What do you do next? Call the headhunters, look in your little black book? Maybe you should consider calling an interim management agency instead.

Although they prefer to be called 'interim continuity managers', these guns-for-hire-at-a-moment's-notice are just that – very well-qualified stop-gaps until the headhunter provides a list of candidates and you can choose a worthwhile replacement.

Martin Wood has been in the interim management business for over two decades and now runs the operation for Boyden Interim Executive in London. 'It's a very niche business,' says Wood. With a core roster of around 100 managers on his books that he terms, 'his loyal, exclusive blood-bank', Woods can supply you with a replacement for your missing manager for most disciplines. 'I have about 20 HR, 20 CEOs, 50 IT people and the rest from marketing and manufacturing' he says. Wood admits that not everyone wants to be an interim manager. 'There's not a lot of talent out there that wants to do this sort of thing, so it is as much talent limited as opportunity limited', he notes. However, many experienced executives, who have made enough money to live on, like it because they can take up challenges that interest them.

'The great advantage of these people is that they have no strings attached, are not trying to ingratiate themselves, so they really tell it like it is. Often, they are just what a business needs.' Woods adds that, 'there are a lot of people we would never recommend, because they are really looking for a job, our stable want the challenge and then move on to something else.' While often it can take two or three years, most assignments are about six months.

A lot of these people work for six months and then take a six month break, and this type of work pattern means that Woods thinks this sort of business is set to take off more and more. 'I meet a lot of 30-year-olds who are intent on managing their own careers,' he enthuses, 'and I think that interim management may be exactly what they would be good at.'

How are employers thinking differently?

If employers the world over are having to think in different ways about how they deal with the talent shortages, just what are they working on to try and improve the situation? What lessons are they learning? What directions are they taking? Here are some dispatches from the people wars battle front.

In practice

Graduate windfall

Germany faces a shortfall of 150,000 plus software engineers. Although he may have acted a little late, Hasso Plattner, a co-founder of SAP has created the Potsdam-based Hasso Plattner Institute, whose graduates will start to hit the market in 2003. Guess where they will all be heading for? But did Plattner get this idea from another software entrepreneur, Bill Gates, who has already seen the fruits of the IT college he founded? Expect to see more and more companies deciding to 'grow their own graduates' as the talent wars hot up. You can exchange free tuition for a guaranteed period of work after graduation.

Stay and merge with us

Mergers and acquisitions unbalance and unnerve people, but management professionals are increasingly urging scared staff to buckle down and enjoy it. Brad Thomas, a VP of executive resources at Citigroup (where Citicorp and Travellers have just merged), notes 'A merger is a great time to learn a great deal,' he says, 'you are living in a construction zone and watching a business come together. It is invaluable experience, that smart people realize gives them an important skill set that is marketable if they need it.'

Mickey Mouse gets grey hair

Those grey panthers in the workforce are being pounced on by top corporate big game hunters. Think that Disney stands for youth? Think again. The majority of the workforce at Disneyworld are now retirees from other corporations. At GE, they found that it really is cheaper to retrain veteran engineers than employ new ones. In UK supermarkets, there is a war that has nothing to do with price. They are finding that customers prefer talking to staff who are over 50 and so, the battle is on to employ more. One retiree of 62 was employed to rollerblade around the shop checking prices!

So how was it for you?

So concerned are they to make new recruits happy, that German engineering giant Siemens has instituted a programme that tracks the attitudes and perceptions of recent arrivals in the first six hours, six days and six weeks. 'It is what happens at the very beginning of their employment that affects their mind-set,' says a spokesman, 'we want to make sure that they are turned on, not turned off.'

We do it our way

Motorcycle manufacturer Harley Davidson's spectacular turnaround has been well documented. One thing that is not so well known is that its employee development programme not only focuses on how an individual's needs can match the needs of the firm, but is entirely run internally. 'What we sacrificed in polish, we gained in genuineness and commitment,' says Margaret Crawford, director of employee development.

Clone me!

Founded in 1886, consulting firm Arthur D Little is anxious that new recruits don't think that it has a stodgy, conformist image – a surefire way to scare away young talent these days. Log on to its website and the first thing you encounter is a statement that says, 'We treasure diversity in our staff and are committed to maintaining it, without imposing an Arthur D Little mould on our consultants. We do not want clones and we will not produce clones.' An interesting way of distancing yourself from some other consulting firms who seem to make a science out of hiring in their own image.

Step this way

Can you go too far in making the working environment exciting for the employees? TR Fastenings, an engineering firm in Sussex, UK encourages staff to behave in odd ways. Strange dress codes, dancing on desks and surreptitiously inserting pop song titles into conversations with clients are all applauded. The company's sales manager explained that, 'during a presentation to staff about our corporate plan, the CEO burst in dressed as Hitler and goose-stepped around the room to prove he was a fanatic'.

Give me five

Conscious of the trend toward work/life balance, Deloitte Consulting – where many of the staff travel as a matter of course – have instituted the 3-4-5 rule. Basically it comes down to three days with a client, fourth day in the local office and the fifth day in the home office. 'That way, our consultants can get home weekends,' explains a spokesperson.

Hold the marshmallows

Faced with employees that count the money, rather than worry about clients' needs, the president of the World Bank, James Wolfensohn has sent his top 300 managers to business school to make them 'think more like employees at Burger King'. Groups of 15 are being sent on a six week management course, rounded off by a week spent in the field, 'not in a hotel, but living in a slum with a non-governmental organization'. Mr. Wolfensohn said that the real problem of changing the bank's culture lay not with top management, but the 'marshmallow middle'. To tackle the problem, he removed 150 line managers from their jobs and made them reapply. They might not be happy but workers at other levels have been delighted.

Go home and stay there

Even in Japan, workers are taking the work/life issue more seriously. Virtually all major Japanese corporations now insist that employees take their two-week holidays and they are not meeting any resistance. Prior to the recession, many Japanese would forgo their holidays for the love of the company – not any longer it seems.

Have a great weekend

In Belgium, a printing firm has come up with a revolutionary work week – it only lasts a weekend. Volunteer workers (and there is a waiting list) at Casterman, a printing firm in Tournais, have been working two shifts of 12 hours each since 1986. The working week for the 40 press operators is compressed into one weekend as well as two consecutive nights and one Friday every fortnight. The system is reported to work well for both employees and the employer. The workers have a whole week to do as they please and during the weekend the atmosphere is more relaxed. A survey by the firm reported a 92 per cent satisfaction rate amongst the weekend workers and 60 per cent said that the work regime had a positive affect on their health.

Cold shoulder

Firms across the US are learning that the colour of employees' offices has an impact on whether or not they are happy at work. The Color Association of the US, asked workers what colour they would like their offices to be, if they had a choice: pale greys, soft reds and pastel yellow topped the poll. And a word of warning; workers dislike cold or strong colours, which they associate with new technology. They want their workspaces to be softer and warmer.

Tie-breaker

In a break with tradition that has the whole industry talking, Japanese electronic firm, Hitachi, has adopted a casual dress code for all employees who don't deal with the public. Not only are the sober ties, white shirts and grey suits getting the boot, but workers are no longer required to address supervisors by using their title, but simply use the person's name. Hitachi say the moves are 'part of a series of measures designed to revitalize staff'.

Super-stock

British supermarket chain Asda (aquired in 1999 by US giant WalMart) created a share fund where employees could pay in from a minimum of £5 to a maximum of £250 per month for five years. Those that invested their £5 a month netted £30,000, those that paid the maximum, £750,000.

Gradual employment

At telecommunications company Nokia they tie down talent through creating temporary positions for students, helping them with their doctorate or Master's degrees, on the understanding that once they graduate they can join.

Sorry, I've a headache

Research by Audience Selection in the UK shows that different reasons for illness give clues to employees' mental health. Migraine sufferers tend to be happy in their work, while the food poisoning line is deployed by staff who are unhappy and likely to be trying to signal for help.

Watch your language

Two-thirds of large corporations say that they now recruit throughout Europe and put a premium on language skills and mobility as the top employment criterion. Seventy-three per cent have ambitions to be employers of choice across Europe, not just in their own countries.

Happier customers

Finland's national airline, Finnair, tore up its media advertising budget and poured the money into training staff. The company had the idea that, as it was a small carrier, any advertising it did was lost money, but making all its people better would mean happier customers. The idea paid off, customers love it and retention rates have soared.

Friendly fun

It started with hard-pressed IT companies looking for programming talent – now it has spread to consulting too. Bring a friend to work days (and weekends) are becoming commonplace across the US and Europe. The top earner I heard about was a $50,000 sign on, split between the employee and the new recruit. That's how to become best buddies.

The bane of your life

Consulting firm Bain keeps a database of 2,000 former employees and sends them a newsletter and annual reports. Reason? A great source of business and leads for talent.

Sponsoring gets tough

Companies are finding that work experience programmes and summer jobs don't always lead to signing on talent. Prudential Insurance discovered that its programme – and others – need to be a lot more competitive these days. It found that, such was the pressure to grab students, that top line consulting firms were touring the top 20 schools and 'sponsoring' any student enrolled on a business programme; happy to financially support them for two or three years.

Going Dutch

Currently, one worker in three in The Netherlands is part-time, as the country records a huge increase in this category of jobs (66 per cent in ten years) to over two million. The reasons are a changing economy and more women in the work force who want to work less than 35 hours a week.

Zurich is people

Rolf Hüppi, head of Zurich Financial Services (ZFS), realizes that in a service industry like ZFS, it is the people who make the difference. He says, 'capital and information are almost commoditized. What will make the difference is talent that is superior to that of the competition. Without the requisite talent we won't be able to achieve any of our strategic goals.'

He, too, has a phrase for his organization, 'Zurich truly is people.' But it doesn't stop there. 'This is not just a slogan, it is a statement of fact. Therefore this is the number one priority on my personal agenda.' And this isn't simply a fad or phase he's going through either. For him, 'people have always been important'. And looking back over the past ten years or so he recalls, 'we understood quite well the kind of people (skills, education, etc) we needed. The mix of talent was fairly stable because the environment and the success factors in the industry were stable.' However, today, he explains, 'the environment is changing not only at an unprecedented pace but also in unexpected ways. The very definition of what constitutes our industry and what it takes to be successful is increasingly ambiguous.' This, as we all know is nothing new, being competitive has always meant changing the rules of the business game. However, as Hüppi points out, 'not only is this happening faster and faster, the game itself is changing, a bit as if you were playing soccer today and need to be a successful dance group tomorrow'.

His advice to corporations facing a similar challenge – and, today, that means everyone, in every industry in every region of the world – is to attract 'a much broader mix of talent including talent that exists only outside our industry'. CEOs take note, or you'll be left on the playing field and will have no one to play with – they'll all have gone to the dance.

Meaningful contribution

As you can see, every winner in the people wars has a unique way of treating employees, adding value and meaning to their working lives. This openness, this flexibility is the key. Certainly not all employees are treated the same, but they are all accorded their own dignity and clearly recognized as making a meaningful contribution. Remember, not all of us ever want to be the CEO, we don't even want to be a manager or supervisor. But, in today's world we can vote with our feet and leave. We don't really want all that hassle, but we can. What's more it is getting easier to do every day. The opportunities can be tempting. So we must find ways to convince our employees that ours is the best offer they will get. We may not pay top money, but people will have fun working here and grow as well. The key to winning this part of the war is to look at your entire organization, see where things could be better – there will be a lot of them – and get down and do it.

Think temp – think flexible

Recognizing that younger people today don't necessarily want the same type of work commitment as their parents, even stuffy professions like banking are realizing that to get the right talent, they need to be much more flexible in their thinking.

In Norway, the Norskbank has teamed up with interim firm Manpower (even to the extent of taking a 15 per cent stake) to create an organization called Bankpower. In Germany, staid Deutsche Bank belied its image by doing the same and teaming up, again with Manpower, to attract talent it would not otherwise have access to.

'Firms like Deutsche Bank recognize that they have to do something to get the types of people they need and give those people the flexibility they want,' says Manpower's marketing director for Europe, Lyndon Evans. (This is mirrored in CitiGroup's US experience in building e-commerce.)

Elsewhere, according to Evans, 'temporary work can really mean full-time work, it's just that people can organize their lives in a way that suits themselves – not the employer'. Evans notes that 'temporary work' is probably a misnomer these days as it is becoming a major part of the economy in many countries, accounting in some cases for up to 5 per cent of a nation's working time.

In another trend, 'some graduates are moving to temporary work assignments,' reports Evans, 'so they can try out different companies. In countries like Norway, people will work nine months and then take three months off.' This trend is yet another that employers should take into account when looking to attract talent. Failure to make room for these sort of emerging work patterns will exacerbate staff shortages.

The other move is that employers are also going to have to take into account the way emerging technology can change how a workforce reacts to opportunities. A lot of employers want the flexibility of temporary or part-time workers. If they say to a housewife, 'would you like three hours work a day?', she'll most probably say yes. But, if they then say, 'well you'll also need to travel for one hour each way,' then she'll most likely say no. The solution to this – an innovation that is going to bring thousands of new people to the workforce – is to install the technology in their homes at a stage where it makes economic sense. It can be a real boost to your talent base. For example, a mother will put her kids to bed and do three hours of inbound help calls. Available and inexpensive technology brings to employers a whole category of talent that had previously been marginalized. It is a tremendous opportunity and needs to be quickly understood and taken on board by employers.

Points to ponder

- Temporary work is taking on a new dimension fuelled by people needs and technology. Consider how best you can use it in the future.

- When you are interviewing potential employees, make sure you know who they are meeting and what the message is going to be. You don't want demotivated or 'off message' employees getting their views across.

- To recruit today's young talent, older managers must change their views and understand what motivates these people.

- Is your HR group equipped to be talent scouts, searching for the best and signing them up?

- If you aren't getting a lot of, 'can I come and work for you?' requests, you had better question why not.

- Are you still fixated on clearing out older workers? Beware they are going to be in short supply. Think carefully before you let them go.

6 | It's all about development, reward and communication

We're overpaying him, but he's worth it.

Samuel Goldwyn

There are highly successful businesses in the United States. There are also many highly paid executives. The policy is not to intermingle the two.

Philip Wrigley

There is a tendency to want to admit that this is the chapter where I have put everything that didn't quite fit into the simple formula of 'Attract, Develop and Retain'. But that's not really accurate. The problem is that there are three areas that, while separate, are vital to the whole process of attracting and retaining talent.

- Development – or talent will most surely leave.
- Communicate: say what's happening – or they'll take the new found talents you have helped them develop and go and get a better paying, more rewarding job elsewhere.
- Reward – or talent won't stay long either.

Many organizations – most it would seem – treat these three areas in splendid isolation. Trainers train, compensation people play around with slide rules (oh yes they do!) and communications people watch their budgets being cut. So it was as an attempt to try and get some recognition that these three – albeit soft – areas have some sort of link, that I have put them together in one chapter.

Sadly, all three of these areas seem to be deeply vulnerable to both the short and long-term economic shocks that most businesses go through. Apart from the advertising budget, training and communications are usually the first victims of any CEO casting about for instant savings to improve the bottom line (later in this chapter you will find my own theory of communication). But, if we are to believe that there is a new world of work out there, where people expect to be challenged, developed, well compensated and informed, then these areas must, by default, become critical. So, binding them together for a common purpose wouldn't seem such a bad idea either.

training and communications are usually the first victims of any CEO casting about for instant savings to improve the bottom line

Maybe, just maybe, it is time for some brave managers to seize the moment and put reward, development and communication together. If they need any ideas, I know a lot of people who would be only too delighted to help them.

Development – where it's going and why

As we have seen earlier, there are some CEOs who think that a stack of currency is worth more than improving someone's skill set, but hopefully, they are a dying breed. Elsewhere, amongst major corporations, CEOs see executive development as a critical factor in keeping their organizations healthy, wealthy and wise. So much so, that the Association of Executive Search Consultants (AESC) were 'astounded' by a study it commissioned in 1998 that interviewed 300 top managers and discovered that, 'by overwhelming pro-

it is time for some brave managers to seize the moment and put reward, development and communication together

portions, today's corporate leadership believes executive development is very much worth the effort'. The AESC report went on to comment, 'with all of this discussion of declining loyalty, shortened tenures and future CEOs looking outside of their current corporations for their big chances, is there really any benefit to corporations spending resources on executive development? Surprisingly, the answer is yes.' It went on to say, 'Responses in this area are about as close to a complete consensus as you can get.'

But not for long. Asked if it was a good idea to make those major investments in development, most admitted they hadn't actually done much about it, although it was a good idea.

Worse was to come. When AESC tried to find out just how much time and interest the CEO put into development, 76 per cent of them said a lot. Sadly, 56 per cent of their top management and 60 per cent of their HR directors disagreed.

This, of course, is where the wheels come off the executive limo. This is where perception meets reality on a winding country lane and there is nowhere to hide. We are back to that issue that CEOs don't ever have time to think about people. We know from observation, interview and interrogation that they don't; which is one thing. But for them to think that they actually contribute a massive amount of their time and intellectual force, when they most obviously do not, is another. It is a potentially dangerous illusion. It is an illusion that can worm its way into the dark depths of a business doing untold damage. Especially where CEOs latch onto management flavours of the month.

Intellectual capital

In a paper on intellectual capital, Patricia Seeman, the organizational adviser on intellectual capital to Zurich Financial Services and her co-authors use a hypothetical case to explain why it is that terms like 'intellectual capital' and 'knowledge management' are not well understood in our businesses.

Seeman writes: 'The CEO of an international pharmaceutical company declared three years ago that his firm needed to become a learning organization. But he issued the directive without explaining how it related to the company's business strategy, what he expected the outcomes to be, or who would be responsible for leading the effort. A series of "cool", knowledge-related initiatives quickly sprung up, but they had no links to the business, or common understanding of what was to be achieved. As a result, they quickly fizzled. Within a year, the concept of knowledge management had lost credibility and was being ridiculed throughout the company.'

Many of us will be old enough to remember other initiatives that CEOs dabbled in – the words 'quality circles' still make me shudder 20 years later ('we had posters and t-shirts and the CEO was excited for a whole week'). In today's world, where knowledge is key and where constantly developing that knowledge is vital to our corporate health, the dabbling CEO is about as safe as a pyromaniac with a flame-thrower. We must be able to harness the knowledge in our businesses and we must be able to look up to the CEO and his immediate team and expect not just some distant commitment from their ivory tower, but that they are setting an example day-by-day: 'walking the talk'.

The right mix of talent

Seeman and her colleagues encapsulate the need for people and the need to win those people wars in a very neat paragraph; 'the purpose of managing human capital is to ensure that the business has the right mix of talent at the right time to implement the firm's corporate strategy. Human capital raises questions about the company's current level of individual skills compared with the competition. Where will the talent for the firm's five year plan come from? How will management attract, retain and develop these individuals?'

Get it wrong, as many CEOs seem to have done (although frighteningly they think they are doing pretty well), and you won't have to ask the question. Talent – even not very good talent – is in shorter and shorter supply and votes with its feet in most cases. Announcing ludicrous people initiatives, whether knowledge management, being a learning organization or creating human capital, that have no real thought behind them, is not just stupid, but it will do an exceptionally fine job of terrorizing or terrifying your talent. Most people can put up with quite a bit, but when respect vanishes, people do too.

A lack of appreciation

Don't agree? Let's look at a Roffey Park Management Institute report *The 1999 Roffey Park Management Agenda*. 'The factors that would make people leave the organization were directly related to the things which motivated them', says the report. 'The most commonly cited factor that would make people leave the organization was a lack of appreciation, which was cited by two-thirds of the respondents.' However, just behind – and CEOs please note – 'poor management was stated by 65 per cent'. The Management Agenda then asked if the respondents, 'faced any dilemmas in their careers at the moment?' The majority (57 per cent) said that they did. The main dilemma? 'Grappling with whether to stay with their current organization', for the main reasons of, 'poor management and lack of recognition'.

So we can safely say that not only are managers not going to put up with a great deal of stupidity, miscommunication and muddled thinking from the top, they are already evaluating their future options. Fail to give them real development that has a use (in their present job or to make them more marketable longer term)

> **managers are not going to put up with a great deal of stupidity, miscommunication and muddled thinking from the top**

and you seriously risk losing these people at the dawn of the greatest organizational talent famine that we have ever experienced: not the time, one would think, for conducting whacky organizational experiments.

Miracle management snake oil

But, not only do employees at all levels not fully believe in the actions of many CEOs, they also think that they pay lip-service to organizational 'sinecures' that – as with Patricia Seeman's hypothetical example earlier – have little to recommend them in adding any intellectual weight to the business. Unfortunately, it seems to be the prevailing view, that top management comes up with a new idea and then drops it on an unsuspecting organization and expects it to be some kind of miracle management snake oil that will solve all problems, motivate the masses and keep their noses firmly to the grindstone.

Linda Holbeche at Roffey Park, wanted to know the truth about whether this was really the perception of the rank and file. Were 'these values often perceived to be more of a public relations statement than a reflection of reality?' What she found was that, '79 per cent of the respondents indicated that their organization did have espoused values which it claimed to practise. These values covered a range of statements including:

- integrity
- fairness
- develop people to their full potential
- respect for others
- strive for excellence
- equality for all
- support others
- customer focus
- honesty
- people valued as greatest asset
- team-working
- empowerment
- creativity.

The results bore out the scepticism which surrounds organizational value statements, with the majority of respondents (61 per cent) indicating that espoused values did not match the actual values. 'The main discrepancy between the two,' says Holbeche, 'was caused by management not "walking the talk", which was cited by 76 per cent of respondents.'

espoused values did not match the actual values

Flickering lights of sanity

But surely not everyone is bad at this? There must be some companies that are trying? The answer to that is, yes, of course there are. Out there in the dark, there are quite a lot of flickering lights. One assumes that, like moths drawn to a flame, that's where the talent migrates to.

Indeed, as I have made clear in example after example, companies are doing their best. Often budgets aren't as big as they could be – or should be – but people are making progress. What they need to do a lot more of is invest these development processes with some kind of monetary measurement to get top management's attention. Because there is no getting away from it, honing skills and developing your talent are the only ways to renew your business.

According to some US studies, in 1970 it took about 15 years for half of your work skills to become obsolete. Today, it takes about three years. Therefore, if you fail to renew the skills of your people, you cannot stay in business for long. Making them redundant as they become obsolete and bringing in expensive, trained up talent isn't an economic option for most businesses either.

Building a global team that delivers

At car manufacturer Volkswagen, the issue has been not just attracting and keeping talent, it has been to broaden it rapidly from a German-centric organization to one that has room for and actively encourages talent from all over the globe. Volkswagen sets particular store by the creation of a global junior management programme that has become so prestigious that employees are clamouring to get onto it.

Designed around the idea of getting people from different nations and parts of the business, each intake has 30 people which break down into six groups of five. Rather than sitting listening to lectures all day, the groups are asked to come up with a problem that is really important to the business and then solve it. Each person in the group is allowed to spend 40 days on the issue – 20 days working directly on the project and 20 days at Ashridge (a UK management school). If they need more time, they have to sacrifice weekends and vacation time.

The uniqueness of the programme is that the 'owner' of the problem is a senior Volkswagen manager who really needs the problem solved. The process includes a final presentation by each group to the main Volkswagen board and can make their career. So far, the programme works extremely well and is a great way to develop talent. Over 80 per cent of those on the programme have been moved to more senior positions within a year.

At Zurich Financial Services, they have developed a special programme for their operations in the Far East. Like the Volkswagen project, it is designed to be a lot more than just classroom interchange. Called the 'Asia Academy', it is administered by the Australian Graduate School of Management in Sydney, which is the 'home campus' for the programme. Again, it is based around teams solving problems and getting to know each other across the region – a vital element of the programme's goals, which seeks to build both synergies and talent pools in Asia as a way of deepening employee commitment.

German airline, Lufthansa, has created the Lufthansa University, where it intends to invest as much knowledge into staff as it possibly can. Its head of HR, Tom Sattelberger says pragmatically, 'our strategy is to increase investment in training and development in good times, with a view to maximizing the marketplace abilities of our staff'. A nice way of saying, 'here's a set of skills you'll be able to use when you choose to leave us or we choose to let you go'.

In the UK, car-parts firm Unipart has created Unipart U, its corporate university that aims to, 'develop, train and inspire people to achieve world class performance. Opened in 1993, the 'U' as it is known is the first area seen by any visitor to the group's head office in Oxford and has become an integral part of working life: employees enter and leave

a technology training centre, opened to reduce the level of 'techno-fear' in employees

the company every day through the 'U'. They are also encouraged to teach in it as well as learn. In addition to the university, Unipart has also created an IT training centre called 'The Leading Edge'. 'The Leading Edge,' says Unipart, 'is a technology training centre, opened to reduce the level of "techno-fear" in employees.' Employees are encouraged to drop in any time of the day to try out new software packages; explore new techniques, such as multimedia and PC teleconferencing; or simply to surf the Net. Unipart says that it has, 'become a centre where learning about IT developments is coupled with an enthusiasm to use technology to help free the creative potential of all employees'.

'We have to invest in developing people. It is a must if you want to see them still here next year', says Gaby Boone, senior manager of the Europay Academy, just outside Brussels in Belgium. Europay, the European arm of MasterCard, employs a young (average age 34) workforce, many of whom are technology graduates. 'Of course we train them and other companies steal them,' laments Boone, 'but if we didn't provide development opportunities, we would be running an even greater risk.' Recognizing the need to be linked to the latest ideas, on a global basis, Europay not only links up with MasterCard in the US to share training ideas, but has joined an alliance of corporate universities that includes Motorola, GE and Hewlett-Packard. On the back of interactive training modules that it has created for its customers through its intranet, it has also pioneered *PC Privé*, where employees can have a PC installed at home (partly paid for by the firm) that allows them to do on-line training as well as e-mail. Current plans call for employees to have five training days a year – to a value of around $3,000. Boone believes that Europay is becoming known for training and that it does help recruitment. 'New people expect to get training and development from us, there is no doubt about that,' he says, 'at our induction programmes you here people saying, "well this is a good start, but I want more".'

Wanting and expecting more is a guiding principle of one of the oldest corporate universities – Motorola University (MU), which has been in operation since 1989, and has set itself ambitious targets to keep ahead of others in the race to push more and more knowledge around its global business. Mike Staunton, head of MU in Europe, says that MU – like other leaders – is now in the process of moving on, becoming much more of an organization dedicated to knowledge management rather than just training. As he explains, 'in 1998 we began a top to bottom reorganization of MU. Our goal is to create an integrated, global learning organization that can provide training to everyone at Motorola worldwide, be part of the value chain of doing business with Motorola and be the change agent of the corporation.' And, while others are still thinking of training in classrooms, MU and others are moving on to the second generation of corporate university – a virtual learning experience. Under the slogan, 'Right Knowledge Right Now', MU is using its vast technology resources and global infrastructure as a key enabler in getting knowledge to and from the workforce, wherever it may be. Using intranets for interactive modules, e-mail to deliver text files, interactive video and CD-ROM technology, it is able to let Motorola staff browse its total offering in a seamless, timeless fashion. This is backed up by classroom sessions, but can also include special presentations by senior executives that can be accessed in real-time by staff all around the globe. Staunton makes it clear that MU is a bottom-line operation, it is part of the business, not some nice-to-have, add-on function. 'Our mission is to be the agent of change within Motorola,' he says, 'and in doing that, we become part of the value chain of doing business with the company. Our job is to support business managers through leadership and management development in the global marketplace and to foster business growth through timely organizational renewal, global brand equity management and knowledge management.'

MU's Staunton makes it very clear that organizations must look to what technology can do in terms of reach, speed and sophistication – failure to do that will leave unprepared organizations falling further and further behind in the knowledge and skills race. After 18 years of providing focused training and development, MU says it has learned a thing or two about how to do it better than its competitors. Its suggestions should be heeded because they illustrate why, in today's business, training and development cannot be seen as a standalone issue and must be part of corporate strategy, delivering knowledge solutions across the organization.

- Keep close to the business environment and the customer.
- Understand the business environment as well as what the business does – especially in high-tech industries.
- Be proactive – not reactive. Our approach is to be a business partner – don't wait, you can't afford it.
- Technology is an enabler, not a negative – use it. Web-based training is the future and knowledge management is now the key opportunity.
- Training is an investment not a cost – aim to get that mindset into your organization.
- Don't be afraid of change – embrace it and turn it to your advantage.

Once again we see a split between those that see what talent needs to get the job done and those that create meaningless initiatives that have little to do with today's reality. Development today is all about communicating vision, values and knowledge as rapidly as possible around your business. It is about skilling and re-skilling people – even in the remotest location. It is exciting, vibrant and – for those that implement it fully – a whole new strategy where technology drives and knowledge thrives. Let us hope that many more CEOs get the message before it is too late, before the best have already made up the new rules and are already marching forward.

Communicate, communicate, communicate

Once in a seminar, I said that 'the road to hell was paved with the first editions of company newsletters – there is never a second one'. I got an unexpected, rousing round of applause. The reason for it was that I had hit a raw nerve for a lot of people. In company after company, across every kind of industry, there are torn up pieces of one communication plan or another littering the corridors. Part of the problem is that in many companies no one knows where to put communications. At various times I have seen responsibility for employee communications: rest in its own little niche; taken by a powerful top management advocate; as part of an, at the time enthusiastic, CEOs private office; live under the human resources umbrella; and, most illogically, reside in the marketing department. The truth is that employee communications – apart from being a management oxymoron – doesn't seem to comfortably fit anywhere. At best, it is looked upon as a necessary evil at worst it just doesn't happen.

Smart managers don't take responsibility for internal communications, they steer well clear. No one, in the history of private enterprise, ever made their name on the back of informing the employees about anything. It is one of the poisoned chalices of the corporate world.

> No one, in the history of private enterprise, ever made their name on the back of informing the employees about anything.

The problem has been that top management, like top politicians, have a desire to keep people in the dark and therefore much of what corporations spin out of employee communication's departments is interpreted with cynicism – not to mention ribald humour and even complete disbelief – by staff who have heard it all before.

Carefully crafted corporate copywriting is dismissed as beautifully bound bullshit by the masses – they just refuse to be impressed, when a few days, weeks or months later they are to find out the real truth, not the management version of it. In reality, naming the department 'Corporate propaganda' wouldn't be a bad idea. The other part of the problem is that communications is vital, but companies never spend much money on it. Also, it is one of the first things to go in a budget squeeze along with training, advertising and PR.

Based on 30 years of trying to get corporations to take employee communications seriously and make it part of long-term motivational strategy, here is my corporate communications theory. Anyone who would like to add to it is welcome to put their ideas on our website at www.johnsonandjones.co.uk

Beware the employee survey

Let's call our company the Acme Corporation. It is doing pretty well, business is booming, profits are up, the stocks are up, the top management is feeling good. Someone decides that an employee survey should be conducted to find out what people are thinking. The CEO agrees. 'It will show the people that we really care – call the human resource department and ask them to set it up.'

Three months later, some 600 pages of data has been produced. The survey shows one employee need above all others – better communication. (I have been involved in hundreds of employee surveys in the past three decades and 'better communication' is *always* at the top.)

When informed of the survey results, the CEO decides to use a staff newsletter to inform the workers of company activities and a member of the marketing team is asked to produce it.

So poor Bill gets given the poisoned chalice of trying to pick his way through the political and hierarchical fiefdoms that make up the company – a thankless task. Finally, weeks late, having been pored over by anxious executives who should have better things to do with their time (not to mention the corporate legal department), the first edition of the newsletter is produced. Six months have now elapsed since that fateful decision by the CEO to conduct an employee survey. Unwittingly, or should it be unthinkingly, the CEO has triggered a deep pool of resentment, by totally failing to address directly all the other concerns that the employees raised.

Carry out employee surveys at your peril; you raise expectations that something will happen. When nothing does, employees *know* you have something to hide, even if this is not actually the case.

At this point too, the market is now rocky, business is down, cash-flow is getting tight. The CEO and his team are looking around for quick savings and the newsletter is axed. It is an easy hit to make and it suits them; they don't really want to tell too much, especially now.

Now fast forward two years. Business has picked up, and many staff have moved on, including the CEO. The new CEO, feeling altruistic that day says, 'let's have an employee survey and see what the people in the organisation think'. The process is about to begin all over again.

Communication – a major imperative

Is the Acme Corporation scenario described above fact or fiction? Sadly, it is fact and it has happened in too many places. Employee communication is a flawed business. Many have written about it, but few ever do it right. However, in this new world of work, where knowledge and the sharing of that knowledge become a major competitive advantage, honest, accurate communication must be an imperative. If we are to energize our people, we must inform them. And if we do not do it, today's technology means that employees will do it themselves – there are no secrets anymore. Please tell your CEO that we live in an increasingly transparent corporate world where there are no hiding places – no room for secrets. So again, we have very little time to get this one right. Communication, fast, accurate, easy to digest, user-friendly, global is going to be a major factor in building your business in the 21st Century.

Communications strategy at Siemens

Here's a view from one company that really is endeavouring to achieve an effective communications strategy, Siemens. It states that 'Communication is the heartbeat of an enterprise; what is communicated, when and how and by whom are all variables that define organizational character and culture. The new communications strategy at Siemens is directed toward much greater transparency.' It adds, 'The change in communications style was supported by a **clear, concise, consistent messages, which are listened to and heard in the same way in different parts of the world** change in those responsible for it, as the task moved from its traditional home in the human resources department to an enhanced staff in corporate communications.'

Clear, concise, consistent

International Survey Research (ISR) in Atlanta observes that in the battle to go global, 'the principal method for achieving commitment and alignment is the art and science of communication. When organizations move from a transitional to a transforming dynamic, employee reactions to communications improve markedly,' it says. 'For the pugitive, transnational company this is a daunting objective. It requires clear, concise, consistent messages, which are listened to and heard in the same way in different parts of the world.' It adds, 'It also requires a sensitivity to local norms, nuances and nomenclature, which ensures that these same messages are not only heard, but understood, in the same way wherever they are delivered. Further, effective communications is a two-way street. That is, leaders not only have to send messages in a consistent and culturally astute manner, but they also have to receive signals from employees such that they really hear what is being said. And, at the same time, they must be able to integrate these inputs into their thinking, without compromising the clarity and coherence of the global message.'

Manfred Kets de Vries, a professor at the business school INSEAD in France, takes that view further. 'In any communication of change, leaders must focus on clear compelling reasons for change, lest employees feel tradition is being abandoned for naught. To further guard against that fear, leaders should build on aspects of the existing culture that are appropriate for the new organization.' He adds, 'A dedication to honest, focused and persuasive communication pays dividends to those spearheading a change effort.'

The difficulty is that few companies do so to any focused, consistent degree. Somehow communications always seems to be an afterthought – then messages get garbled and confused. It is little wonder employees around the globe insist that they haven't a clue what is going on.

Nick Winkfield is the head of European operations for Wirthlin Worldwide, a market research firm. He has been involved with employee communications for almost 40 years. Recently, he became concerned that companies weren't doing enough to ensure that the messages they were sending out were being properly understood. He also recognized that, as companies became ever more international in their operations, it was getting harder – despite new technologies – to mould a message so that it would be understood by all, in the same way.

This is Winkfield's view of how we should look at the messages we are sending out to our staff and why, in an era of turf-wars for talent, it is even more crucial to get it right.

'"Think global, act local" has become a marketing mantra. But inside the company, just as out in the market, it is not always easy to find the right balance. Managers must have the entrepreneurial freedom to develop their businesses in different markets, but always within the boundaries of corporate values and objectives. Motivating managers to maximum performance within these boundaries, requires consistently effective communications.' Winkfield goes on, 'So how should you communicate with your key managers in order to achieve the optimum combination of alignment with corporate values and individual motivation to perform?'

The nine stages of a message

According to Winkfield, there are nine 'stages' that a message goes through. It must be:

- sent
- received
- understood
- believed or trusted
- believed to be important to the company *and then:*
- felt (more than just believed) to be relevant to the manager personally
- held at the front of the mind and acted on continuously (corporate values and goals)
- 'stored', then retrieved and acted on when necessary (operational information)
- communicated to teams, customers and other external contacts.

As Winkfield explains, 'You can be pretty sure your message is being sent – but do you really know that it is completing the course? And if you do know that it is still in the race after hurdle five (most messages crash out at this point), what can you do to ensure that it clears hurdles six to nine?' Winkfield suggests that, 'if your message is not making it, the reasons can include the following.

- Key managers attend the global briefings, cascade meetings and so on. Although they may learn and absorb, they go home and carry on as before.
- Junior managers and employees complain that they do not know enough about corporate values, goals or strategies to do their jobs well.
- The intranet and other innovations (*see* pages 200–204), are admired and then left unused.
- Printed communications are read, believed, thought to be useful and then forgotten.
- Messages that are "not relevant now" are lost forever.
- You are surprised and frustrated at how long it takes to get any real response to your initiatives.'

Delayering and devolution of power

Winkfield says that, 'all of these are increasing problems for large and especially multi and transnational businesses. Why? Partly because the rapidly changing business environment demands ever faster responses; and partly because of organizational change: while delayering and devolution of power have removed many of the barriers to fast communications they have at the same time weakened the traditional channels of communication and new channels (e.g. intranets) are not yet being used to full effect.'

To be effective in a global world, Winkfield believes that you have to overcome a mass of challenges, 'especially when different national cultures are impacting on the corporate culture (and its subcultures). And this is even more difficult in the wake of mergers and acquisitions.' He notes that, 'it can be just as hard to change if you have been successfully doing the same things for 100 years, but can see far reaching changes coming around the corner'. In Winkfield's view, 'these challenges need a combination of motivational and behavioural research, hands-on communication skills and a real understanding of international management issues.'

As he points out, doing this right, 'doesn't come cheap, but the benefits of reaching your key talent and influencing their behaviour fast, comprehensively and effectively, do not need quantification. The bottom line will say it all.'

Mergers and acquisitions – the communications nightmare

A whole book could be written on how to handle communications in the midst of a merger or acquisition. Much depends on the type of merger (friendly or hostile) and just how much culture clash can be expected as top managers try to integrate.

The other issue is where the merger takes place, as national laws or habits can mean that one firm's approach can't or won't be the same as another. Suffice to say, there is one big lesson that I have seen in every merger situation – companies stop the communication process far too soon.

Many consultants speak of the 100-day rule, where you have all the paraphernalia of the communication in place, spend vast sums and then – just as the message was beginning to be understood – you roll up the carpet. This is not just wrong, it is plain dangerous.

As Linda Holbeche of Roffey Park Management Institute, who has carried out in-depth studies into mergers and what goes wrong, says, 'Six months into a merger it often looks very different. The board think they have told the employees about the merger and the communications consultants have departed. But restructuring is now underway and this is the time when people out in the business really need to know what is going on. When is there bit going to integrate, relocate, restructure? When, if at all, will their own job be affected? How will the jobs in the new structure at middle and junior levels be appointed (now all the senior ones have been done)? Where is the promised new pay system?'

Communicate at every step

Holbeche's advice is, 'communicate at every step – even when there is no news. This is a critical process, akin to giving oxygen to an anaesthetized patient. If business leaders want their organization to survive the trauma of merging and to recover fully, they must ensure that there is a steady flow of high-quality communication.' She adds, 'Stopping this flow temporarily or prematurely can be just as devastating as oxygen starvation.'

The intranet as a communications tool

Around the globe the use of intranets (private corporate computer networks) is quickly changing the way we communicate, teach and motivate our employees. Many knowledge-driven industries now boast that 100 per cent of their employees are on-line in one way or another. But as with anything new, there are right ways and wrong ways to manage it – especially in getting the right messages communicated and understood on a global basis.

Optimum benefit from an intranet

Tom McGuire, founder of Clarus, a Brussels-based communications consultancy, and a leading expert on the use of intranets by multinationals, offers the following ten tips on how to get the most out of this outstanding communications tool.

- Manage an intranet as a company asset, with leadership shared between an IT owner and a content owner. The return on any intranet depends on its content input, technical infrastructure and software applications. Its stock of knowledge will rise faster than the number of authorized users in the workforce. For best results, a senior IT manager and a top corporate communications manager *must* have technology and content responsibilities respectively. Working jointly, these colleagues provide the shared leadership to define policies and secure resourcing for sustaining an intranet that fully reflects the culture and values of the organization.

- Form a multi-discipline team to develop and launch the intranet with a sense of purpose, based on an agreed plan. An intranet is a global tool. To be successful, the company's culture must be stronger than any country's or region's culture. To start-up and maintain the quality and level of information on the intranet, companies should identify managers from multiple disciplines to take the lead – notably IT, HR and corporate communications. Founding 'Intrapreneurs' should be drawn from different regions of the world. The core team provides the simplified applications that let all employees become content creators (within secure limits to ensure corporate culture and content quality).

- Define the job of an intranet webmaster, who is usually more technically minded and skilled, and make it a full-time job. This person is the system administrator and responsible for technical support, maintenance, uploading servers, domain name conventions, control and supervision of operations and service, among other activities. A good intranet webmaster is agile with computers and skilful through practical experience. While there may be a single intranet webmaster in a company, many employees in departments and groups install and maintain an intranet server as part of their jobs.

- Standardize and simplify the intranet's structure so that navigation, information access and presentation of content are user-friendly. There is no 'right way' to do this. The structure of an intranet should mirror the needs of its users: the overall number of employees, worldwide, who can access the firm's intranet and who typically work in a multinational myriad of clusters, circles, networks and task-forces. Create user groups to define and drive an intranet initiative. These groups serve as a steering committee to promote intranet usage, recommend applications and overcome obstacles and misunderstandings that often arise in cross-company collaboration. Some of the benefits of a standardized intranet are reduced administration, ease of use and significant time and cost savings.

- Be mindful that content falls into quadrants, with one axis going from general to specific and the other from static to dynamic. Although an intranet is a tool for everyone, not all will benefit in the same way. For example, a company news centre is of general interest and highly dynamic, but details of an upcoming conference for financial managers is specific and should include input before, during and after the event.

- Ensure that IT issues surrounding an intranet are resolved and consistent with corporate IT standards. An intranet should capitalize on a company's overall investment in hardware, systems and software. Small communities of intranet users will quickly compromise corporate IT platforms and services if they are allowed to persist in pioneering their own IT solutions. To create redundant databases, introduce renegade content engines or install publishing applications incompatible with corporate standards is short-sighted and potentially damaging to the organization. When an intranet is properly fitted within the corporate IT environment, its total cost of ownership is mostly related to people, namely more than 85 per cent of total cost is training, development and content management – the remaining 15 per cent is hardware and software.

- Establish guidelines for design of intranet pages, frames and navigation, consistent with corporate identity standards. Every company promotes its own identity – internally and externally – through the uniform use of its logotype and other graphic design elements. A good intranet is harmonized fully with the 'look and feel' of the company's identity. Whatever intranet page is being viewed, it should be recognized as exemplifying the corporate identity. Graphic design guidelines for intranet should encompass the home page, so-called frame sets (subsections of the screen), sidebars and navigation buttons, to name a few aspects of what users see when they click, scroll and keytap their way around. Design elements should speed location and presentation of information, not crowd or clutter it. Layout should be attractive, but relevant. Content is the most important aspect.

- Develop guidelines for technical and content issues, including processes and procedures, and regularly update them. Comprehensive guidelines that address fundamental topics associated with the utilization of an intranet are central to its success. The user group is everyone with access. Who owns the structure? Who owns the content? What is the role and responsibility of the Webmaster? What is the procedure for developing new applications? Who can publish content and what is the process for doing so? The founding intranet team should draft and issue version 1.0 of such a guideline document at the outset, which is signed and approved by senior management where possible. Over time as the intranet grows in size and complexity, the document should be revised and updated.

- Define the profile of an intranet editor, who is usually content-minded and skilled, and make it a full-time job. Given the importance of content in making the intranet fully effective as a knowledge and communications tool, companies should appoint an intranet editor. The editor ensures that content policy is respected and adhered to. This means communicating intranet principles, clearance processes and publishing guidelines. For example, a dedicated editor not only oversees authorization of various contributors, but also innovates ease of use, formulates answers to frequently asked questions (FAQs), maintains facts and figures and ensures the integrity of numerous feedback channels. An editor controls the highest levels of information and content structure, including ownership of the corporate news centre.

- Demonstrate to employees that top management embraces a globally operating intranet by relating it to the company's vision. Making an intranet the backbone of internal communications signals that top management is committed to open exchange of ideas and information. This means reserving a prominent site on the intranet to feature the CEOs goals and messages. What is the company's ambition? How do individual employee contributions fit into that vision? An intranet is an already proven method to increase motivation and supportive behaviour. It facilitates cultural transformation, builds understanding for the impact that changes will have on everyone's job and focuses on strategic issues and programmes. Employee pride and satisfaction increase when supported by an effective intranet operation. Busy people (who today often operate from multiple locations) have less time for other – more outmoded – means of communication.

Communication isn't what it used to be

There is no doubt that every last one of us needs to learn the lesson that communication isn't what it used to be. IT technologies mean that it is in the hands of everyone – and that in turn means that it needs careful, sensitive management. In many companies, an unhappy or confused employee with enough technical knowledge can find the way to send a message to every employee (and probably every client as well). No organization can run that risk.

Equally, in this world of instant communication, we have to accept that introducing ideas first in one region and then another is laughably obsolete. When we make global decisions, we have to back these up with global announcements that take into account the complex needs of our people, wherever they are. To add to McGuire's list, I would say that webmasters need to be both organizationally aware and politically aware, with a deep understanding of the impact messages will have on the global population of their business.

This is a book about talent and how you hire it, hone it and hold it. I have no idea where some of these people we will need in this world of instant communication will come from, or what all their skills should be. All I know is that you don't see many right now and there are no job descriptions or even job titles – the term 'webmaster' doesn't begin to cover the function. What I do realize is that companies are going to have to take employee communication seriously for the first time, partly for the selfish reason that unless they do, they will lose people. Offering that argument to a CEO will guarantee that communication is back on the top of the agenda.

But there is one last point that needs to be emphasized about communication – that the revolution has struck. The electronic age of the Web and the Internet and intranet has made a complete difference to how (and how quickly) we communicate. Wise managers who understand this change can create powerful new methods to reach employees wherever they are – instantly. We all need to be sure that we understand what this ability to communicate can do for us and our organizations, because it is something that no one has ever experienced before. Ignoring the electronic communications revolution is like saying that the railway will never come to your town. It is there already and is being used by energetic start ups who are able to build global cultures and send global messages at the stroke of a key.

> webmasters need to be both organizationally aware and politically aware, with a deep understanding of the impact messages will have on the global population of their business

Managers in stodgy industrial giants who think that appointing a webmaster will solve the problem are wrong. Many of their competitors in the people wars have CEOs who have their own web sites, communicate on-line for an hour or two each week with any employee who wants to be heard and instinctively know how to use this new medium. If you want to win the people battles, first do a little spying, log on and see what's happening out there. Then, when you are suitably scared, do something about it.

So what are we going to pay for all this talent?

A great number of the people we have talked about are going to be expensive to take on and cost even more to hold. What is evident from all my investigations is that the price for top talent is spiralling ever upward – even the mediocre are going to do pretty well in the scramble to grab much needed knowledge and can-do workers into our organizations. However, this is not a book that seeks to discuss in detail compensation levels for different groups in different industries in different regions of the world. What I think is important for business leaders is to know where the major trends are most likely to take us.

Pay trends

- The biggest emphasis on total compensation is giving equity to managers – and adding pay for performance to traditional salaries.
- Even 'family' companies see the need to hand out stock to hold onto key executives.
- In high-tech companies, stock eligibility is now deep in the organization.
- Global companies mean global jobs and a global system of reward.
- Even in highly taxed European countries, pay for performance is making an impact. The challenge is to find the best way to make it work – for the company *and* for the individual.

Perception of reward

Some of the points above might be obvious, others less so. Let us begin with the one that so many still get wrong – that perception of pay is predicated by place. We have heard a great deal so far about work/life balance; this is also true when it comes to reward. It is really important for any CEO or HR professional to keep in mind that what is perceived as a good deal by one person will be of little interest to another. Giving a huge bonus to a Belgian, Spanish or Scandinavian executive is purely to fuel the coffers of the national tax regime – the executive will see little of it. Do the same in the US or the UK and you will get a totally different reaction.

Reward as a motivator depends solely on what works in a particular country and the social perception of it. Drive a large Mercedes or BMW in Scandinavia and you will be looked down on – the cultural attitude is that you don't show off your wealth and it is ecologically unsound too. In the US, where success is much more in-your-face, driving a large, powerful car is a sign that you have made it.

One senior HR manager with a long history of operating on international assignments wearily explained. 'How do you make a manager in New York with a huge stock option plan understand that his counterpart in the Netherlands is quite happy living in a tiny house in the suburbs of Amsterdam on one third of the take-home pay and commuting to work on a bicycle? Then again, how do you also explain that his opposite number has no plans to work after five in the afternoon (three on Fridays) and is going to take a full month of his six or seven week vacation allowance in his caravan in Spain in August?'

Force-feeding

One of the worst things that has happened in the name of globalization, is that companies – and I have to say they are mainly American – who still confuse 'going global' with being American everywhere, force feed what they perceive as things that are good for you. Because of this, employees have had dumped on them, bonuses that awarded 80 per cent to the local tax people, stock options that they had to pay tax on and medical and personal protection insurance that they don't need. What many US companies still need to take on board, particularly in Europe, is that the culture and social structure are vastly different.

Another key issue for HR professionals and reward specialists is that talent shortages are not only driving up pay and perks, they are also ensuring that you can never really know what the market rate is from one month to the next. Shortages in IT-related and marketing functions are now getting so critical that rates change almost daily.

Salary surveys – once a safe indicator of rates for the job – are basically useless as the time taken to gather and analyze data makes them obsolete long before they are published. Even subscribing to on-line information is becoming suspect.

Add to that the fact that anything outside of major markets is going to be seriously flawed and you have a situation where hiring is done by the 'seat of the pants'. No wonder the price for recruiters with negotiating skills is at a premium.

Money for mercenaries

The other concern that CEOs of companies with poor reputations are going to have to face is that the only way they will get talent will be as commodity talent buyers, or 'body-shoppers', having to pay huge amounts to buy what they need as they will be unable to attract. The other downside is that they will be hiring mercenaries who are working just for the money, with no loyalty and a well-ingrained habit of following the highest bidder at a day's notice. Many companies will bring this on themselves by not creating the right sort of work environment, spawning a culture of zero loyalty and short stays.

Talking of highest bidders, there is every expectation that salaries, bonuses and severance pay for those at the top are going to increase. Buying top talent certainly won't get any cheaper. Certain jobs are going to have a global price tag attached to them.

Guaranteed net salaries

Another trend that is hard to pin down because it verges on illegality, is the rise (particularly in Europe) of the guaranteed net salary. Basically, what happens is that companies, desperate to employ high-performing or scarce talent, will agree to pay a net amount to an executive over a period of years. This means that it is up to the company to work out how it handles the tax and other obligations. This can amount to a great deal of total compensation to be paid, when you realize that top-earning executives in Scandinavia or the Benelux earning $1 million could have a social security and tax burden that would multiply that figure by three. Eager to save as much of that social burden as possible, companies and their lawyers are investigating such deals as 'consulting' assignments for overseas subsidiaries, split work weeks and other loopholes.

An American pay model

But overall, what is certainly clear is that the rest of the world is moving to an American pay model. This may be out of efficiency, or may be out of greed but the trend is clear. Whether a family-owned company in Portugal or the European operations of a US multinational – pay trends

It is clear that the rest of the world is moving to an American pay model

have come a long way in just the last five years.

Indeed, as some of those recent global mega-mergers (e.g. BP/Amoco, Daimler-Benz/Chrysler, Deutsche Bank/Bankers Trust) have served to emphasize, when you are faced with major pay disparity between Europe and the US, the only way to solve it is by paying everyone at the top end: both for salaries and stock options.

Four key trends

For today's executives – and not just for those at the very top – there have been four distinct trends that are sweeping old methods aside, changing forever the way we get compensated for our work. Simply put, these can be summarized as moving from:

- pay the position *to* pay the person
- pay for seniority *to* pay for performance and leadership
- fixed pay *to* variable pay/more risk
- internal performance measures *to* value creation measures.

Global pay rates for global jobs

Much of this change has been driven by globalization. While many companies still just talk about it, there has been a revolution taking place, as formerly standalone industries have seen their operations merge and blend into a virtually seamless whole, creating global price tickets for jobs.

Business areas like financial services, IT, the media and much of consumer electronics are getting closer together. Elsewhere, retail businesses are joining up with other businesses. What this means is that there are now truly global jobs that fit into the new infrastructure of the truly global company. And global jobs have one thing in common. Whether you live in Europe, Asia or America, there is one price, one reward band (usually high) for that job. Be a senior e-commerce specialist and you can name your price, and it's the same if you live in Palo Alto, Brussels or Tokyo. And for those who live and work at this global level the rewards can be exceptional – but the risks (literally putting your money where your mouth is) are high too. If you cannot create value in the business you just don't get paid.

Basically, there are four drivers to rewards in the global job:

- the focus is on real operating income and cash flow (not 'traditional' accounting perceptions of performance)
- rewards require a 'competitive' return on shareholder investment
- no incentive is earned, until the competitive return has been exceeded
- stock price movement (in the upward direction!) is in many cases mandatory too.

Incentive-based reward

It is not only top performers who are seeing their compensation patterns change. Down in the engine-room of virtually all businesses, new, incentive-based reward systems are finding their way into everyday business life. Without them, you risk losing your top performers. In fact, today, even mediocre talent is asking for – and getting – better deals.

Four other developments are impacting the way people get rewarded in the European company of today. In essence, we are moving from:

- historical performance comparisons *to* peer company comparisons
- focus only on the numbers *to* focus on holistic view of executive performance
- cohesive pay structures *to* flexibility to recruit talent
- compensation that equals cash and pension *to* encouraging employee share ownership.

Much of this is solidly linked to stock performance; giving employees at all levels equity in the company is becoming the rule rather than the exception.

While there are those who seriously doubt that this trend will really work – believing (perhaps rightly) that any performance management programme only encourages the wrong and narrowly focused behaviour – most companies find that the pressure to change their compensation methods is just too great to resist. So, expect total compensation which includes a large slice of employee ownership, to become the norm. Failure to take that into account will mean putting your best people at risk, as more and more companies make this a routine part of their compensation programme. If you aren't doing it already, the chances are it is almost too late and another battle in the people wars will go to someone else.

A word to the wise

So now we all have our instructions. Develop our talent, communicate to our talent and pay our talent. That triumvirate is going to have a great deal of attention lavished on it in the years to come. Does anyone have all three in the correct balance? It seems too early to say, but if ever there was a case for admitting that the 'soft' issues were going to have a big part to play in the corporations of tomorrow, this is it. Only these issues aren't that soft anymore – they are a crucial part of the ammunition you are going to need to win that war for people.

Aligning your talent with business needs is going to be hard work. The only consolation is knowing that if you don't do that, you won't have any talent to worry about.

Points to ponder

- Employees don't come to work just to do a job – they expect development and an organization that will pay them to hone their skills.

- We live in a transparent world; communication takes on a critical new importance that CEOs need to understand and act upon.

- The communications revolution is spurred by the Internet, failure to make use of this fully will impact on your ability to win the people wars.

- Reward systems are changing rapidly. Pay for performance is the norm and you must be a part of it.

- Equally, one size does not fit all. What motivates in one part of the world is a turn-off in another. Companies seeking global markets must understand local cultures better.

7 | Getting your business ready for the battles to come

Delegating work works, providing the one delegating works, too.

Robert Half

In the space age, the most important space is between the ears.

Thomas Barlow

If you think that you're already having difficulty attracting and retaining business talent, this is just the beginning. All the forecasts point to a global drought of can-do people that is going to last a minimum of a decade. That's ten long years of fighting hard to get the best and keep them on your side of the battlefront.

So, it is pretty obvious that, unless you are a company that people are queuing up to join, you are going to have to work very hard on your image and reputation. In researching the talent issue, it became clear that there are three criteria that distinguish the companies that top talent want to work with. They are recognizable by:

- the way they are able to engage and involve their employees.
- their focus on personal development.
- their acceptance and promotion of the work/life balance.

Furthermore, all the companies I have encountered that are getting the people part right, seem to realize that they have to develop and maintain their own, personalized, set of plans, policies and procedures to make all this happen. They know there are no hard and fast rules: what drives one person to work with you and stay for a while won't be the same for another.

Similarly, it would seem that all the companies that are successful at attracting and keeping their talented employees, do so on the basis that each and every member of staff knows what the employment agreement is.

There are no hidden traps in the agreement – it is truly an agreement between employer and employee that suits both parties at the time. As long as the employer keeps to its side of the bargain and offers a great place to work, challenge and constant development, the employee will give of his or her best. Employees will see it as a 'place worthy of their investment'. But, the employer must realize that needs change over time. To be successful with people today you need to know how their wants and desires are evolving and treat them as individuals not as part of a group.

There are no hidden traps in the agreement – it is truly an agreement between employer and employee that suits both parties at the time.

People issues on the strategic agenda

As the war gets bloodier, more and more senior managers are realizing that it is time to get people issues onto the strategic agenda, that the attraction *and retention* of talent must become a core competence of the organization. Without the right people, trying to be a dynamic, innovative company, just won't be possible; you will literally starve your ability to grow through a shortage of people-power.

Five ways to increase innovation

Human resources consulting firm Hewitt says that, based on its own research of top companies, there are 'five ways to increase innovation' that are all related to the people you have around you.

Culture

Company culture should:

- be more open and tolerant
- involve more risks and mistakes
- move faster.

Leadership

Leadership can be improved through:

- more trust
- support
- autonomy
- encouragement.

Work activities and relationships

Work activities and relationships thrive with:

- more flexibility
- greater use of teams
- networks
- effective communication.

Advancement opportunities and development

Increase workers' opportunities with:

- more training hours
- more types of learning; employees are responsible
- different philosophy; less succession planning, leaders and entrepreneurs emerge.

Total compensation

Compensation can be improved with:

- more rewards and recognition for ideas and innovation
- broader use of incentives and benefits
- less individual differentiation; no penalties for mistakes.

That is the way all of us are going to have to think if we are to have a fighting chance in the battles to come. It is the only way that our businesses will be seen as talent-rich. And as we have seen already, talent attracts talent, because everyone wants to be on the winning side.

Look to alliances

Just as no individual today can know everything, so the same applies to a business. Success in the future will not be just based on what you know, but on who you know. Can you partner with another company to make it better, deliver it faster, or create a totally new service? To do that, we will need an increasing number of talented people in our businesses who know how to seek out alliances, understand the art of negotiation and are able to coach, coax and coerce.

Share your talent

We will also need business leaders who are pragmatists, who understand that you can't always have 100 per cent of a talented individual, but may have to share them with others. Today, we are seeing the emergence of a new breed of management talent that will take its abilities around a range of corporations, not working

> you can't always have 100 per cent of a talented individual, but may have to share them with others

solely for the highest bidder, but giving a little to each. Consultants have done this for years, now it is the turn of talented individuals too. If you want the top people, you may well have to be prepared to share them with your competitors. Remain flexible in your thinking.

And, while many people seem to feel that the role of a CEO has become a lot more difficult, the better among them would replace the word 'difficult' with 'challenging'. Talking to CEOs for this book, it was encouraging to realize that – although some do seem out of touch with market reality – when it comes to the battle for warm, talented bodies – many of them think it is the very best of times to be at the head of an enterprise. As Rolf Hüppi, the chairman and CEO of Zurich Financial Services says, 'the upper echelons of large corporations demand passion and commitment above and beyond the call of duty'.

A clearly defined balance

But it is also for CEOs to realize that while they and their top teams may have that inner drive and eat and sleep their business, many of the people that they need are content to do an excellent job, but need another life too. To my mind, the recognition of this – that the average person in a corporation needs a clearly defined work/life balance – is a major step to building the kind of culture that employees are going to demand in the next century. No matter how hard we try, we will not be able to bully and coerce talent into working harder and longer hours. People power, on the basis that they know they are in ever shorter supply, has come to business. Our CEOs had better learn to deal with it.

Invalid belief

A paper by Roffey Park Management Institute, *Balancing Life and Work*, describes this revolution admirably. 'The imbalance between work and life has been shown to be heavily dependent on the long hours culture,' they say. 'This is tied up with a belief that productivity is associated with long hours – a belief which is invalid. Organizations need a different measure of commitment at work which considers an individual's output, rather than just the visible time they spend in the workplace.' They continue, 'Graduates and other high-calibre employees are increasingly asking for more flexible arrangements. The shifting values of the future workforce play a crucial role in the balance equation and the research clearly indicates that younger generations increasingly aspire to balanced, varied lives. This value shift is not gender specific, both men and women desire fulfilment outside of work. Companies which are responding to this desire for balance will have a stronger advantage in the struggle for tomorrow's best qualified workers.'

> There is a belief that productivity is associated with long hours – a belief which is invalid

As a young corporate lawyer explained to me, 'I'll work five nights in a row to midnight, but when I am not busy, I'll take a day off. I expect my employer to accept that.' If we, as an older generation, fail to take these emerging lifestyle needs into account, we will lose the talent we have worked so hard to attract.

That same young lawyer was told that, 'I would have to wait four years until I could get a transfer from London to our firm in New York. Four years is too long to wait, so I quit. I already have three offers to go and work there, all with interesting work, all for more money.' That is the voice of today's reality. We have created a work culture where speed is of the essence. Can we be surprised when the talent in that culture is in a hurry too?

Beyond Generation X

Not to dwell too much on the younger manager, but CEOs and the rest of top management are going to have to learn what makes them tick, i.e. what motivates them. Perhaps they could start by scrutinizing the list below.

Claire Raines' book, *Beyond Generation X: A Practical Guide for Managers*, lays out the generation X work ethic for all to see and explains why. 'Generation X, she says, is:

- self-reliant: they spent a lot of time alone as children
- sceptical: witnessed pollution, crime, racial tensions and AIDS
- financially aware: given money to handle household matters while parents worked
- balanced in terms of work and personal life: watched their workaholic parents
- reluctant to commit to an employer: watched their parents get downsized
- flexible with life-stage boundaries: getting a 'real job', buying homes and marrying are coming later
- unimpressed by authority: saw their heroes dismissed
- techno-literate: were the first generation to grow up with computers
- comfortable with diversity: are the most diverse generation, ever.

Raines then takes those traits and applies them to what it means for your business when these people get their hands on it. And its too late to worry, you employ these people already. The Generation X worker is:

- flexible: ready to adapt to new people, places, circumstances
- comfortable with information and technology

- outside-of-the-box thinker and worker (remember there is no box)
- independent
- managing as much of his or her own time as possible
- goal-oriented
- entrepreneurial
- creative
- eager to prove him or herself
- wanting to see results, every day
- trying to invest in self, create security from within.

A predictable work schedule

What you need to do is adapt your business to meet the needs of these workers so that you can profit from their talent and enthusiasm. As consultants PricewaterhouseCoopers discovered in their 1999 International Student Survey, 'a key factor that respondents believe would facilitate a balance between personal life and career is a working schedule that allows them to see their family and friends on a predictable basis'. But the survey showed that this new generation understands the rules as well. 'While students all over the world make balancing work and personal life their top career priority, they are willing to work hard for it. On average, respondents expect to work at least 47 hours a week at their first jobs.'

Of course all of this depends on quite a lot of issues, including opportunities to work in very different ways indeed.

God-like expectations

As John Hunt, professor of organizational behaviour at the London Business School, pointed out in the *Financial Times* in 1998, 'if we confront young people with god-like lists of what is expected of them, then we are certain to fail to find or develop them'. Hunt continues, 'We should not be surprised if fewer and fewer young men and women will see their future in global organizations where the expectations of their interpersonal or leadership skills are grossly overblown.' He then adds, 'Why should they bother? Why tolerate this humiliation when running a small consultancy two or three days a week in the booming management development industry could provide more fun, more freedom, as much or more wealth and – importantly – realistic expectations of what they might achieve?'

You have been warned

Then again, there is another aspect to this new world of work that employers must take into consideration. If how well they are being developed is high on the 'wish list' of employee expectations, just what that development has been and where, is going to be a new badge of office: how well trained you are will accord a hierarchy of boasting rights in the workplace. Get sent to INSEAD or IMD and you can really strut your stuff. Do a distance learning MBA with some obscure business school and maybe you should just keep quiet.

Want to reward your best young talent? Think long and hard about how they want to be developed and how grateful you want them to be.

Those that won't make It

The other group that needs dealing with in a considered fashion are those that just won't make it to the end of your journey. Companies are finally recognizing that how they deal with unwanted employees strongly impacts how they are viewed by would-be workers. Certainly, in today's world an increasing number of candidates want to know before they join what happens if it doesn't work out. Because of this, guaranteed severance pay is rising – dependent usually on how eager the company is to employ the person.

Elsewhere, apart from the now almost standardized use of outplacement if things go wrong, companies are offering stress counselling, picking up fees for tuition and training classes, and extending medical coverage. One firm I talked to turns losing your job into a business proposition – offering a $5,000 success bonus if you get reemployed within three months.

The haunting subject of succession

Despite the fact that business is an ever more complex world to operate in – or maybe because of that – CEOs and other top managers still seem to be dragging their feet when it comes to having viable succession-management polices. While many CEOs will tell you that they have a company-wide succession plan, such are the rapid arrivals and departures in a modern corporation that keeping it relevant is a time consuming, almost full-time business. Sadly, this role of monitoring succession plans is often given to the wrong type of person to administer. Then it becomes just that, an administrative process, rather than a dynamic review of options and opportunities.

One industry that sees the effects of poor succession planning at close range is executive search (usually, because they are called in by a panicked board of directors to urgently find a new CEO). Based on its global experience of filling senior appointments in the aftermath of sudden departures, headhunter Korn/Ferry has fixed views on what is going wrong in the corridors of power. 'There was a time,' it says, 'when most organizations had several individuals ready to step in if a vacancy appeared in a key position. But, today, most companies have reduced management teams so drastically that they have limited reserves to draw on. As a further complication, the boxes on their organizational charts, once occupied by veteran players, now hold new recruits.'

Also, surveys I have drawn on for this book, show that most top people are planning a much shorter tenure that their predecessors.

Obstacles to succession

Korn/Ferry go on to list ten key 'obstacles to effective succession planning'.

- Denial: this is rooted in the fear of ageing and death; the reluctance to relinquish power to the next generation; the refusal to acknowledge that the company is losing momentum.
- Command and control leadership: a company may have a charismatic leader who has no intention of giving up control – and undermines efforts to put an effective succession plan into place.
- Dependence on a number two: there is an heir apparent lined up, but there is a falling out with the CEO, or the next in line gets tired of waiting.
- Deferred planning: the company has a young, healthy CEO – or assumes that when the time comes, it will go outside for new leadership, so there's no need to worry about a succession strategy.

- Dissension: Board members disagree about who should succeed the CEO, whether outside or inside candidates are best, or what the criteria should be. Or there is tension between the board and the CEO that prevents a realistic strategy taking shape.

- Failure to develop talent: the HR function has been so severely downsized – or so removed from corporate strategy – that succession planning, and the whole realm of developing talent within the organization, is given a low priority.

- Delegated responsibility: the job of drafting a succession plan is delegated to someone in the organization who lacks authority, is out of the loop on overall strategic planning and cannot align this critical function with other decisions that determine the organization's future.

- Distraction: the company is so busy fighting fires and trying to stay competitive in a very tough marketplace, that management succession is simply overlooked.

- Downsizing: the management ranks are so depleted that there are few candidates to step in when key positions are vacated.

- Dummy planning: a business may have an elaborate management succession plan that has little to do with reality, and will not stick when the time comes to use it. A 'pretty picture book' of internal candidates is useless unless the skills or leadership training needed are regularly assessed.

What kind of business are you going to build

Who succeeds the present CEO is going to depend a great deal on exactly what kind of business you want to build.

In a world where so much emphasis is now placed on the use of technology as an enabler of business opportunity, the type of person – their skills and visions – may well be very different from the CEO you would have chosen just a few short years ago.

Additionally, the type of organization structure is going to be very different to accommodate the needs of those younger generations who have a different view on how work should be prioritized.

As Belmiro de Azevedo, president of Portuguese industrial giant Sonae, whose business includes everything from mobile phones and supermarkets to wood pulp, says, 'Our people move up on a zigzag career process. They may be the general manager of a small company today and finance manager of a big company tomorrow. We like to lead by example and transmit our values by how we act – you cannot achieve this by writing memos.'

With a slate of senior managers under 40, and a mobile phone company where employees have an average age of 27, de Azevedo is certainly backing the youth vote. 'We have a common vision,' he says, 'we believe that change and an open mind are very important. Sadly, at present, too few companies have this asset.' He adds, 'I like to think that the top 100 people in Sonae are all unorthodox people. Here, the rising stars will get the green light to grow and the smartest will overtake the more senior people. At Sonae, we look on this as a kind of internal sport.'

It works, the atmosphere at Sonae's Porto headquarters is electric – the turnover virtually nil.

Global performance criteria

Dutch electronics giant Philips, takes a more organizational approach to what it wants its future leadership culture to be. Hayko Kroese, HR director for its components division, notes 'although we have always nourished top skills within the company, we have no great tradition in providing standards for how to apply this professional knowledge...before, it tended to be different in each country and each division.' He goes on, 'People were using different words for the same concepts and, secondly, the criteria being used for top leadership were becoming obsolete. To become world-class it is extremely important to develop global criteria for outstanding performance, so our business leaders know what it takes.'

This is how Philips defines what a leader needs to have for the 21st Century: it makes a useful inventory when going shopping for top talent. See how many of these attributes your next list of candidates possesses:

- Show determination to achieve excellent results: Philips expects its managers to develop a vision of where the business should be going, translate this into challenging goals and take active ownership and accountability for getting there.

- Focus on the market: external input and excellent business knowledge are prerequisites for developing a vision. In addition, profound market knowledge, customer insight and a broad perspective on the business are keys to success. This also implies the ability to think strategically.

- Find better ways: true value creation means that you have to make it happen in your organization. Put the systems and processes in place and manage them. Manage profitability and champion change – use each and every opportunity to improve business processes. Leaders optimize key processes by finding ways to get things done faster, more efficiently and more effectively in cooperation with others.

- Demand top performance: those in a leadership role are expected to turn the vision into achievable targets and act as role models for top performance. They show direction and lead by example while addressing difficult people issues when they should be addressed.

- Inspire commitment: true leaders can persuade their teams to share the same vision, demonstrating excellent communication and influencing skills. They win commitment at a rational and emotional level, apply an understanding of people to motivate and inspire colleagues, and so get the best out of them.

- Developing self and others: leaders raise the capability of the organization by continuously developing themselves and others, creating a learning organization in which knowledge is actively managed. True leaders prove to be masters in giving and receiving feedback and help others to improve through coaching and mentoring.

These six points offer a valuable insight into the types of leadership talent that organizations are going to expect and demand in the years to come. But with a shortage of these kinds of people, it also serves to illustrate that the battles for talent are going to be bloody and long.

Where does HR fit in?

Most managers I have spoken to view HR's role as somewhat ambiguous in the talent wars to come. Their feeling is that it has not evolved sufficiently fast and is still not a part of the strategic process, having been relegated to a support role. True, as we saw in earlier chapters, there are some HR professionals who have broken out of that mould, but these seem to be few and far between. Several managers I spoke to cited three key reasons why HR's survival was in doubt:

- web-based technologies short-circuit the HR function entirely
- line organization assumes HR's role
- outsourcing of HR services.

How much these will happen and how fast, is open to question, but there is a strong feeling in many corporations, especially as the talent issue gets onto the CEO's action list, that a new structure will appear. More proactive, more combative than any HR department to date, it will be strategically staffed to have one purpose, to attract and above all retain talent, as we saw with the example of IBM or at PricewaterhouseCoopers where they have appointed a 'global leader of human capital'. As we begin to see employees as real monetary assets, a function of this kind will be seen to have a critical business purpose. Those that are put in charge of it will be the rising stars of the corporation.

What about the shareholders?

And those rising stars are, of course, going to have to deal with that most vocal of external groups – shareholders. As we have seen, most CEOs already feel that pressure to perform in the short-term, seriously jeopardizes their ability to carry out long-term investments and strategies. Will this ever change? With stock markets in the West riding on an all-time high (that many say is unsustainable) you could say, 'not right now'. But, in a world that is now at the mercy of events way beyond the power of a single corporation to correct, we may well have to see some changes.

Hopefully, one day, CEOs with real visions will be able to plan for the longer term, and ignore those quarterly results. How likely this is remains to be seen, but research by the Association of Executive Search Consultants (AESC), found that 'shareholder focus is seen as having a major negative impact on a corporation's ability to serve other stakeholders: this is particularly true among future CEOs'. The AESC study goes on to comment that, 'respondents openly acknowledged that the current shareholder

a new structure will appear that is more proactive, more combative than any HR department to date

focus in corporate America has a significant downside. First, it places intense pressure of CEOs, creating short-term expectations many would consider unreasonable. Second, and more broadly, members of today's corporate leadership believe this shareholder focus has reduced a corporation's ability to serve the interests of other important stakeholders, namely employees and customers.' The survey summed it up as follows:

Q. *Has the empowerment of the shareholder and the focus on short-term results hampered a corporation's ability to serve the interests of other stakeholders, such as employees, communities, customers . . .?*

Current CEOs   62 per cent say yes
HR Directors   74 per cent say yes
Future CEOs   77 per cent say yes

Shareholder showdown

So, maybe tomorrow's CEO will challenge the shareholders to a showdown, insisting that a focus on the short-term is the wrong strategy in the success-critical battle for talent.

The AESC study makes it all too clear that its findings, 'serve as a clear warning that US corporations need to do a better job of preparing executive talent for the future and also strengthening the long-term commitment on the part of senior executives to the company.' And they have sound advice for top managers contemplating the future success of their organizations. If you are a top manager or CEO, I suggest you read this very carefully, it is an excellent (research based) summation of all the issues that I have covered.

- *Executive development.* It's worth the investment. Even though investing significant resources in executive development may appear futile, due to shortened tenures and a lack of long-term commitment among many, it is still worthwhile. Corporate executives (particularly up and comers) still believe it is a useful investment, helping to grow the general pool of capable corporate leaders and also helping to instil loyalty among executives.
- *Fast track training programmes.* These are seen as a key way to develop executive talent. Unfortunately, most corporate executives acknowledge their company's lack in this area.
- *Get the CEO directly involved in executive training.* Taking ownership of the programme allows CEOs to personally instil their vision in their people and, most importantly, breed loyalty throughout the organization. Up and comers are clearly crying out for this sort of personal mentoring. While CEOs may think they are doing this already, they need to be encouraged to

do more (despite their already overburdened schedules). In the long run, a more loyal and long-term executive staff makes the job of the CEO that much easier.

- *Power sharing.* This should be looked at as the primary tool in building commitment among valued staff. It is the single most effective thing a CEO can do to ensure a satisfied and loyal senior staff. Interestingly, even generous compensation packages are not believed to be as effective.

- *Shareholder focus.* Don't get lost in it. Remember the other key stakeholders necessary to your company's survival and success.

- *Quality of life enhancers.* Look to these to keep the best and the brightest and minimize the 'opting-out' phenomenon.

As the AESC study concludes, 'it is certainly worth the effort. In the end, as most would agree, successful businesses in the 21st Century will be those who prove superior in attracting and retaining the best leaders.'

Prepare your forces

Here are some other ideas that you might want to consider in preparing your forces for the talent battles ahead.

- How good are your internal and external recruitment teams? Do they really know who they are looking for? Do they really know the long-term strategy of the company?

- How do you differ from your competitors? What are the unique elements of your job offer? Why would I want to work for you rather than another company? Can you encapsulate that in 25 words or less?

- Do you conduct in-depth exit interviews to discover why employees are leaving and do you use this information thoroughly and painstakingly to plug the holes where talent is leaking from the business?

- Have you considered creating a new organizational structure where the attraction and retention of talent is elevated to a strategic role, putting a senior manager in control with the twin mandates of seeking out and tying down at all costs the talent you need?

- Do you know who the top companies vying for the same talent as you are? What are they offering that is different from you?

- Do you know who the top companies stealing your talent are? Why is your talent leaving to join them?

- Do you have full knowledge of the positions and skills that are totally critical to your business that you would 'pay to stay' (until they can be replaced) or 'pay to hire' under practically any circumstances?

- Have you ever called job candidates who refused your offer to find out why?

- Have you asked headhunters which are the companies they target to fill assignments in your industry – are you on that list?

- Are your top managers fully empowered to make an offer and hire talented executives or specialists if they 'accidentally' come across them?

- Are you equipped to share top talent with others? If not consider it, it could be a way to keep hot-shot soldiers on your side.

- Have you the right sort of managers that can forge alliances and joint-ventures, adding value to your business?

- Are you as flexible in your recruitment and retention strategies as you need to be? If not, change them.

- Do you have a top management team (honestly) that really walks the talk and has the confidence of the employees? If you haven't you might need to change them or at least get them to acquire new people skills.

- Are you using technology to improve your communications to employees at all levels. Don't leave it to others, information and message control is a vital part of the people wars.

- Lastly, make certain you understand the new demands for life/work balance and get your management systems adapted to these new needs.

It is only by asking and honestly answering questions like these that we can even begin to consider winning the people wars.

Most managers that I know are scared stiff that the answers to these questions will reveal huge holes in their ability to hire, develop and nurture business talent. My answer to that is, 'you had better know just how bad it is as soon as possible'.

If our internal recruiters are not fit to hire the people we need, let's make them better. If our search firm doesn't know as much about our business as we do, let's change them – there are plenty more eager to have a go. What this battle for the best is going to take is an admission from many of us that we are fat, complacent and not in very good corporate shape. We are getting out of breath and out of ideas and we haven't even come to the real battle yet. Ideas – mixed with a good dollop of honest assessment – are going to be one of the keys to winning these wars for talent. We are going to be living in a world where the commodity we have become used to – corporate cannon fodder – is going to be in ever short supply. Those people that we have a poor record of dealing with either honestly or decently are going to get their revenge, if we don't move quickly. It's difficult enough to fight the enemy outside, dealing with revolution and counter-insurgency inside is harder still and much more organizationally exhausting.

We're talking talent

Of course, you could pray that technology will come to the rescue and mean that we don't need all those people anyway. Forget it. We are talking talent here – and believe me, you'll want it and you'll be surprised just how much you are prepared to pay for it.

Nick Winkfield, head of Europe for market researcher Wirthlin Worldwide, has a sane view on all this. 'If car makers were hit by steel shortages and escalating prices,' he points out, 'they would have a choice: either price themselves out of the market, or redesign their cars and make them out of less steel, more plastics. Faced with a shortage of leadership talent companies have a choice: either pay the price or redesign themselves so that they can function effectively with fewer leaders, more managers.' Perhaps that is our organizational destiny?

Think like you used to

Somewhere in the process of researching this book, I was told a story by someone who suggested that there was a simple way to review just what you needed in terms of talent for the future. It went something like this. 'All of us have a day-to-day view of our business, it is never really much more than that. We solve problems, we fight fires, we think we set strategy for the future. But what we do every day is based on the knowledge we have of the business. It is based on our likes or dislikes, and our prejudices. The last time we really saw our organization without any of our own prejudices and misconceptions was the first day we were employed. We arrived, we saw, we became involved. What all of us need to do, is walk out of the door as though it was our very last day. Then, we need to come back as though it was our very first day. If you were arriving as CEO, or vice president of marketing, engineering or finance, what would you do with this organization? Where would you take it and who would you want to help you get it there?'

It may be unlikely that you'll ever do that, but my advice is put down this book and go home. Tomorrow, walk into your business as if you had never seen it before; like it was your first day. Assess all those people; make an assessment of who you need to win the war. I can promise you one thing: wars have two sides, winners and losers. If you don't do that – or something equally drastic – you know which side you'll be on don't you . . .

Bibliography

Aligning the Global Management Team: Nick Winkfield, Wirthlin Europe, May 1999.

Balancing Life and Work: Roffey Park Management Institute, 1998.

Behind the Mask: The Real Face of the Human Resources Function Today and In 2002: Management Centre Europe, February 1999.

Big Headhunter is Watching You: *Business Week*, 1 March 1999.

Breaking Through Culture Shock: Elisabeth Marx, Nicolas Brealey Publishing, 1999.

Building and Retaining Global Talent: Towards 2002: Mike Johnson, Economist Intelligence Unit and Hewitt Associates, April 1998.

Building Intangible Assets: A Strategic Framework for Investing in Intellectual Capital: Patricia Seeman, David De Long, Susan Stucky and Edward Guthrie, Classics Knowledge Management, MIT Press, June 1999.

'Building Trust': W. Chan Kim and Renée Mauborgne, *Financial Times*, 9 January 1998.

Chief Executives in the New Europe: Association of Executive Search Consultants and London Business School, November 1998.

Companies of the Future: Universum Top 100, Universum AB, 1998.

Compensation and Benefits Review: Amacom, March/April 1999.

Compensation Trends in Europe: Neil Irons, Hewitt Associates, the 31st Management Centre Europe, Global Human Resources Management Conference, London, April 1999.

Employee Commitment Replaces Loyalty: MORI Human Resource Research, Summer 1997.

Employee Retention: New Tools for Managing Workforce Stability and Engagement: Corporate Leadership Council, 1998.

Executive Advantage: Association of Executive Search Consultants, July 1998.

Finding and Keeping Great Employees: Jim Harris and Joan Brannick, Amacom, 1999.

Getting a GRIP on Tomorrow: Mike Johnson, Butterworth Heinemann, 1997.

Getting the Most out of Your College Recruitment Efforts: DBM (Drake Beam Morin Inc), May 1999.

Global Executive Demand Grows: Korn/Ferry International Index, 1999.

Globalisation and Employee Satisfaction: International Survey Research, 1998.

The Golden Book of Management: Lyndall Urwick, Amacom, 1984.

How Much Did That Last Bad Hire Cost You?: DBM (Drake Beam Morin Inc), May 1999.

'HR Consulting Market Set to Grow': *Financial Times*, 12 March 1999.

HR Focus, Special Report on Recruitment and Retention: Amacom, 1999.

Initiative for the Retention and Advancement of Women: Deloitte and Touche Tohmatsu International, 1997

International Student Survey: PricewaterhouseCoopers, June 1999.

Intranet: A New Tool for Managing Human Capital: Tom McGuire, Clarus, May 1999.

'Job Satisfaction is the Key': Terry Neill, Managing Partner, Change Management, Andersen Consulting, *Focus*, Zurich Insurance Company, second quarter 1999.

Labour Market Flexibility: Rachel Kelly, Manpower Inc., September 1998.

Learn to be a Leader: Mondial, Philips' Worldwide Internal Magazine, May 1999.

The Learning Organisation: Unipart Group, February 1999.

Lessons from the CEO: World Economic Forum, Davos, February 1997.

Managing: Harold Geneen with Alvin Moscow, Doubleday, 1984.

Managing Mergers, Acquisitions and Strategic Alliances: Sue Cartwright and Carl L. Cooper, Butterworth Heinemann, 1997.

Manpower Argus: June 1998 to June 1999.

Mergers and Acquisitions: Getting the People Bit Right: Roffey Park Management Institute, October 1998.

'Overworked and Overpaid: the American Manager': *The Economist*, 30 January 1999.

'Programming Jobs: What, Where and How Much?': *Dr Dobbs Journal*, Spring 1998.

Retention of Key Talent is Critical to Long-term M&A Success: Watson Wyatt, March 1999.

Roffey Park Management Agenda: Roffey Park Management Institute, January 1999.

Sacred Cows Make the Best Burgers: Robert Kriegel and David Brandt, Warner Books, 1996.

Similar Worker Attitudes Across Cultures: Gemini Consulting, September 1998.

Skills Assessment, Job Placement and Training: What Can Be Learned from the Temporary Help/Staffing Industry?: Jobs for the future, February 1997.

The State of the Job Market Around the World: DBM (Drake Beam Morin Inc), May 1999.

Strategic Rewards: Creating Financial Capital Through Human Capital: Watson Wyatt, May 1999.

Supercharge Your Management Role: Mark Thomas and Sam Elbeik, Butterworth Heinemann, 1996.

The Talent Solution, Aligning Strategy and People to Achieve Extraordinary Results: Edward Gubman, McGraw Hill, 1998.

Technology Fast 500 CEO Survey: Deloitte and Touche, 1998.

'The 100 Best Companies to Work For': *Fortune* magazine, 11 January 1999.

'Those That Can Teach Leadership': John W. Hunt, *Financial Times*, 2 December 1998.

'Tomorrow's Business Leaders': Mike Johnson and Peter Spooner, *Chief Executive*, September 1979.

Top 100: Global Banking and Securities Industry Outlook: Deloitte Research, 1999.

The Vital Difference: Unleashing the Powers of Sustained Corporate Success: Frederick G. Harmon and Garry Jacobs, Amacom, 1985.

'The War for Talent': *The McKinsey Quarterly*, 1998, Number 3.

'What is Trust?': *Management Review*, July/August 1998.

Who We Are At Work / Job Satisfaction High as workers Adjust: Shell USA, 1999.

Winning the War for Talent: Watson Wyatt, April 1999.

The Year 2000 and Beyond – Are You Prepared?: Dennis Coleman, PricewaterhouseCoopers and Robert Weinman, Prudential Securities, Conference Board Employee Benefits Conference, March 1999.

Index

Abbott Laboratories, 25
AC Nielsen, 134, 136
acquisitions *see* mergers & acquisitions
Acuff, Tom, 12, 71, 80–1
advertising, 97–8
Aetna, 133
air travel, 35
Alahunta, Matti, 16
Alcan, 87
alliances, 216
Amazon.com, 153
ambition, 158
American Express, 132133
American Management Association (AMA), 45
Andersen Consulting, 4, 155
AOL, 77
Apple Computer, 157
appreciation and recognition, 186–7
Arthur D Little, 174
Asda, 176
Asia Academy, 189
Association of Executive Search Consultants
     (AESC), 124, 161, 184, 225–6
AT&T, 2, 41–2
Audi, 10
Audience Selection, 177
audits, 146–8
Australia, 8, 41
Autosil, 110–11, 168
Azevedo, Belmiro de, 222–3
Aziz Corporation, 152–3

Bain, 178
Bang & Olufsen, 16, 78
Bank Boston, 133
Barclays Bank, 73
Barrett, Matthew, 73
Bauer, Eddie, 78
BBC, 80
Belgium, 156, 176
Bell, Chip, 153
Ben & Jerry, 104, 131
benefits, 84–6, 153
best practices, 70–1
Billings, Gary, 54, 166
black economy, 31
Blandy, Yann, 93
BMW, 59, 78–9

Body Shop, 77
Boone, Gaby, 190, 191
Boonstra, Cor, 73
Boucher, Peter, 53–4, 72
Bouwens, Jacques, 102, 104, 168
Boyden Interim Executive, 172
brainstorming, 147
Brandt, David, 131
Brecker & Merryman, 8
British Airways, 59
Brotherston, Ken, 92
Brown, Dick, 73
Brussels, 8
Buchert, Dennis, 83
Building and Retaining Global Talent, 20
Burgeois, Tim, 62
burn-out, 13
     see also stress
Burston Marsteller, 131–2

Cable & Wireless, 73
Cadbury, Dominic, 171
Caliper, 166
call centres, 112
Canada, 36
car park test, 40
Carasso, Marino, 130
career paths, 41
career plans, 41
Case, Steve, 77
Casterman, 176
Cathay Pacific, 105
challenges, 120–1, 124
Chase Manhattan, 132
Chevron, 133
chief executive officers (CEOs), 18, 152
     assessment questionnaire, 162–6
     changing priorities of, 161–2
     concerns of, 19–20
     salaries, 11–12
     tenure of, 17, 124
chief information officers (CIOs), 70
child-minding services, 27
China, 10, 18
Chivers, Ann, 109
Cisco Systems, 75
Citibank, 53–4, 103, 120
Citicorp, 77

Citigroup, 115, 173
Clarus, 200
climate control, 127–8
clock punchers, 63–4
Coca-Cola, 157
colleagues, 124, 170
Color Association, 176
commitment, 124, 227
communication, 164, 183–4, 192–204
    and delayering/devolution, 198
    employee surveys, 194
    intranets, 200–3
    and mergers, 199
    stages of a message, 197–8
commuting, 107
Compaq Computer, 73
confidence of managers, 53
conflict handling, 165–6
Conforti, Silvio, 56–7
consultancy industry, 6–7, 89
convergence of business, 30
Cooper, Cary, 57
Coors, 133
Cordeiro, René, 169
corporate universities, 189–92
Crawford, Margaret, 174
Cruisers, 144, 145
culture, 15–16, 78–9, 82–3
    and mergers, 59
    and innovation, 214
    and reward systems, 206
Cunard, 106
cynicism, 99

Da Silva, Pedro Sena, 110, 168
Daniëls, Marcel, 87
Darcy, Keith, 82–3, 119, 123
DBM, 41, 96, 139
de Azevedo, Belmiro, 222–3
delayering, 198
Dell Computer, 153175
Deloitte & Touche, 8, 84–5, 135, 175
Delta, 157
demographics, 2, 171
DERA, 109, 134–5, 136
Deutsche Bank, 180
development, 18, 183, 184–92, 215, 226
    appreciation and recognition, 186–7
    corporate universities, 189–92
    intellectual capital, 185–6
    mix of talent, 186
devolution of power, 198
DHL, 23, 34
dislike of the boss, 122–3
Disney, 79, 173–4
downsizing, 11, 13, 55
dress codes, 176

e-commerce, 115
Eastman Kodak, 133
Ebbutt, Tony, 58

eclipse, 129
Economic Intelligence Unit (EIU) report, 20–1
Eddie Bauer, 78
EDS, 16, 34
ego, 57
Egon Zehnder, 169
Electrolux, 106
employee charters, 167
employee involvement, 13–14
employee surveys, 194
empowerment, 164–5
engineering graduates, 7
Equitable Life Assurance, 166
Ericsson, 105
Europay Academy, 190
European Graduate Survey, 92–3
Evans, Lyndon, 112, 180
Executive Demand Index, 19
executive development see development
expatriates, 136–41
    and mergers, 139
expectations of job-seekers, 88, 94–5
Exxon, 77

Fahey, Liam, 28
family life see work/life balance
Fannie Mae, 133
Federal Express, 106
Felix, Peter, 66
financial services, 72, 99–100, 159
Finnair, 16, 177
Fiorina, Carly, 26
flexibility, 31, 115, 128
Fokker, 31
Ford, 133
4Bs, 123
France, 98–9
freedom charter, 167
Frese, Hanneke, 97, 153, 155
fulfilment seekers, 63

GAP, 34, 78
Gates, Bill, 113
Gateway, 105
Gemini Consulting, 12, 40–1
Geneen, Harold, 127
General Electric, 2, 120, 173–4
general managers (GM), 32–3
General Mills, 157
General Motors, 113
Generation X, 18, 91–3, 218–19
German Engineering Association, 7
Germany, 35–6, 122–3, 173
Geva Institute, 122–3
Gingher, Deborah, 169
Girlfriends, 132, 133
glass wall, 26–7
global managers, 10–11
Global One, 61, 97, 121–2
global pay rates, 208–9
goals, 41

Goffin, Christian, 51, 87
golf-days, 85
Gonçalves, Jorge Jardim, 156
Goth, Günther, 15, 161
graduates, 29, 55–6, 92–6, 173
    attracting, 96
    expectations of, 88,94–5
    salaries, 7, 8, 95
Granada, 128
Greenberg, Herb, 166, 168
greying population, 28, 170–1
groups, 127
Grove, Andy, 17, 146
guaranteed net salaries, 207
Gustafson, Eric, 70, 170
Guy, Philip, 109–10, 170
Gymboree, 78

Harley Davidson, 174
Harmon, Fred, 157
Harris, Jim, 104
Hay Group, 36
headhunters, 7–8, 80–2
health and safety, 33
Heresniak, Ed, 43
Hessler, Pierre, 40
Hewitt, 171, 214
Hewlett-Packard, 26, 75, 130
high achievers, 63
Hitachi, 176
Hoechst, 129
Holbeche, Linda, 121, 122, 187, 199
Honda, 59
hours of work, 42, 121, 219
human resources (HR), 48–56, 224–5
    attitudes towards, 51
    consulting market size, 62
    failure of, 50–2
    management disciplines, 51
    and mergers, 60
    proactive approach, 54
    re-labelling of, 52
    strategy, 55–6, 60
Hunt, John, 219
Hüppi, Rolf, 108, 178–9, 216
Hyundai, 79

IBJ Whitehall, 82–4, 119
IBM, 49, 113
ICO, 109–10, 170
ideal employers, 92–3
IKEA, 16
illness, 177
image, 77–8, 158
Inacom, 75
incentive-based rewards, 134, 209
India, 5–6, 154
industry swapping, 69–73
information technology (IT) industry, 4–5, 67, 154
innovation, 214–15

Intel, 157
intellectual capital, 185–6
interim management, 172
International Survey Research (ISR), 195
Internet, 74–5
intranets, 200–3
Ireland, 9
ITT, 127

Jacobs, Gary, 157
Japan, 10, 91, 175
job losses, 30, 34, 46–7
job satisfaction, 155
job security, 34, 42
job-hopping, 107
Jobs, Steve, 17
John Deere, 106
Jones, Alan, 103–4, 120
JWT Specialized Communications, 74

Kennedy Information (KI), 62
Kets de Vries, Manfred, 196
knowledge management, 185–6
Knutson, Anders, 78
Korn/Ferry, 19, 70, 75, 92, 169
    CEO assessment questionnaire, 162–6
    on succession planning, 221–2
Kotilainen, Pii, 16
KPMG, 6
Kravcisin-McClain, Nancy, 25
Kreigel, Robert, 131
Kroese, Hayko, 223
Kuijpers, Rob, 23

ladder climbers, 64
Lamielle, Serge, 147–8
language skills, 177
Laura Ashley, 77
law firms, 23
lay-offs, 30, 34, 46–7
leadership abilities, 159, 162–4, 215, 223–4
The Leading Edge, 190
learning provision, 65, 90
lesbians, 133
Levi Strauss, 77
lifestyles *see* work/life balance
living for the business, 125
location, 76–7, 105–7
Lopez syndrome, 113
Losers, 145
'love affair' syndrome, 73
loyalty, 1, 14, 39, 43–4, 89
    see also trust
Lufthansa, 190

McCaughey, Patrick, 100–2, 142
McDonald's, 91
McGuire, Tom, 200
McKinsey, 8, 18, 40
Malaysia, 10
management audits, 146–8

Management Centre Europe (MCE), 51–2
management style, 24–5
Manpower, 75, 99, 180
Marks and Spencer, 130
Martino, Rick, 49
Marx, Elisabeth, 103, 126, 139–40, 152, 158
MasterCard, 70–1, 86–7
mental health, 177
mercenaries, 206–7
Merck, 157
mergers & acquisitions, 13, 47–8, 56–60
   and communication, 199
   culture clashes, 59
   and ego, 57
   employee fears, 59
   and expatriates, 139
   human resource strategy, 60
   and job losses, 30
   learning from, 173
   management audits, 146–8
   roles, behaviour and attitudes, 58–9
messages, 197–8
Metcalf, Julian, 134
Michl, Michael, 70, 86–7
Microsoft, 34,113,132
Midland Bank, 132
minorities, 28
Mintzberg, Henry, 13
mix of talent, 186
Mobil, 71, 72, 77
Mollett, Guy, 27
Monsanto, 132–3
'Mother Duck Syndrome', 33
motivation, 61–2, 124, 165
   and reward systems, 205–6
Motorola, 191

NCR, 133
negotiating skills, 165–6
Neill, Terry, 155–6
The Netherlands, 8–9,36, 93–4, 178
networking, 168
Neumann International, 80, 146–8
new-age companies, 34–5
Nike, 34, 78
Nokia, 15–16, 177
Noortman, Wim, 51, 87
Norskbank, 180
Northwestern Mutual, 157
Norway, 180
Nyström, Win, 28

obsolete skills, 188–9
office colour, 176
oil industry, 71–2
on-line recruiting, 74–5
O'Neill, Michael, 73
opinions of employees, 125
Oracle, 7, 134
organizational development (OD), 50
Origin, 76, 129

outsourcing, 53, 142
over 50s, 28, 170–8
overseas assignments, 136–8

Pape, Christian, 170
part-time working, 178
Pattyn, Didier, 28
pay trends, 204–5, 207–8
   see also reward systems
paycheque cashers, 65
Pearson, 26
Peat Marwick, 135
people management policies, 119
performance, terminations for poor performance,
   16–17
Performance Dynamics, 47, 87
perks, 84–6, 152–3
personal development, 17
personal goals, 41–2
   see also work/life balance
personal sacrifices, 42–3
Philips, 73, 106, 130, 223
Phones4U, 97–8
Pickering, Robert, 76
Pieper, Roel, 73, 76
Plattner, Hasso, 173
Portugal, 110–11,128,156,168–9
power sharing, 227
Pret à Manger, 134
PricewaterhouseCoopers, 8, 17, 219
private sector, 9
Procter & Gamble, 102
'project dandelion', 119
promotion bonuses, 134
Prudential Insurance, 77, 169, 178
public sector, 9

Raickmann, Thierry, 147
Raines, Claire, 218
Reckitt & Coleman, 73
recognition and appreciation, 186–7
recruitment policies, 88
Reed Elsevier, 73
Reed, John, 77
rejection package, 104
relationships, 215
Renault, 59
repatriates, 138–9
reputation, 77–8, 82, 158, 160–2
reward systems, 122, 205–10, 215
   American model, 207–8
   cultural differences, 206
   global pay rates, 208–9
   guaranteed net salaries, 207
   incentive-based rewards, 134, 209
   mercenaries, 206–7
   and motivation, 205–6
   pay trends, 204–5, 207–8
   perception of reward, 205–6
   promotion bonuses, 133
   severance pay, 220

see also salaries
risk takers, 64
Roffey Park Management, 24, 42, 58, 121, 186, 199, 217
Rothwell, Bill, 69
Rover, 59
Runzheimer International, 35
Russia, 95–6

safety, 33
salaries, 10, 18, 22
    of chief executive officers (CEOs), 11–12
    of graduates, 7, 8, 95
    salary surveys, 206
Sandmark, Gunnar, 61–2, 97, 122, 142
SAP, 34, 97, 173
SAS, 85
Sattelberger, Tom, 190
Savage, Richard, 134, 142–3
Scandinavia, 16
Scardino, Marjorie, 26
Scottish Power, 85
security, 34, 42
Seeman, Patricia, 121, 185, 186, 187
Service-Ware, 128–9
severance pay, 220
Shanahan, Bill, 160
shared values, 83–4
shareholders, , 225–7
sharing talent, 216
Shell, 62–5
shopping for talent, 112–13
Siddall & Company, 152, 170
Siemens, 7, 15, 134, 161, 174, 195
Silicon Valley, 5, 7, 17–18, 98, 129
Singapore, 10, 18
ski-days, 85
skills
    mix of, 186
    obsolete, 189
    transferring between industries, 69–73
smiling faces, 91
SmithKline Beecham, 60
software engineers, 4–5, 67, 154
Soho Foundry, 157
Sonae, 128, 223
Southwest Airlines, 16, 153, 167
specialists, 29
Spencer Stuart, 169
sponsorship, 86
    of students, 178
spouses, 103–4, 135–6
spying, 113–14
stages of a message, 197–8
Staunton, Mike, 191
Stephane, Jean, 60
stress, 35–6
    see also burn-out
stretching people, 120–1, 124
succession planning, 25, 152, 220–4
Sun Microsystems, 7, 31, 113, 153

surveys, employee, 194
swapping industries, 69–73
Sweden, 133–4
SWIFT, 135–6
Switzerland, 36

T-shirts, 98
taking back staff, 91
teams, 127, 189–92
telecommuting, 137
temporary work, 180
terminations for poor performance, 16–17
Thomas, Brad, 53–4, 120, 173
Thomas, Mark, 47, 87–8, 156
3Com, 130–1
TIAACREF, 158, 160
time stress, 35
TR Fastenings, 174–5
tradition, 79
training, 91, 130, 177, 226–7
    see also development
trust, 43–4, 45–6
    see also loyalty
'turn-off' factor, 24–5

Unipart, 190
United States, 4–5, 8, 9, 12
    hiring American CEOs, 73
Universum, 94

values, 97, 121, 187–8
    shared values, 83–4
van Ballaert, Sonia, 156
Virgin, 77
vision, 84
Volkswagen, 135, 189
voluntary simplicity, 29
Volvo, 133–4

wages *see* reward systems; salaries
'walk the talk' managers, 14, 40
Watson Wyatt, 9, 171
webmasters, 200–4
'well-being' industry, 8
Welsh, Jack, 2
Wetfeet.com, 94
Willey, Keith, 152, 170
Williams, Roy, 52
willingness to work, 65
Winkfield, Nick, 43, 45, 196–7, 198, 229
Winners, 144
Wirthlin Worldwide, 43, 196, 229
Wolfensohn, James, 175
women, 26–7, 42–3, 102–3
    ladder climbers, 64
    lesbians, 132
    spouses, 103–4, 135–6
Woods, Martin, 179–80
work activities, 215
work colleagues, 124, 170
work days, 177

work experience programmes, 178
Work Family Directions, 41
work/life balance, 41–3, 87, 89, 175, 217–18
worker types, 63–5, 144–5
working hours, 42, 121, 219
workplace
    office colour, 176
    safety, 33

World Bank, 175
worries of people, 44–5
Wright, Lance, 55–6, 71–2

Xerox, 131

Zurich Financial Services (ZFS), 107–9, 119,
    178–9, 189